KEEPING AUSTRALIA ON THE LEFT

A Catamaran Odyssey Around Australia

MARK STEWART DARBY

Hellgate Press
CENTRAL POINT, OREGON

Published by Hellgate Press/PSI Research
© 1999 by Mark Stewart Darby

All rights reserved. No part of this publication may be reproduced or used in any form or by any means, graphic, electronic or mechanical, including photocopying, recording, taping, or information storage and retrieval systems without written permission of the publishers.

The names of some people in this book have been changed to respect their privacy.

Editor: Kathy Marshbank
Illustrator: Eric Hansen
Cover Designer: Steven Burns

Please direct any comments, questions, or suggestions regarding this book to:
    Hellgate Press/PSI Research
    Editorial Department
    P.O. Box 3727
    Central Point, Oregon 97502-0032
    (541) 479-9464
    (541) 476-1479 fax
    info@psi-research.com e-mail

Library of Congress Cataloging-in-Publication Data
Darby, Mark Stewart, 1957–
    Keeping Australia on the left : a catamaran odyssey around
Australia / Mark Stewart Darby.
    p. cm.
ISBN 1-55571-508-7 (pbk.)
1. Darby, Mark Stewart, 1957– – – Journeys. 2. Tom Thumb (Catamaran)
3. Voyages and travels. 4. Australia – – Description and travel.
I. Title.
G530.D26 1999
910'.9165'7– – dc21   99–37417
                                                                                           CIP

Printed and bound in the United States of America

First Edition 10 9 8 7 6 5 4 3 2
Printed on recycled paper when available

Contents

1 Daring to Dream 1
2 Crossing the Bars
   Sydney to Southport 21
3 Cane Fields and Beaches
   Southport to Mackay 37
4 Cruising the Islands
   Mackay to Cairns 55
5 Cape York and Beyond
   Cairns to Weipa 73
6 Into the Never-Never
   Weipa to Gove 89
7 Arnhem Land
   Gove to Darwin 101
8 Pearls and Great Sandy Deserts
   Darwin to Port Hedland 115
9 Mining and Lobsters
   Port Hedland to Perth 129
10 The America's Cup
   Perth 149
11 Windy Cliffs
   Perth to Victor Harbour 159
12 A Winter Port
   Victor Harbour 173
13 The Great Southern Ocean
   Victor Harbour to Lakes Entrance 187
14 The Passage Home
   Lakes Entrance to Sydney 205
   Epilogue 223

Acknowledgements

Thank you to family, friends, sponsors and the people of Australia who all made this trip possible. Special thanks to all involved in encouraging and supporting the sharing of it through this book.

To Sponsors and Supporters without whose assistance the trip would not have happened:

Cottee's General Food
Classic Yachts, Western Australia
Damart Thermal Clothing
Eureka Tents
Kraft Australia
Kodak Australia
Grand Prix Sailing
Glad Bags
2GO Central Coast Radio
ICI
Jo Hopkins
Jonathon Sceats - Sunglasses
Line 7
Marlin International - Lifejackets
O'Neill's Wetsuits
Paddy Pallins
Pier 21, Fremantle
Roche Products Pty Ltd - Vitamins
Samuel Taylor – Aerogard
Sanitarium Health Foods
Smiths, Ann & Wade
Smith & Nephew Australia – Nivea Skin Care
Speedo
Suzuki Outboards, WA
Tekna diving equipment
Trek Outdoor Australia (who designed and built the Catcan)
Ulmar Kolius sails, Western Australia

About the Author

Mark Darby is a trainer, educator, project coordinator, and manager. With formal qualifications in Parks and Recreation Management, he has led and coordinated outdoor education-based programs throughout the world. He instructed courses for Outward Bound Australia and lectured in Leisure and Tourism Studies at the University of Technology, Sydney.

In 1984 Mark established the selection program that recruited and placed over 1,000 young Americans on the British-based youth program, Operation Raleigh, for a four-year program of science, medical and community service projects throughout the world. During the past eight years he has been a program director and team leader for the Canadian-based organization, Youth Challenge International. He has coordinated international groups of youth on community development programs in South and Central America and the South Pacific and established the Australian branch of the organization.

Mark is currently a Director of the Australian Youth Ambassadors for Development Program, an Australian government initiative placing 500 young Australian professionals on development assignments in the Asia Pacific region. Mark currently lives in Canberra with his partner, Cate, and daughter, Amelia, always drawn back to weekends at Tathra, on the beautiful south coast of New South Wales.

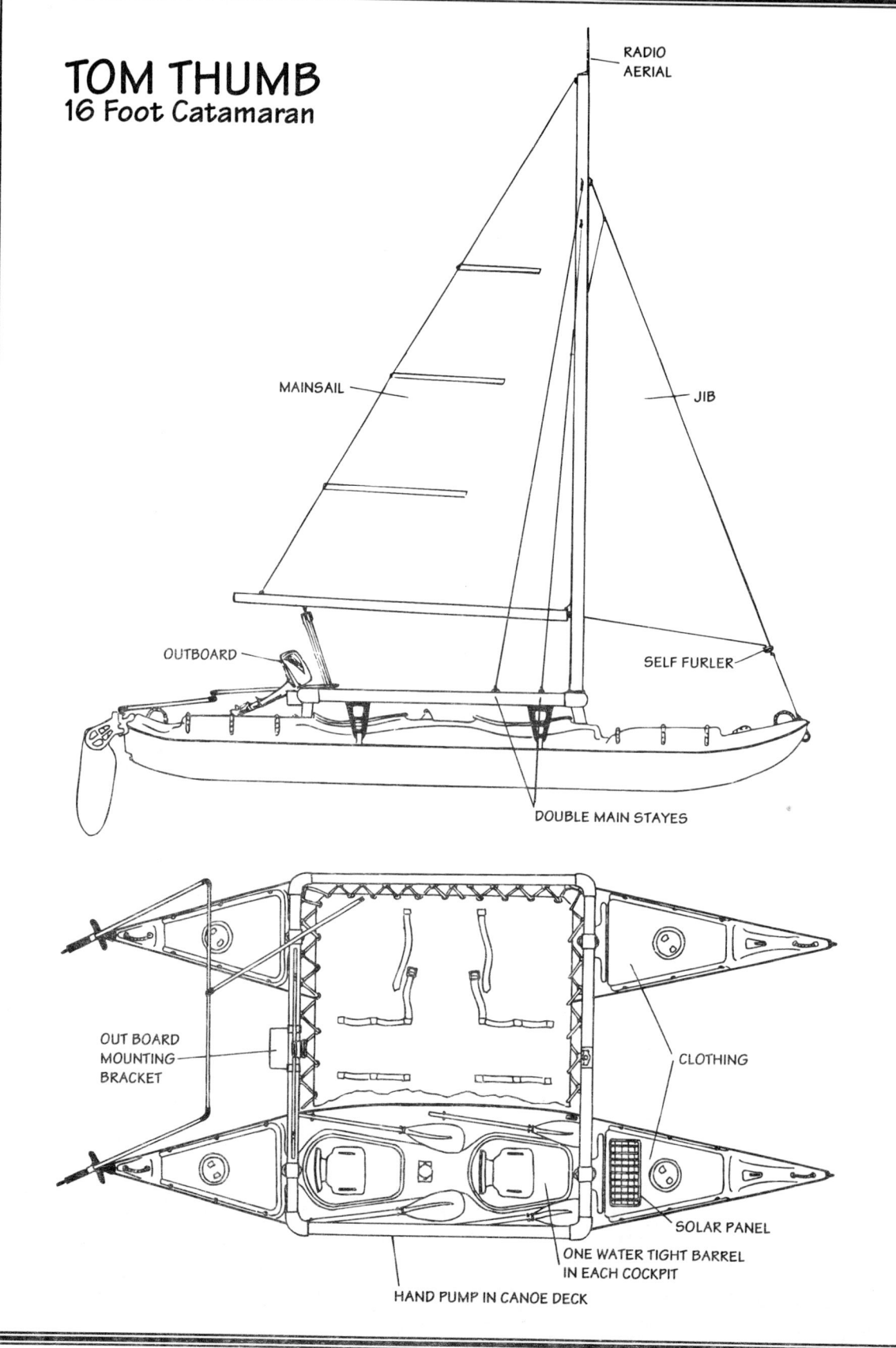

Chapter 1

Daring to Dream

What on earth were we doing here? A dull, grey, tidal sea stretched off into the distance. It was early morning and already too hot to stand on the sandy beach. Sea salt and sunscreen had baked onto our faces and large black March flies drew blood from their bites. In so many ways we were wishing ourselves away from this harsh reality and each other.

One hundred and fifty days of travelling and here we were in the middle of nowhere! Not even halfway around this bloody country! And asking "Why? Why are we doing this? Who is it for?" Good planning, stubbornness and the occasional bit of luck had gotten us this far. We had survived several stressful months of preparation, followed by the hard reality of five months sailing the Australian coastline in our 16-foot open catamaran, *Tom Thumb*. Over this time the two of us had barely been further apart than the two square yards of *Tom Thumb's* trampoline deck. Now, thousands of miles north of our home port, Sydney, on Australia's northern shores, the heat and effort were taking their toll. We were desperately tired, mentally and physically. The natural beauty and wonders that surrounded us had ceased to be an antidote to the days of salt spray, baking sun and winds that rarely blew in our direction. Neither of us wanted the trip to end here. We had dared to dream and now our dream was daring us.

Our thoughts were churning inside but neither of us wanted to be the first to voice them, yet we both realized that something had to be said. "What does this mean to us? It's our trip and our lives," Sue pleaded. Words flooded forth between us on this lonely northern beach as we debated the question we thought we knew the answer to. Why were we making this trip? Were we giving up the whole trip now to retreat and seek help for our tired boat and small broken outboard motor? Would this be the end? Were we letting sponsors, friends and family down to turn back now? It had taken Sue's tears to make me face the fears I had also entertained, but hadn't been willing to acknowledge. The wilderness of northern Australia was no place to enter with broken equipment. For the next month through the harsh, uninhabited Kimberley coast we would rely on the outboard to help find our most precious supply — fresh water.

Sue turned and walked off down the empty beach. She returned an hour later and without saying much we packed *Tom* and set sail to return to Darwin and find help. We managed a weak smile and even a slight laugh as we headed back across Fannie Bay to the Darwin Yacht Club we had left only yesterday. The favorable breeze seemed to say we were going in the right direction. Exhausted, yet somehow relieved, I found myself reflecting on what had brought us here in the first place.

It was strange to think back two years to when I had first met Sue. During a university student conference on the Californian coast, a group afternoon walk along the local beach had petered out to just the two of us. We ran, skipped and hopped along the beach like children, rejoicing in the familiar sounds and smells from our childhoods played out on opposite sides of the Pacific Ocean. It was a wonderfully refreshing afternoon, feeling the wind and waves, the sand between our toes and salt on our faces. A friendship grew from that common touch of the sea. Heads turned when we arrived back late for dinner, but we didn't offer an explanation. I smiled at the thought of where that day had led us.

My interest in sailing had grown as a teenager learning to race catamarans near my home at Terrigal, a beachside holiday town just north of Sydney. Catamarans were fast and fun and I enjoyed the thrill of the wind and surf. I remember spending a lot of time upside down in the water, but it sparked an interest and a certainty that I would come back to sailing at a later stage in my life. Working as an instructor for Outward Bound and youth adventure programs I had been inspired by the value of personal challenge and outdoor adventure.

The idea of touring around Australia in a small catamaran had been a dream shaped over time. I'd met an Australian sailor who had attempted to race a 16-foot catamaran in the Sydney to Hobart Yacht Race, followed by racing long distances along the American coastline in the "Hog's Breath 1000" and other events. What a way to see Australia! A catamaran could be surfed ashore to camp yet provide enough stability to carry equipment for up three or four weeks. The dream and plans grew from there. When Australia won the America's Cup yachting race in 1983, breaking America's 132-year-old record, I joined in Australia's celebrations. Boyhood memories of black-and-white, late night television broadcasts of the classic Australian yachts, *Dame Pattie* and *Gretel,* doing battle for the cup off Rhode Island had captured my spirit. I knew I had to be in Perth in January 1987. This was sailing history — the America's Cup was being contested outside America for the first time ever!

However it was my work in America with the international youth expedition program, Operation Raleigh, that gave me the belief that anything was possible. While talking to American youth, and their very concerned parents, across the country about the virtues of a three-month project of science and community service in developing countries and isolated sections of the globe, I met an incredible range of international explorers and adventurers. At a meeting of sponsors in Houston a business executive commented that "Operation Raleigh was a collection of extraordinary people." He was quickly corrected by a young participant. "No, we are just a group of ordinary people who do extraordinary things. Anybody can do it if they believe in themselves." As I shared my ideas of sailing around Australia, support and advice from friends and colleagues helped to shape its reality.

At least two people would be needed to manage a 16-foot boat and there was a question of safety in the isolated areas of Australia. Given the length of time we would be spending together, as well as some romantic notions, the preference was for a female companion. As plans for the trip came together in late July 1985 the question of "whom" became a priority. I didn't dare think of asking Sue! After a fun-filled three months together we had parted at Christmas with no promises as I went off to work in North Carolina. We had stayed in touch as she completed her studies and worked the summer as a whitewater raft guide and naturalist in the mountains of California. We were due to meet in August when I would be flying back to California for work. I knew Sue was seeing someone else. A weekend at Point Reyes was to be our final farewell, a chance perhaps to wish each other health and happiness when we parted. I procrastinated for weeks deciding whether I should, or had any right to, ask her. I would just have to wait and see.

Sue looked great. Working the summer as a whitewater raft guide had left her fit, healthy and confident. There was a sense of fun and ease in us being together. The moment was perfect as the sandhills, surf and seagrass of a lonely windswept Californian beach were wrapped in a spectacular sunset. Bread, cheese and a bottle of wine…

"Sue, I have a business proposition for you. Remember that sailing trip I've been talking about? The boat is for two people. Would you come with me?"

She fell over laughing. Stunned silence and some more red wine.

"You're serious aren't you?" she eventually asked.

"A proposition," I repeated. "I'm asking you number one because you are female, number two because you are American and number three because you are Sue."

Out stumbled the words amidst the sunset and red wine on the Point Reyes sandhill. Arrogantly I told myself, she has to make this trip for herself. In many ways I felt I was proposing marriage. Sue was still laughing and shaking her head. I wasn't sure this 22-year-old Californian would be prepared to pack-up and leave her life and America for the southern shores of the Pacific, especially with some crazed Australian.

"Don't worry, I'll put it all in writing and mail it to you so you don't feel it was a bad dream and to assure you that it is a serious proposal."

We didn't mention it to Sue's parents that week, although we both nearly choked when her father mentioned some interesting Australians they had just met who'd sailed the Australian coast in a small catamaran. I thought I was hearing things, but amazingly enough we were to meet Sandy and Ginty Anderson during the trip. A friend's comment on the way home to North Carolina said a lot. "She's a nice girl Mark, you seem so natural together." "I hope so," I responded, "because I have just asked her to sail around Australia with me."

I sent off the written proposal to Sue to assure her it wasn't a moment of craziness brought on by red wine.

> *Enclosed is an outline of an expedition I would very much like us to share. The pay is lousy, the work hard, and the hours unbelievable. You'll eat sand and salt for a year, have days of gale force anxiety and days of windless boredom and above all have to put up with me! The returns on this personal investment are yours to discover. The final decision I know will not be an easy one, but please understand, either way our friendship shall always remain.*

The following month was a blur with work, without a thought for the sailing trip until I noticed a familiar return address on a letter in my in-tray. With sweating palms and knots in my stomach I opened it. It was from Sue's mother, written with tears in her eyes at 2:00 A.M., after being told by her daughter that she was off to Australia to go sailing for two years. She was coming! I felt like jumping for joy but was sobered by Sally's emotional outpouring as she battled to come to terms with her daughter's decision.

> *For our part it will be the longest two years of our married life waiting to hear that you are both back safe and sound. What will this adventure mean in your lives except to say that you did it? Is that enough for a whole year of surviving each day of ocean, rain, sun, wind and the unknown? This would be so easy for us if we didn't care. Our trouble is that we care too much. If I keep writing I will be sending you a bucket full of tears. Take the very best care of our daughter that you possibly can.*
>
> *Sally & Joe*

I felt excitement, yet a responsibility — this trip would affect many people's lives. At the bottom of my tray was a card from Sue.

> *I cannot really describe how I feel since my life has been turned upside down, thanks to you. I realize this is most likely the biggest decision in my life and only I can make it. I know this project is going to*

be a lot of hard work, long hours and lousy pay, But Mark I know more than anything I would love to take part in this with you. Yes!!

And oh, by the way, I told my parents.

I called California to check, "Are you sure?"

"This is a once in a lifetime opportunity, and a chance to do something for myself", Sue said over the phone, "Let's do it!"

I realized that the trip had started. It was going to happen. Someone else shared my dream. Now the challenge was to *make* it happen. My parents received a five-page letter trying to explain what we were planning, begging their understanding and hoping they could give their moral support. Parents! You spend so much of your formative years trying to desperately break away, staking your claim for independence. Just when *they* have got used to the idea of leading their own lives, you once again land on their doorstep asking more than you would of any close and trusted friend. We were both grateful to have parents still together, something uncommon among our peers. We would learn much about them during the trip, building respect, love and friendship that we had previously taken for granted.

The initial estimate of what the trip would cost varied between $20,000 and $30,000. "Double it," was the advice marketing friends gave. We had $5,000 between us! Our evenings were spent feverishly writing letters to potential sponsors and researching a growing list of necessary equipment. Our Operation Raleigh friends helped develop and sponsor a letterhead for us. The expedition name, "Circumcontinental Challenge" was a mouthful and the basis of a few good jokes, but the letterhead was professional and I am sure opened doors for us that would normally have been closed. Our friends had T-shirts printed featuring our logo. We had expedition T-shirts even before we arrived in Australia or had a boat! Meanwhile Sue negotiated the writing of articles for her local paper and tracked down a few potential sponsors.

The farewell in December from Sue's family was enthusiastic if not somewhat daunting. A gathering of about 40 people all politely offered their best wishes, undoubtedly convinced Sue was being led astray and would come to her senses soon.

"Let's face it," said Sally, "Sue was a surprise to me at forty-five (giving birth to her), and I guess she's gone on being so." Meanwhile, Joe contemplating his adventurous youth traveling the railroad boxcars across America during the depression, dryly added, "I guess my past has just come back to haunt me through my youngest daughter." We hugged and said our good-byes with words we all had to believe in, "We'll see you in 18 months when you come down and see us sail back into Sydney."

We arrived in Australia in time to celebrate the New Year, 1986, with a hard four months of full-time preparation ahead of us. Based on winds and seasons and the minimal preparation time, we set our departure date for early May that year. My parents, who had not seen me for nearly two years, welcomed Sue into the family and provided us with accommodations in their work studio, a converted dairy. This was our base to further research the trip and start collecting our growing list of essential equipment. I was daunted enough by the list let alone imagining where we would fit it aboard.

Finding a suitable boat was our first challenge. We wanted a catamaran that was sturdy, able to carry up to three weeks' food and ten days' water, and yet light enough to land on a beach and be pulled up the sand by two people! This was after all a tour of the Australian coast as much as a sailing trip. Of all the boats I had seen or sailed none easily fit this criteria, except for those which were custom built. Fate, however, had a hand and months earlier my father had chanced upon a unique catamaran, called a Catcan, in a Sydney design display center. According to its promotional material, its hulls were actually two fiberglass two-person kayaks. "Beautifully made," according to my father. After writing from America to the company who designed and made them, Trek Outdoor Australia, we were anxious to meet them as soon as possible.

It was hot and humid, and the buzz of cicadas filled the air, reminding me I was back in Australia. We stood on the front porch of a Federation style house in the southern suburbs of Sydney bearing a large sign "Kirrawee Lodge." I wondered if it was the right address. It didn't seem to be the kind of place one would go to buy a boat. We tapped on the tattered screen door and waited. I stuck my head inside and almost collided with a dark, curly-haired fellow in work overalls, who, after a polite, "hello" ushered us into his dining room that doubled as an office. As soon as we were seated he rushed off into the back room to answer a phone call. We sat looking at some rather odd photos on the wall — large trucks, grain silos and army commandos in a variety of canoes as well as a collection of service awards which stood on the mantelpiece of a boarded up fireplace.

After his phone call we had the pleasure of meeting Peter Pool, the director, designer and chief salesman of Trek Outdoor Australia, essentially a one-man show. He looked us over rather sternly, knowing the nature of our visit. At the end of our explanation about what we were trying to do, Peter turned to Sue and asked, "Why do you want to do it?" He smiled politely at her rehearsed response about challenge and personal interest. "Come on," he said, and led us through the house to the rear garage. Supported on trestles were a number of large fiberglass hulls at various stages of construction. We were skeptical at the idea of a makeshift catamaran being constructed from kayaks. Standard racing catamarans feature sleek narrow, banana-shaped hulls to cut through the water and prevent the bow from nose-diving. These 16-foot kayaks were three feet wide, with symmetrical V-ed hulls concaving down to a flat bottom. Two open kayak cockpits and small, watertight flattened deck sections bow and stern provided plenty of storage. There was no doubt that they were well built and extremely tough. We poked around, pushing and prodding, contemplating the shortcomings of such a tiny vessel as Peter expounded on the virtues the Catcan. With a group of friends, Peter had just finished an expedition in similar kayaks down the remote Daly river in Northern Australia, filming for the television program *World Around Us*. We were sufficiently impressed to arrange a test sail with Peter for the following week.

When we arrived promptly on Wednesday morning Peter had obviously been reflecting on what we had proposed.

"You guys are for real aren't you!" he remarked.

"Yes, it's a choice between this boat and another catamaran and we are leaving in May."

"Well it had better be the Catcan," said Peter, "because it is the only boat that'll make it."

The test sail was in twenty knots of wind with two old kayak hulls put together and "bits still to work out," according to Peter. The sails, a small mainsail and self-furling jib, totaled eleven square yards and allowed steady sailing without a trapeze. Without spray skirts to cover the cockpits ("none made up yet") they quickly filled with water and we continually worked the hand bilge pumps. But despite the weight of Peter, Sue and I, plus two cockpits totally awash, the Catcan still sailed! It was hardly at racing speed, but it was enough to convince us it would do the job we had in mind. So began an incredible friendship and wonderful support from a person who often mothered us and shared vicariously in a journey he had obviously once entertained as his own.

Construction of our boat was continually delayed. Peter insisted upon refinements in construction to ensure that the Catcan was equipped to take on the forces of this trip. Extra reinforcement of a foam sandwich on the bottom of our hulls and aluminum plates within the fiberglass to reinforce the brackets and the trampoline mounts all took time. Peter's fiberglasser was also a perfectionist and, knowing what this boat was for, he took special care and extra weeks. The wait was frustrating but the extra effort and time would prove worthwhile during the year ahead. It had been years since I had done much sailing and Sue had only had one brief season of crewing a catamaran. We both grew impatient to learn how to sail and tune our boat. Peter's never ending dry humor and casualness always helped ease the tension. His ultimate compliment to Sue was made during one of our many visits, "I wish there had been a few birds like you around when I was your age."

We did get some practice sailing on a friend's catamaran at the entrance to Hawkesbury River north of Sydney. In good winds on a sunny day we circumnavigated our first island, Lion Island, a few square miles in size. I didn't dare point out to Sue the large fin of a shark cutting through the water just yards away. Our next circumnavigation was to take much longer. We reassured ourselves that we had a few thousand miles up the slightly calmer and populated East Coast of Australia to practice our sailing before we got to the isolated north and rough southern oceans.

While waiting for the boat we worked full time preparing ourselves and gathering equipment. We started a fitness program of swimming and jogging almost every day. I taught Sue how to bodysurf in case we ever capsized while trying to get the boat ashore in a big swell. We enrolled in the Ships Officers' Medical Training Course for two weeks at Sydney Hospital. It was an intensive program, which refreshed our first aid skills and confidence in handling injections, minor stitching and the variety of drugs we would carry. Hands-on experience was a useful requirement of the course. Sue attended to the daily treatment of third-degree sunburn on the breasts of an English tourist who fell asleep on Bondi beach while I helped to stitch up the head of a construction worker who hit himself with his own hammer! We met some wonderful characters and fellow sailors among the staff. They provided excellent advice and assistance in making sure we were properly prepared for any medical emergency.

We had just enough funds to set out, thanks to wonderfully supportive friends and family. But, since we planned to sail into the middle of the America's Cup in Perth, we felt it was worthwhile trying for some sponsorship. We spent months typing letters, developing a professional sponsorship package and identifying potential corporate sponsors. We received advice from professionals in the field of sponsorships as well as some marketing managers and eventually developed a package we were satisfied with, but time was short and we had only a few sponsors. The rejection letters were mounting. As we realized that we may not have a major sponsor, we became tougher negotiators. When accepting a 'No' for dollars we immediately responded with requests for equipment.

A major difficulty in gaining the attention of prospective sponsors was our lack of profile and track record in sailing. If we passed this barrier they often related tales of how they had done badly in past sponsorships. "It sounded so good," stated one marketing manager. "One of the most exciting projects I had ever heard of, climbing unique and isolated peaks in South America. We happily provided a large quantity of film with a book and film documentary in the offer. It turned out their photographer wasn't very experienced and all the rolls came back blank!" Other tales of sponsorship included providing equipment but never hearing of the project or people again. We vowed to keep in touch with our sponsors and hopefully prove that at least we were trying to be professional in our approach.

Peter Pool was convinced we should organize filming of the trip for a documentary so we spent time talking to the documentary staff of the television program, *World Around Us*, about their experiences and even acquired a waterproof super 8 camera. The prospective cost of $3,000 to $4,000 for film stock put that project on hold and we settled for still photographs and a year's supply of Kodak slide film, which we faithfully promised to expose. My local radio station, 2GO, in Gosford was a great supporter and in exchange for a tape recorder we agreed to phone them with monthly updates from around Australia.

It was a difficult time for Sue, being so far away from home and friends. This was compounded by my being totally obsessed with making the trip a reality. Sue hated typing letters and making phone calls more than I did. As time wore on and the sense of urgency developed, Sue became more confident in forcefully stating her requirements, or skillfully negotiating the donation of another piece of equipment. Despite the pressures at the time we can still reflect in wonder at some of the amazing people we met and the enormous amount we learned about marketing, sponsorship, the business world in general, and our own abilities even before we started the trip.

Before we left California, Sue had tracked down Jack O'Neil, of O'Neil Wetsuits, as a potential supporter. After lengthy negotiations we eventually arranged a personal meeting with Jack at his home in Santa Cruz. A convertible E-type jaguar in the driveway indicated something more than the ordinary suburban house. We were ushered through the door by a smartly dressed woman. At the top of the stairs the Pacific Ocean and the famed Santa Cruz point-break filled the large picture windows. We accepted the offer of coffee, cleared clothes and papers from the dining chairs and table and sat staring out at the sea as we waited. A figure eventually emerged up the stairwell. Wearing faded blue jeans, a crumpled T-shirt and an old leather jacket, topped by tousled hair, with a beard and a black patch over one eye, he extended a hand in our direction. "Hello. Jack O'Neil." We were both momentarily too stunned to move, but eventually stumbled to our feet to introduce ourselves.

Keeping Australia On the Left

After grabbing a cup of coffee Jack joined us at the kitchen table, his back to the view he had obviously lived with for many years. "Well, what is it you are thinking of doing?" he asked, sipping on his cup. We began our carefully rehearsed presentation about a trip for which we didn't even have a boat at this stage. He listened patiently before asking us a couple of questions about our experience and intentions, and then talked about other projects he was involved in sponsoring including world windsurfing teams and explained how most of his limited budget was tied up in that. I felt our first rejection coming. "Of course, we don't have control over our Australian distributor, but I'll give them a call and I'm sure we can work something out. Here's the name. Contact them when you get back to Sydney. Good luck with your trip." Jack stood, giving us the sign that our time was up. We shook hands and were ushered back through the maze and out the front door. Sue and I just stood shaking our heads in the driveway next to the Jaguar.

"Do you think that means yes?" asked Sue.

"I don't care," I said. "It was worth it just to meet Jack."

Back in Australia the people we met in our search for support and sponsorship were just as colorful and diverse. From Rear Admiral Ian Knox, Head of the Australian Navy, to the very fashionable Jan Murray, a publicity and promotion agent, and wife of a federal government minister. Jan had admitted on the television program, *60 Minutes*, to christening her husband's new ministerial desk by having sex on it with him and leaving her panties in his ash tray. She truly believed in the notion that any publicity is good publicity. We were anxious as to what she would advise us to do to generate interest in our sailing trip! The Rear Admiral was rather more practical and productive with letters of introduction to his Patrol Base Commanders in Northern Australia.

Support came from sometimes unlikely sources. Solarcells, a company, located behind an auto repair shop and sharing an office with a rock-and-roll band provided our solar power. The marketing manager of the high profile drug company, Roche, grilled us with questions before offering a year's supply of vitamins. Marlin Lifejackets gave us made-to-measure jackets. "Go for it! But please don't drown in these, it's bad publicity!" was the parting comment from their Marketing Manager. Basic essentials such as a year's supply of sunscreen from ICI, an assortment of Kraft food including Vegemite, which Sue had acquired a taste for, and Glad bags for waterproofing our gear, were also gratefully accepted.

Researching the coast of Australia for our type of sailing trip was more difficult than expected. Good anchorages for larger yachts are indicated on charts or sailing guides, but we were more interested in what the shoreline was like as we would be landing our boat on the beach each night. We talked to many people who had only been legendary names to me before. Malcolm Douglas, a noted adventurer and documentary maker of Australia's north, gave advice on crocodiles and filming. Paul Caffyn, the first person to paddle around Australia in a sea-kayak, provided invaluable details of how to tackle the more daunting stretches of unbroken cliff line on the Western Australian coast and Great Australian Bight and drew sketch maps of inlets and landings. The commander of Norforce, Australia's northern defense forces, also offered to spend some time with us when we reached Darwin, to indicate where the freshwater sources lay on the isolated Kimberley coast. This knowledge could be critical on this section of the coast where we did not expect to see anybody for perhaps thirty days. No one would follow us along the coast providing ground support. After we left my home port of Terrigal we would be on our own and that meant a lot of detailed planning now. Being unprepared could mean failure, or even worse.

We walked out of a marine shop with two heavy rolls of charts that mapped the entire Australian coast. Many hours were spent poring over them with anyone who was interested and able to give advice about the best ports and beaches to visit. However, books of aerial photos of the coast became our best way of assessing protected beaches suitable for landing and we could then relate them back to the charts. Other books on cruising the coast gave warnings of the dangers of river bars along the East Coast. After a month of such research we were totally overwhelmed with information.

We then carefully packed the relevant data for each section of our trip. Supplies of dried food, vitamins, sunscreen, film, and books were also carefully packaged into 23 boxes destined for a schedule of towns around Australia. My parents would mark our progress and mail each supply box.

After leaving in May, we planned to be in Perth by January and back in Sydney within that year. Our postmaster, at my parents hometown of Wamberal, would follow our trip in detail. He knew how important these boxes were and would do his best to ensure their safe arrival.

Finally the boat was completed. The bright yellow hulls shone. Each hull had a flat watertight section in the bow with plastic screw down lids, which became our wardrobes, holding the majority of our clothes. Behind this was one of the four trampoline mounts, which were metal castings that fitted into rubber mounts and were supported right through to a locating hold on the floor of the hull. This gave enough support to withstand the twisting and turning of the trampoline as it held the two hulls together. The trampoline was further bracketed by two smaller supports to the outside of each hull. All brackets were held by locating pins that could be quickly removed in an emergency to free the hull, so it could be paddled away as a kayak. The large twin cockpits had mounted seats that divided up the storage area of the hull and stopped equipment rolling about. These cockpits were covered with black neoprene spray covers. Hand operated bilge pumps assisted to keep the hulls relatively dry. We carried two sets of clip-together kayak paddles that could be stored either on deck or in brackets on top of each hull. Each stern also had a flat-decked, watertight hold that usually held boat supplies such as repair kits and fishing gear. The outboard bracket hung off the back of the trampoline between the rudder system. Leaving nothing to chance, Peter had double-stayed the mast to support a mainsail and furling jib. Because of the weight and shape of the boat, it did not need trapeze lines to help crew hang off the sides. We had sacrificed speed for sturdiness. The four square yard, open trampoline between the hulls would be where Sue and I would spend most of our time in the year ahead.

It was ours! We towed our new boat back to Terrigal, anxious to spend some time on the water. Our first test sail was full of expectations. However in light winds the jib cleats jammed, the rudder pin fell out and we rammed a moored fishing boat in the middle of the bay. It was a disaster. I was swearing and cursing at everything in sight, including Sue, as we floated backwards into the shore. It was ludicrous to think that we were planning to sail out of

Sydney Harbor in six weeks time! We had our boat, but we were far from ready.

> *Projects of this nature, when operating in the minds of young men (and women), are usually termed romantic; and so far from any good being anticipated, even prudence and friendship join in discouraging, if not opposing them. Thus it was in the present case: so that a little boat of eight foot in length, called Tom Thumb, with a crew composed of ourselves and a boy, was the best equipment to be procured, from the first outset.*
>
> *Captain Matthew Flinders*

This excerpt from the journal of Captain Matthew Flinders (1774-1814), Royal Navy, described his original exploration of the Australian coastline with his friend George Bass. In many ways it also suited our trip and thus we found a name for our small vessel — *Tom Thumb*. Flinders and Bass ventured not far south of Sydney in their *Tom Thumb*. George Bass, however, went on to survey a large section of the southeast coast of Australia in small whaling boats, providing conclusive evidence of the existence of a strait, now called Bass Strait, between Van Diemen's Land (Tasmania) and New South Wales (the Australian mainland). In 1801 Flinders returned in a much larger vessel, the *Investigator*, to become the first person to circumnavigate the island continent, confirming its name, Australia. As testimony to his skill and commitment as a seaman and surveyor, many modern charts for more isolated regions still rely on soundings and coastline charting made by Flinders on that voyage. Considering he was in his early twenties at the time it is an even more impressive achievement. We hoped that in borrowing the name of Flinders' vessel we would also share some of his spirit for adventure.

The pressure was building as time raced toward our deadline of May 3rd, the date we had set as the last possible day we could leave Sydney, to be followed north by the winter and make it to Perth in time for the Cup. Sue's letter to American friends captured much of what was happening,

G'Day Mates!   26 April, '86

The final frantic moments have arrived before setting sail on the 3rd of May. We are up to our eyeballs in equipment and food, trying to sort it all out into the right boxes for the year ahead. I have finally given in to writing mass produced form letters. You have all been so wonderful about writing and I think of you everyday. So I apologize, but between pouring Tang powder drink mix into plastic bags and running back and forth to Sydney there isn't much time.

Let me bring you up to date with what is happening down under. Yes, we finally got that mystery machine called a boat! It was a month-and-a-half overdue, but here it is and a true beaut! The name of our little boat is "Tom Thumb" after the first vessel of an early explorer, Matthew Flinders. In fact, it was the only boat that Matthew Flinders ever had that did not leak! So we have taken that as a good omen. Since this is the first boat of its type, we've received some funny looks and even more amazed faces as we tell people what we are going to do.

Sponsorship, ahh, yes. This has been on the minds of many. We have been very successful in getting heaps of gear donated. Just yesterday Mark and I received a year's supply of Speedo swimwear. We have suits in every style and color. Mark has some darling red ones with little boats on them. However, even with all this gear we are still looking for a cash sponsor. We've tried everything from A to Z, sent over 60 proposals, had numerous meetings, all to end in, "No, sorry! It certainly sounds exciting. Best wishes and good luck!" As the song says, "When the going gets tough, the tough get going," or should I say "sailing" in our case. We have both entered the condition of debt, which we feel is better than not doing the sail. We've worked too hard and dreamed too long to let the small matter of money get in the way.

Well mates, I hear Mark asking, "Where is the wrench?" I hope this letter finds you all well and happy.

Love, Sue

Our collection of supplies had expanded. The basic supplies consisted of our clothing in the front hatches of each hull, fishing and camping supplies to be used regularly in the rear hatches, sleeping bags and tents stuffed in garbage bags tied behind seats, two twenty-gallon and four five-gallon fresh water containers, five gallons of outboard fuel, and four water-tight barrels holding food and general supplies below decks and one for emergency on top. Our emergency barrel contained an emergency beacon (EPIRB), torch, flares, compass, two gallons of water, two days emergency food, first-aid kit, fishing gear, emergency stove and matches. We also had a ten-channel 27-MHz radio powered by a solar panel and a motorcycle battery to store the energy with an aerial up the mast. On deck behind the mast, strapped to the trampoline, was a large waterproof bag containing charts, the day's food, our O'Neil wetsuits when not in use, two blow-up rollerbags to help haul *Tom* up the beach, a sea anchor, an ordinary anchor, and for the occasional calmer day, a waterproof radio/cassette and reading material. When fully loaded *Tom* wallowed, rather than sailed, but then we weren't racing around Australia.

When it appeared that we were going to meet our departure date, my parents had a farewell party at home with family and friends. It was a nice thought, but I did not want to be there. There was still so much to do and politely answering continuous questions for which I didn't have answers was not my idea of fun. I was feeling stressed and frustrated. One minute I remember reaching for dessert, the next I woke up in bed two hours later with a splitting headache. I had apparently collapsed and had a fit. Sue had quickly come to my aid. Family had somewhat calmed down by now, and guests had long since departed, offering their sympathies and concern. "Mark, you have to see a doctor. Don't you think that would be wise?" my father calmly suggested.

I grimaced at the thought of well-meaning medical advice saying I should not go on the trip. However, at the insistence of Sue and my parents I agreed, even though everyone knew I would not give up on this trip. I had experienced a similar fit ten years before followed by every test under the sun which all proved inconclusive. I was certainly not going to change my life now, "just in case something might happen!" Sure enough, the local doctor advised me to "reconsider" the trip and I politely said thank you and left, assuring Sue and my parents I would take it much easier from here. They knew I wasn't about to postpone anything, especially not this trip. "At least I know what to do," said Sue, having lived with a friend who was epileptic. We didn't talk about it again.

One final point we hadn't quite got around to organizing was how Sue was legally going to stay in Australia for the next two years on just a three-month visitor's visa. It was one of those things that would just happen once the details of the trip were worked out. After many urgent letters, phonecalls, a visit to my local Federal member of parliament, Michael Lee, a letter to the U.S. Ambassador to Australia and a full medical checkup, a two year extension finally came through the day before we sailed!

May 3rd arrived and it was a case of now or never. I had spent the previous day with Peter Pool bolting on the last minute pieces, somehow believing we were ready, as Sue rushed around town buying final essentials. In a torrential downpour we met at Rose Bay on Sydney harbor's southern shore. Sue was dripping wet and laden with supplies. We set the mast and launched *Tom* to motor around to the Royal Cruising Yacht Club at Rushcutters Bay, where we had arranged to leave him moored for the night. On the way we dropped in to visit our friends aboard *Zebu*, the Operation Raleigh square-rigged ship which was on its way around the world. Having sailed from the Pacific Islands, they looked in wonder at our small boat and wished us luck. We tied up as best we could at the yacht club, on docks made for yachts rather than small catamarans, and were more worried about theft than any damage to our shining new boat. The staff merely shook their heads at the sight of our boat, especially as the modern, multi-million dollar sloop opposite us had a tender, which was the same size as *Tom*, they winched aboard on davits!

Neither of us slept very well that night, knowing that the morning would bring a day that we had only ever dreamed and talked about. It dawned sunny with light northeast to southeast winds forecast. The weather would now be our primary piece of news for the day. The morning was a blur as we motored over to Pier 1 near Sydney's Rocks area for the official farewell. Relatives, school friends I hadn't seen for ten years, and newspaper and TV journalists all said their hellos and farewells. "So, how long have you two been insane?" was the opening question from the Sunday Telegraph journalist. After answering questions like that and posing for a multitude of photos, someone thankfully suggested it was time to go. With final hugs and kisses from friends and family and tears from my mother, even though we would see her again the next day at home in Terrigal, we pushed off through a sea of streamers. "Don't worry, we will find you sponsorship," yelled Jan Murray in a final flurry of promotion and well wishing.

We rounded the corner of Pier 1 and went under the Sydney Harbor Bridge, a symbol in itself of departing Sydney. After looking back to the waving hands and the silhouette of Peter Pool atop a pier like a seagull, movie camera in hand, we turned and looked down the harbor toward the sea. There was not a breath of wind and somehow we had agreed to be towed down the harbor by some of Peter Pool's mates in an inflatable dinghy. It wouldn't have been too bad except they had obtained special permission for a red flare to mark our departure, which now blew back and choked Sue and I, making it hard to see each other, let alone the harbor. *Tom Thumb* bobbed like a cork as we sailed between the towering 60-foot cliffs of Sydney Heads, the most welcomed sight in the world to 1800s English settlers and convicts after months at sea. We dropped the towline, gave our thanks and final farewells and with a laugh, perhaps to mask the uncertainty of what lay ahead, yelled, "See you in twelve months."

I had never sailed out through the heads themselves and was in awe as *Tom Thumb* responded to the sea breeze and we headed out to sea. Rounding North Head and seeing the coast stretch away from us into the distance Sue turned and asked, "where to from here?" I was stunned. After all the years of dreaming, months of intensive planning and frustrations, here we were finally sailing, finally doing what we had spent so long talking about. I looked at the sea now scooting beneath our small, white hulls and off into the distance where the disappearing headlands marked our future. "Left," I replied. "If we keep Australia on the left we should be OK."

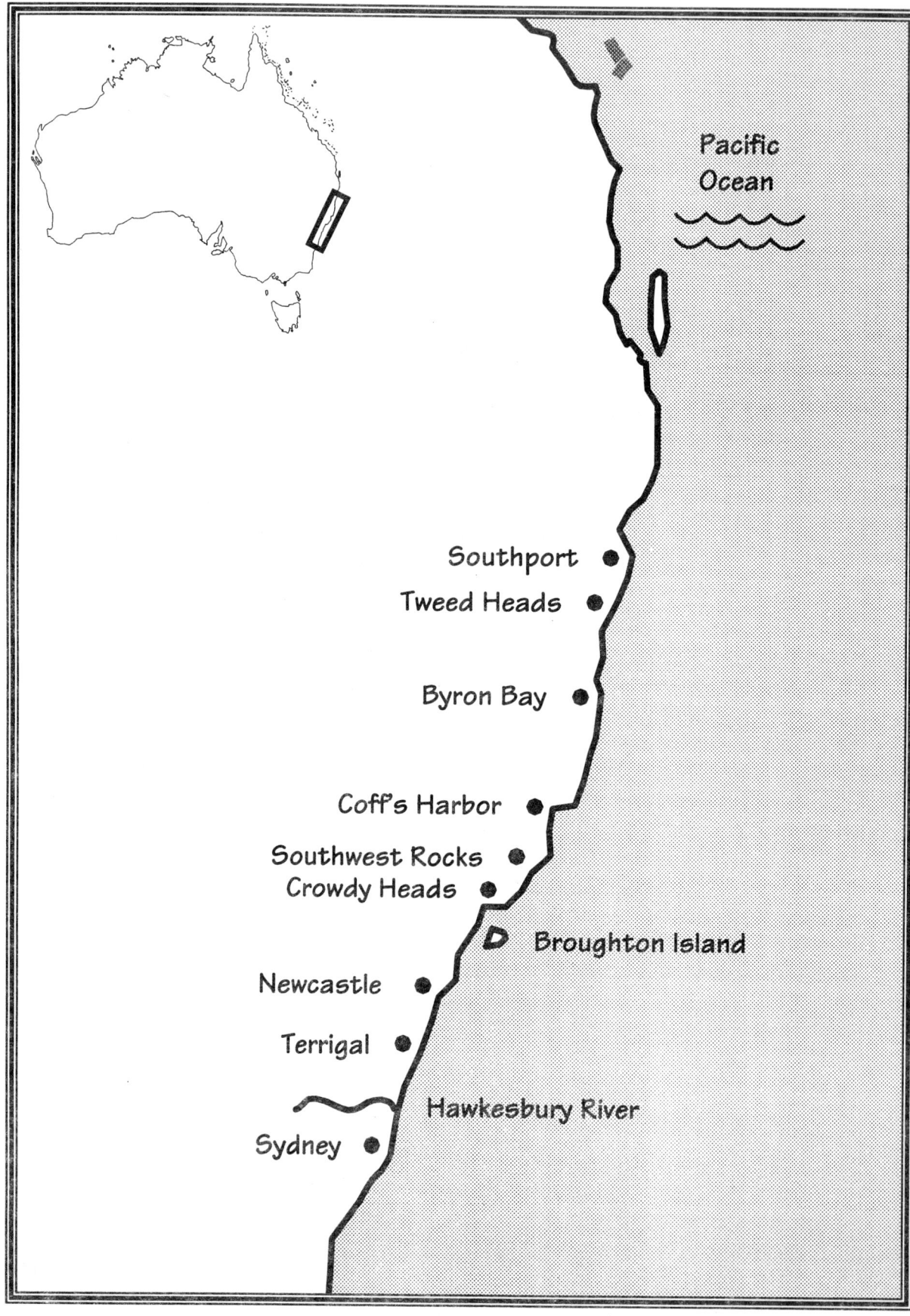

Chapter 2

Crossing the Bars
Sydney to Southport

We shuffled around the trampoline, adjusting cleats and ropes, exploring the four square yards of open space 18 inches off the water that would be our home and transport for the next year. It sagged under the combined weight of us and a large, black, waterproof bag that held all the supplies we needed on hand. This contained a water-proof barrel with our emergency supplies, our chart for that section of the coast, and a few guide books, along with other containers and bags for food, extra spray jackets and whatever else the day might demand.

All was going well with *Tom's* new fittings and last minute alterations as we slowly sailed north past the familiar beachside suburbs of Sydney. He did not sail like any normal racing catamaran, with his two wide, sea-kayak hulls laden with gear. Rather than even attempting to raise a hull clear of the water we planed along with the two upturned bows splitting the swells. In the cool autumn breeze of the afternoon, we were grateful for the calm conditions. Sue began reading our *Cruising the New South Wales Coast* yachting guide and following the chart. It didn't take long before she felt green and took over skippering to help recover.

Due to the latest port strikes in Sydney we had to slalom around anchored container ships held out to sea. The seas were slight with calm winds, so it was strange to hear the media coverage later of an injured seaman being winched by helicopter off one of these ships that afternoon, *In dangerous seas and windy conditions the courageous efforts of the helicopter pilot saved the seaman's life!* We must have missed something! If it was that dramatic we could have pulled *Tom* alongside and taken the seaman onboard ourselves.

"Whatever you do, make sure you are well out from Long Reef," warned Peter Pool before our departure. "Watch out for the Reef ..." The voice was still with me, but I need not have worried. Perhaps it was the farewell champagne and lack of food as we had forgotten to pack any lunch on deck, but we soon found ourselves a good few miles offshore and well clear of any reefs. In fact, we were a bit too well clear of the coast! As the prominent white lighthouse of Barrenjoey Headland came into view, marking the northern limits of Sydney, we headed to shore for our first overnight landing.

Some hours later, with the afternoon sun quickly sinking, we sailed into the protected waters of Pittwater Bay and came ashore next to a suburban park, cafe and seaplane dock. We were still in the suburbs of Sydney, yet we felt in a different world of our own. We carried the outboard and waterproof bag up the beach before struggling with cold fingers to unstrap the trampoline. Then we removed the neoprene sprayskirts from the hull cockpits and dragged our heavier watertight barrels up the beach. I was surprised and concerned to see a few inches of water sloshing around in the hulls and pumped them dry. With most of the weight out we blew up two plastic roller airbags and, placing one under each hull, hauled *Tom* clear of the high water mark. This was to be a daily process and it had taken us half an hour.

We emptied equipment all over the beach, trying to remember where the essentials had been packed. In an attempt to remain inconspicuous while camping on the shores of a suburban park, we opted to sleep on the trampoline under a boom-tent we had invented. As I tied the final knots, two young fellows appeared. "G'day. Are you the two that left the harbor today? We saw you on TV!" So much for being inconspicuous, but at least we did get some media coverage! Sue eventually found the stove and we both anxiously watched the water boil. Our rushed breakfast only twelve hours earlier seemed like another lifetime ago. We happily watched the sunset while shoveling down big bowls full of macaroni and cheese.

In the last of the light we wandered over the sandhills to look at the sea, taking in the peace and the realization that we were finally both back where we loved, to be outdoors. No longer did we have to contend with the pressures of Sydney traffic, business meetings, getting things ready and being frustrated at other people's lack of a sense of urgency. It was now up to us and the will of the wind.

"Are you awake?"

"Yep."

"What time is it?"

"One o'clock, go back to sleep"

"What time is sunrise?"

It was a long, uncomfortable night as we sagged into the center of the trampoline and realized how cold it can be sleeping under a tarp with a clear autumn sky. Thankfully, the sun shone for us the next morning as we heated up a cup of tea and ran around *Tom* to get warm. "How far are the tropics?" asked Sue, rubbing her hands together in thermal gloves.

Getting all the supplies back in was just as confusing as finding them the day before. "It did all fit, didn't it?" joked Sue, as we struggled into our daily uniform of O'Neil Wetsuits, Marlin spray jackets and life jackets and pushed off from shore with sails set. In a fresh morning breeze we broadreached across a calm sea, passing our earlier circumnavigation success, Lion Island, which marked the entrance to the Hawkesbury River. Captain Cook had suggested that it looked like a lion guarding the entrance, and thus the name. Although the Dutch, Indonesian and Portuguese explorers and sailors had all found parts of the Great South Continent before him (not to mention the aborigines who already lived here), it was Cook, a British sea captain, who was credited with discovering Australia in 1770. He was one of the first to chart the east coast and many places still bear the names he gave them.

As *Tom* sliced through the swells, leaving a streaming foam wake, I remembered why I had wanted to sail again! The white main, with three small panels of the Australian national colors of green and gold at its top, stiffened as it caught the full strength of the breeze. The small jib furled out and Sue trimmed its shape as we finally got the feel for our boat. *Tom Thumb* skimmed across the swells, planing rather than slicing like a normal catamaran, although he still gave the same thrill of producing a foaming wake and being one with the ocean. Sue followed the chart, somewhat more easily without the farewell champagne, as we passed headlands, beaches and reefs, transferring our experience of land travel and compass bearings to the water and nautical maps. Neither of us had navigated much on the sea before, but as we were no more than a few miles from shore, we were confident that our outdoor skills gathered from years of hiking would, at the very least, keep Australia on the left.

Our first month along the New South Wales coast would require much patience as the Tasman Sea could build up to large swells of nine to twelve feet within a day as weather systems came in from the west. Regular river inlets with dangerous crossings over their sandy bars were scattered along the coast and did not provide much protection. Rocky headlands separated coves and long stretches of unbroken golden sand, with a backdrop of the Great Dividing Range rising up to 3,500 feet inland. The range flowed all the way up the east coast weaving its way to and from the shore. *Tom* could manage up to a five-foot wave onto the beach, but our landings, dependent on swell, wind strength, and tide, would need to be carefully assessed each day.

We rounded the prominent Cape Three Points, again named by Cook, and looked north as Sydney disappeared behind us. Without us knowing at the time, my parents were at the Cape lookout attempting to spot our progress up the coast. At first they didn't think that the white dot two miles out to sea could be us. When they realized it actually was, they were taken aback by how small *Tom* actually was on the vast, blue background of the Tasman Sea. We turned to head for The Skillion, a headland at Terrigal, and our next landing. This was my homeport — the place where I grew up and the place where I had learned to sail. My parents drove up to the sheltered Haven Beach just as we sailed ashore. There were hugs all around, even though we had only said goodbye yesterday.

We had planned a two-day break to organize the last of our equipment and say a quieter farewell to family. Apart from having hot showers and good food, we were keen to spend some time fine-tuning our equipment and its storage. It rained for the two days and we were grateful for the roof above our heads, rather than the tent.

The departure from Terrigal was even harder than from Sydney. It was the last time we would see my parents for over a year and from here, we were definitely on our own. It was difficult to say very much, or to adequately thank them. Instead of doing just a few laps around the buoys on the weekends, this would be one big lap around Australia! My mother shed enough tears to float *Tom* off the beach. We watched the huddled, waving shapes of my parents until they disappeared from view.

It was a calm, flat day and we decided to run in our small outboard by motor sailing over the slick gray ocean. Despite the steady drone of the motor, there was a strange, dreamlike feeling of passing through a dull watercolor painting, with hardly a splash of water or puff of wind to remind us we were part of it. It was good to have such a calm day to sort out things on deck. We also had time to experiment with mounting chair back-supports to the trampoline to give us some level of comfort.

We passed the coastal towns of Bateau Bay and The Entrance where, as a boy, I had spent many nights prawning with large drag nets, in the shallow lakes. Then, as we rounded Norah Head, the sky ahead filled with dark, threatening clouds and a fresh wind sprang up, bringing in an afternoon chill. We contemplated our options of tacking around the next headland into Catherine Hill Bay or retreating to the familiar protection of Norah Head. We knew there was a protected beach next to a boat ramp about one mile back, so we retreated for the safety of a known campsite.

As we came in to land I leaned over the side, my head almost under water to remove our slotted fins mounted in the hulls. These were part of the original design of the Catcan and, instead of a keel or dagger boards, were supposed to help us sail more directly into the wind. They required much patience, and a solid knock while reaching under the boat to remove them before landing. It wasn't long before they were sent home and we did without them. We quickly popped up our Eureka tent, dried off and stuffed down dinner before the storm hit. After a few flashes of lightening and a splatter of rain we had time for a brief walk around the headland in the fading light. I had often picnicked here and looked further up the coast, wishing I could explore it. Tomorrow we would be venturing to the furthest headlands and beyond, and we would do so again the day after that! It was hard to image this was now our way of life.

The lighthouse on Norah Head is a prominent landmark to coastal shipping even during the day, and one of the few remaining manned lighthouses on the mainland. The lighthouse keeper had seen us turn and come in and was intrigued by our story and what we were planning to do.

"Did you hear the weather alert?" he grinned. "There's been an earthquake in Hawaii! They reckon the tidal waves may reach Australia. Still want to be out in your little boat then?"

Sue was getting used to this dry, cynical Australian humor by now.

The next morning we looked out from our warm tent reassured that the tidal wave had missed us. The day was wet and unsettled, with choppy seas and strong southerly winds, so we reluctantly decided to wait it out. Patience was going to be our greatest test in the early days. At least the lay-off gave me the chance for some routine maintenance, which was just as well. *Tom* had a hole in one hull. It suddenly made sense as to why one hull had been taking in more water and the boat seemed sluggish after a long day. The one-inch puncture had probably happened while taking *Tom* off the trailer in Sydney when he was so heavily laden. Shaking my head at my own stupidity, I realized how lucky we were to have discovered it now and that it had not caused any major damage or a capsize. I pulled out our extensive repair kit of a rivet gun, rivets, spare nuts and bolts, a hand drill, fiberglass repair kit, duct tape and an assortment of spare parts and was glad that we were at least prepared. Half an hour later, after a quick sanding and patch of fiberglass mat and resin, the problem was solved. *Tom* now had one patch and didn't look quite so new.

With calm conditions the next day we motored out to find some wind and eventually sail on to the city of Newcastle. It was a slow meander up the coast past the inlets of Swansea and long sections of empty beach broken by pronounced rocky headlands. We started to get into a routine of sharing skippering, reading charts and guide books, eating and just taking in the view. Seagulls, terns and the occasional school of fish passed by. The swell was up and we waved to surprised surfers at the point breaks. In the cool afternoon the houses and surfclubs of Newcastle's northern beaches came into view. We decided to go into the harbor entrance and find a sheltered campsite. A skyline of cranes and smoke stacks as well as lines of cargo ships out from the harbor, indicated the main industry in Newcastle, a large steel works.

Under the shadows of the skyline we pulled up on a small strip of sand just inside the harbor entrance, backed by a bare dirt parking lot. We shared the beach with a few hardy local families fishing in the afternoon cool. After we made a quick phone call the local press came down to interview us at our first port of call since Sydney. The questions had a familiar touch of cynicism, but they enjoyed our tidal wave story. Eating take-out fish and chips, we admired the fierce red sunset through the smoke of the steelworks before clearing our campsite among food rubbish and used condoms.

It was a cold, foggy night and we were grateful to get away the next morning. We longed to be making distance to warmer waters and the natural beauty of Australia's tropical north. Stockton Bight stretched away into the distance, a 20-mile unbroken stretch of golden sand backed by low bush-covered dunes. A six-foot swell crashed ashore and we were glad to stay clear. It was our best day's sailing yet as we broadreached up the coast surfing the swells all the way. To add to our enjoyment, Sue hooked our first fish while trailing a line, landing a small mackerel on *Tom*'s trampoline. We were tired from a day of continuous sailing, so the tall, rocky headlands of Toomeree and Yacaaba, which marked the spectacular entrance to the natural harbor of Port Stephens, were a welcome sight. We had sailed the coastline of our first nautical chart, leaving only 59 similar charts that mapped the entire Australian coast. We felt proud of our first small step.

The beautiful clear, blue waters of Port Stephens tempted us to stay on and explore the hundreds of miles of protected waterways of the Myall Lakes, but we were still too close to home and felt the need to keep going. After stocking up on supplies in the small community of Shoal Bay, we sailed out the next morning between the high headlands and scattered islands at the port entrance. We had been warned of the tidal current that can run at two knots and produces large waves if running against the wind. Luckily the current and wind was with us and, smashing through the chop, we were soon back out to the Pacific Ocean.

We were headed for a short afternoon sail over to Broughton Island, only a few miles off the coast and about ten miles north. Some locals we'd met at Port Stephens had highly recommended a visit to this national park of just a few square miles. It was a spectacular sight as we sailed through gray choppy swells, the cliff-lined entrance of Port Stephens behind us, toward the distant low gray island. Shafts of sunlight beamed between darkened clouds to highlight the rising inland mountains of Barrington Tops. With not a person, boat or building in sight it was the wildest and most beautiful landscape we had seen yet, but with rising winds and large swells we were grateful that the island was coming closer. *Tom* scooted into the protected and empty beach on the northern lee side of the island and we quickly pitched camp in readiness for the imminent storm. Peering out from the tent through the beating rain, we were moved by the wild beauty of our surroundings as we looked across a low grass island to a wild white capped sea. The isolated sandy coast of the Myall Lakes National Park stretched into the distance, with the Barrington Tops mountains in the background shrouded in black cloud and silhouetted by bolts of lighting.

Sue noted in the logbook, *The storm came in with southerly winds at 15-20 knots, gusting to 30 knots and rough seas. Best part of the day was catching a bream which we had for lunch.* The storm stayed for the next four days. It was a wild scene as plumes of spray leapt off huge swells that broke around both corners of the island. On the second day, concerned that people may be wondering where we were, we ventured off by foot to the holiday fishing village on the other side of the island. We climbed through knee-high grass for over a mile, trying not to disturb the mutton bird burrows hidden along the trail. The southerly wind gusted over our heads as we dropped down a rocky cliff into the small protected Esmeralda Cove.

Weather-beaten timber shacks and fishing boats at anchor made me feel I had just stepped into a documentary on Scandinavia or the Scottish North Sea coast. Men wearing woolen beanies stood around a central shack sharing cigarettes and fishing stories, while women sat on chairs drinking mugs of tea or coffee with children running amongst them. They seemed to be a regular community, going about their usual day. They were rather stunned at our arrival from seemingly nowhere on this wild day. We introduced ourselves and explained what we were doing and after much head shaking and questions of the "Are you serious?" type, we were offered the use of their radio and invited for coffee. The local volunteer Coastal Patrol at Port Stephens happily passed a message on to my parents by telephone that we were OK. When my mother heard that it was the Coast Patrol on the phone she nearly fainted in anticipation of bad news but was relieved to know we were doing well.

The de facto Lord and Lady of the Esmerelda Cove community, George and his wife, Shirley, took us under their wing and told us about the island. The shacks were built by returned servicemen from the Second World War who were offered the opportunity to build their own accommodation on land leased to them for virtually nothing by the government. For some they became a home or base for fishing and for others a cheap holiday place for the family. Many shacks had now been part of the family for up to three generations and there was a strong emotional attachment to them. Although small, most were solid buildings that were carefully maintained with leftover building scraps, their owners usually ignoring building regulations.

However, as with other Australian National Parks, management was now trying to reclaim such buildings and knock them down. George and the community of Broughton Island were putting up a fight, claiming that their radio base provided an important service for seafarers, which we could now certainly support. George mentioned he was off to Port Stephens tomorrow if we needed anything. Sue was happy to have the chance to shop while I was keen to stay on the island and explore. I waved goodbye from the tent as she hiked over the trail early the next morning to meet George. It was nice to have time to read and explore further parts of the island, or just watch the swells foaming past. As night fell I had started to prepare dinner when Sue whooped and rolled down the grassy bank beside me, shopping bags falling around her. She had apparently had a great day with George and three of the local Broughton men, who, after a brief shopping trip, had spent the rest of afternoon in the Port Stephens pub teaching an American gal how to drink Australian beer and play pool. George introduced her as his girl and they lined up glasses of all the different types of draft beer and then drank them all! I laughed, managed to get her to eat some dinner and poured her into bed. She certainly slept well that night, even if she was rather slow to rise the next morning.

That afternoon we were surprised when a Hobie 16-foot catamaran crewed by two young guys came racing around the headland and pulled into our beach. They had sailed over from Port Stephens not realizing how big the seas were when they left the bay. We shared a cup of tea, before they headed off back to the mainland anxiously negotiating the nine to twelve foot swells around the point. We stood on the headland watching them rise and disappear behind each swell realizing how small *Tom* must look on the open sea. We did not hear any emergency calls on the radio so we assumed they made it safely.

The next day we reluctantly said farewell to Broughton Island, which had been a safe and friendly haven, although the seas were still not quite as calm as when we had arrived. With just the mainsail set, *Tom* quickly surfed in the 15- to 20-knot winds and six-to-nine foot swells. It was exciting, if not downright scary, planing down the faces of the huge swells as spray flew off the sides of both hulls, leaving a wide foaming wake. If it was racing it would be great, but this was cruising and we had to get *Tom* through many more miles. I let out the sail and we wallowed off the back of the swells down the long beach and past Sugarloaf Point with its prominent lighthouse above the community of Seal Rocks. Sailing out wide of the headland we didn't have any luck spotting seals on the rocky outcrops through the pounding surf. We huddled under lifejackets and wetsuits, with thermal underwear underneath, dodging the spray in a futile attempt to keep our cheese and salami sandwiches from being soaked. The green hills and mountains rose steeply from the coast, providing a change from the low sand dunes and scrub. After being on the water and hanging on since 7:30 A.M. we pulled into the protection of Charlotte Head early in the afternoon with the assistance of a group of fishermen. After the usual initial speculation from them about our trip we shared a roaring fire and stories into the night. They were doing commercial net fishing for baitfish along the coast. It had not been a good season so far and they were hoping for better luck. It was good to meet people who shared our way of life, camping on different beaches and going with the flow of nature.

The next day in calmer weather we made slow but steady progress before pulling in at Crowdy Heads, a small holiday fishing village and harbor with a beach and sweeping bay tucked in behind the headland. After landing and once again being helped up the beach by fishermen, I went to town for supplies. I returned half an hour later to find Sue huddled beside *Tom* and in tears. She had reached a point of total frustration from not being able to undo her wardrobe hatch cover or pull down *Tom*'s mainsail. "I was scared coming off Broughton Island," she confessed. "I just don't feel comfortable in big swells and winds." I agreed we should have waited another day. Surfing down the face of the swells in strong winds had been hard work and had scared me at times. The *what if's* were constantly going through my head — if we had tipped over in those conditions there was no telling the damage it could do to us and *Tom*. What if one of us was injured, or we couldn't save ourselves, or nobody found us? I told myself our emergency barrel was well prepared and we could always pop off a canoe hull and paddle to shore.

We were slowly coming to terms with the trip and life aboard a 16-foot catamaran. There were days of total wonder and enjoyment, and days of anxiety and hard work. I shared Sue's anxiety inside, but rarely showed it. I felt a responsibility to succeed and a need to stay focused. We were often frustrated with each other — me with Sue's lack of what appeared to be common sense, and Sue with me because I expected so much of her and pushed her. In a low moment we were pleasantly surprised by the welcome of Fred, the Crowdy Heads Surf Club caretaker who offered us a hot shower and dinner at the club which immediately cheered us both up. A salt of the earth surfclub member, Fred shared his stories of travelling Australia, proudly showing off his new VW four-wheel-drive camper in the garage. The next morning dawned stormy and wet and we gratefully took up Fred's offer of a tour around town. Crowdy Heads and the nearby town of Harrington had seen their heyday as shipping and fishing ports, but were now quieter holiday places. The day included a few hours in the local Harrington Hotel enjoying a pub lunch and playing pool while watching the rain come down.

Fred was the ultimate host that evening, insisting we sleep at the club. As we settled in he proudly presented us with two champagne glasses, a bottle of champagne and a television in the comfort of a bedroom. We were stunned and humbled by the hospitality. To help us get away at dawn Fred also insisted on cooking us breakfast the following morning before helping to launch *Tom*. Halfway out through the surf Sue raced back up the beach to give Fred a big hug goodbye. He certainly had put Crowdy Heads on the map.

Conditions were calm as we passed Tacking Point, named by Matthew Flinders while surveying on his ship, the *Investigator,* in 1802. He had noted it as a potential port with a rocky entrance before being forced to tack away. It was later named Port Macquarie by explorer John Oxley, after the then Governor of New South Wales. As in so many settlements of its time it had served as a penal colony for a short period. It was of great importance for new settlers to find safe anchorages for ships, and Port Macquarie had its share of mishaps. With only nine feet over the bar it was hazardous and several ships had been wrecked attempting to cross that bar. An attempt was made to build a wharf further north at Trial Bay as a penal colony project, but it too met with problems from the strong east coast swell. By the time breakwalls were established in the late 1800's at Port Macquarie and many other New South Wales coastal ports, they had become accessible to road or rail anyway.

However this stretch of coast still maintained its reputation for dangerous river bars and lives are regularly lost in big seas.

After a few more days of following cruising yachts up the coast via South West Rocks and Trial Bay we finally pulled into the port of Coffs Harbor. This man-made harbor surrounding some small islands, had the luxury of a yacht club and floating marina. As soon as we had parked *Tom* in the floating docks of the yacht club, Salvador, the skipper of the neighboring yacht, asked if he could help in any way. A cup of coffee with Salvador, his wife and young daughter became dinner and a bed aboard their yacht for the next three days. We were made to feel right at home as part of the cruising fraternity, surrounded by a variety of yachting families and the hospitable yacht club. In between taking stock of our gear and making minor adjustments to *Tom* we happily shared sailing stories with cruising couples and families all headed north for the winter. For yachts, Coffs Harbor is one of the few harbors with a marina on the New South Wales north coast that doesn't require crossing a river bar.

After almost three weeks and 300 miles of successful travel the press questions were becoming less cynical and we began to enjoy newspaper and radio interviews rather than fearing them. Despite being a few days behind schedule we felt proud of ourselves. Coffs Harbor was the mailing point to pick up our first supply box containing sponsored food supplements, a new set of charts and mail from friends and family which were all appreciated. In between repairs we were fortunate to have the loan of a friend's car for a tour around the hinterland of the Dorrigo Plateau, an impressive mountain plateau 12 to 24 miles inland from the coast. It was exciting to see the beautiful gorges and rainforest that we had been imagining when looking from the sea.

For contrast, I also took Sue to the renowned tourist icon called the Big Banana, a 90-foot long, yellow fiberglass construction. It revived my childhood memories of the taste of a frozen chocolate-coated banana on a stick. It also somehow made a statement about the delicate balance in this area between its agriculture industry and the growing tourism market. Back at the harbor we saw a young boy being helped to load a tuna onto his bicycle for the ride home. The fish was almost bigger than the bike and he had apparently struggled for over an hour to bring it onto the rocks on Mutton Bird Island. After some humorous balancing acts someone volunteered to call Mum from the yacht club and arrange for a lift home.

We waited for three days for a southerly blow to pass, yet again, before setting off for our first major geographical landmark, the eastern-most point of Australia. We had three quick days of sailing past some of New South Wales' most renowned surfing beaches such as Crescent Head and Lennox Head, and registered our longest day yet of 60 miles. Sandon River and Evans Head provided beautiful isolated beaches to surf onto and camp at night with no one in sight. I was surprised at how much of the coastline was untouched. In between the small coastal towns, only the occasional four-wheel-drive vehicle visited the coast. For the first time since leaving Sydney we actually sailed for a day without wetsuits, a sure sign we were nearing Queensland and the tropics!

Late that day a shaft of golden afternoon light lit up a high rocky headland, with the Cape Byron lighthouse brilliant white against the iridescent green hilltop. Hovering around this majestic backdrop like a butterfly, was a multicolored hang-glider. I was mesmerized for the moment by this glowing picture. It marked a significant point of our journey as we had made it to the eastern-most point of the Australian mainland. We sailed close by the steep rock walls below the lighthouse and waved to a few surprised tourists. Rounding the headland we carefully looked behind us to make sure we were not going to get swept in by the famed point break that wraps around to a beautiful bay. Byron had become the north coast mecca of surfers, alternative lifestylers, cool well-to-doers and celebrities. It was chic little town that catered to "The California set," as Sue called it — people in search of something and someplace.

We landed at the quieter end of the beach appreciating that some sensible development had allowed for the retention of a wide nature strip along the sand dunes. As we sipped our evening wine and contemplated our day's efforts we chatted with a local couple who mused on the downfall of Byron Bay to "those bloody hippy characters and the developers." We sympathized with their dilemma. Not long after they left we chatted with two fellows wearing sarongs with long flowing beards and carrying an umbrella. They wished us peace in our journey as they departed. We'd had trouble coping with the cultural diversity of Byron Bay and we'd only been here a few hours!

Keeping Australia On the Left

The sail to the northern New South Wales town of Tweed Heads was cruising at its finest, with calm seas and warming sunshine encouraging us. The standard good cruising day would start at first light around 6 to 7 A.M. We would have breakfasted and be on the water within an hour in the early morning off-shore breeze. If we were lucky the breezes stayed with us until a southeast sea breeze came up and blew us ashore in the early afternoon around 3 or 4 P.M., before the sun set at 5:30 P.M. It would be sunny and warm every day as soon as we crossed the state border into Queensland, or so the advertising slogan suggested, "Queensland — beautiful one day, perfect the next!" Perfection has its price however, as we soon found the beauty of untouched beaches replaced by the vacation apartment towers of Coolangatta and the Gold Coast.

Pulling into Coolangatta beach for the night we felt crowded and threatened by these towering edifices shading the beach with their imposing concrete and glass. After the natural beauty of the New South Wales coast they appeared strange and foreign to the beach and sea, with *Tom* perched beneath their glare. The even higher towers of Southport and the Gold Coast could be seen stretching north along the coast. No headlands beckoned here. Any natural beauty had long been destroyed, and we wanted to leave it all behind.

Twelve miles across the bay was the Southport Bar, our passage to Queensland. Peter Pool's words came back to me, "Watch Southport Bar, it's dangerous. Once you are inside it, you are basically inside the reef (the Barrier Reef). If you make it there, you'll make it around Australia." We had continued to hear warnings about this and other bars as we ventured up the coast, most of them now reshaped river mouths with permanent breakwalls. Many experienced sailors had come undone on them before. On an outgoing tide against the swell you could see why, as huge waves peaked out of nowhere to crash through the inlet. There was a strong wind warning for the afternoon as we patiently waited on the beach for the incoming tide to peak. Not wanting to stay a moment longer I assured Sue that by the time we got there the tide would be about right. With just the mainsail set we flew across the bay, screaming off the swells covered in spray as the wind came up to an early 25 knots. It was too late to go back and after an hour the walls of the breakwater came into view. Neither of us talked, not wanting to acknowledge our fear.

Crossing the Bars

We saw some fishing boats going in and then looked again as there were white foaming waves breaking everywhere. I nervously looked at Sue and yelled for her to start looking for the best passage. The wind was getting stronger and I wasn't about to stop. She stood and gripped the mast, peering out over the rising swells. As we leveled up outside the breakwalls we looked at each other in disbelief. The waves we had seen breaking were on the other side of the breakwall and beach area. Before us was a calm flat passage. Our timing with the tide was perfect and we screamed over Southport Bar, waving to stunned fishermen on the breakwalls. We had made it — we were inside the reef and were in Queensland. Now we knew we could make it around Australia.

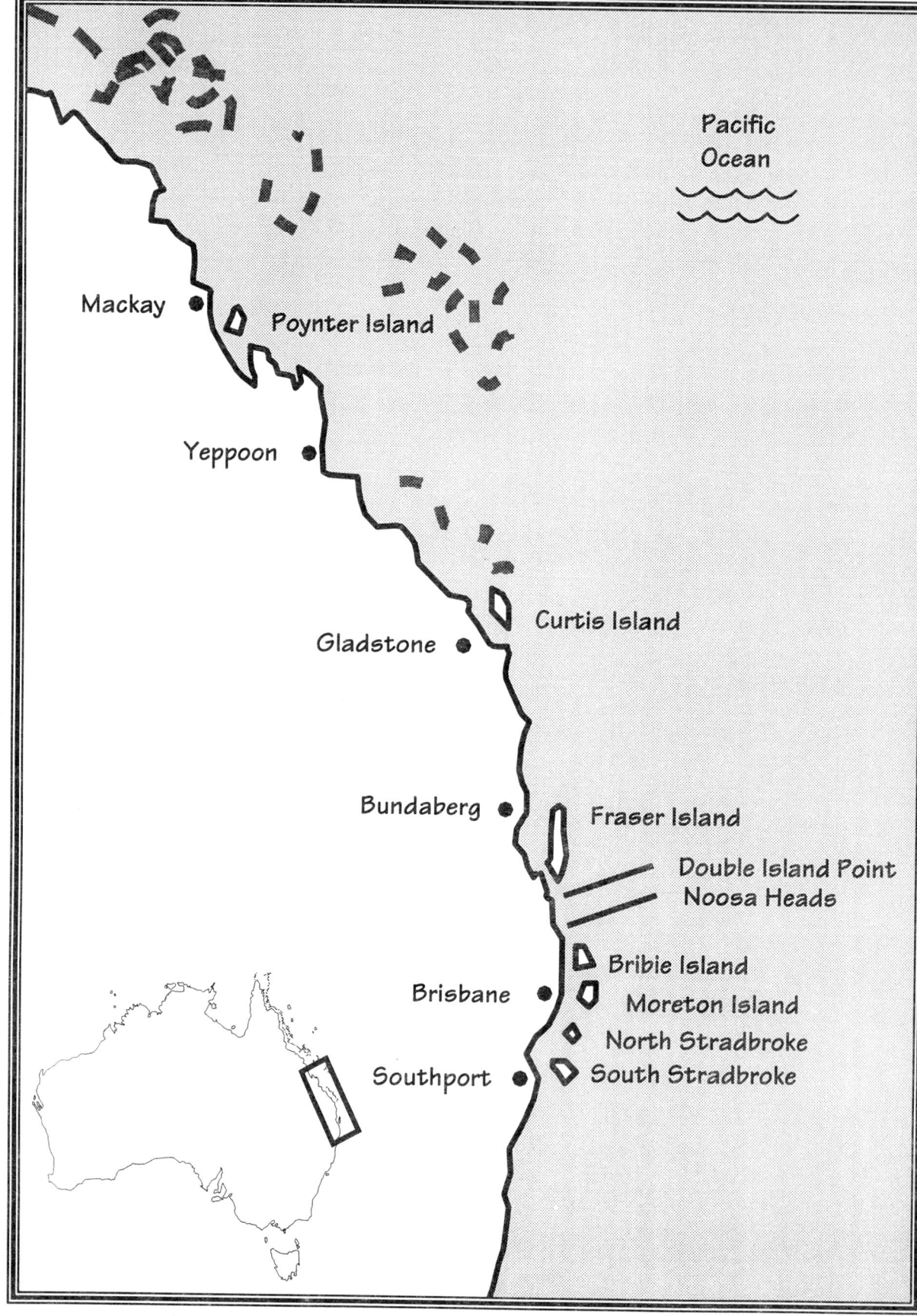

Chapter 3

Canefields and Beaches
Southport to Mackay

The Gold Coast skyscrapers cast long afternoon shadows over the small white structure of the Southport yacht club. We tried to look like we belonged as we tied up at the floating dock amidst millions of dollars worth of yachts. The luxury of a hot shower at the club was worth the $14 for our berth for the night, if we only had a bed to sleep on rather than a wet trampoline. We must have scrubbed up all right as our next door neighbor, Ron, invited us on board his Cavalier 30-T, *RSVP*. You tend to meet all your neighbors when you don't have any walls.

Ron was the ultimate host, offering drinks and a bed on board his yacht for the night. We happily joined him for dinner at a Mexican restaurant, comforted in knowing we were not likely to fall overboard in our sleep if we had too much to drink. We were impressed by Ron's tales of chartering and ocean races, but didn't dare hint at our limited experience. We'd made it to Queensland and we felt justifiably proud.

After a comfortable sleep-in, with many thanks to Ron and yet another lovely hot shower, we headed off for what we expected to be a casual day sailing up the inside of Stradbroke Island toward Brisbane, the capital of Queensland. It was blowing at 25 to 35 knots and the wind was creatively reshaping some newly erected colorful marquees near the Southport bar entrance. A procession of boats continued to pass us, heading for what seemed a crazy passage out to sea on such a windy day.

We realized that today was the official opening of the new Southport Bar, to be conducted by none other than Joh Bjelke-Peterson, the well known state Premier. I tried to explain to Sue who he was in American political terminology. After mixing images of a mid-west farmer and Jesse Fallwall, a southern conservative republican, I gave up. She worked it out for herself over the following months in Queensland.

As the wind howled across the sand spit, undoubtedly filling every glass of champagne with a liberal dose of imported Gold Coast sand, over 100 boats all appeared to be dragging anchor toward the entrance of the bar. We gave thanks that we hadn't sailed into the middle of this the day before. With just our pocket sized jib set we happily left all the celebrations and Southport behind, relishing our first taste of calm inland waters.

Over the next few weeks we would be sailing up inside passages between the mainland and the large sand islands of Stradbroke, Moreton and Fraser. We would rarely enter the open ocean again until we were almost inside the Barrier Reef. Although the reef was up to 200 miles offshore at its southern end, it would give us two thousand miles of welcome protection for the remainder of Australia's East Coast. We weaved our way north through shallow, narrow, mangrove lined passages. Although powerboats overtook us, we quickly caught up again, as we were able to skim over shallow sandbanks while they had to cover extra distance in the channel. It was a pleasant change to be exploring the coast from a calm, inland perspective.

Just as we were enjoying the natural beauty and quietness, the aptly named Tipplers Resort came into view, heralded by some of its spirited revelers out on a local charter boat. Their skipper pointed us out to his guests, who were dressed in the local uniform of thongs, with beer cans in hand. It seemed our reputations had preceded us and a continual stream of questions flowed from our newly acquired friends, intent on their beer consumption, and we decided to climb aboard for a quick drink and lunch. Any temptation to stay longer was cut short by the tourist prices and we departed soon after, back to the quiet of the mangrove passages.

Cutting across yet another isolated bar we were surprised by the presence of an Air-Sea Rescue helicopter on the beach, apparently treating someone for an injury, and ready to fly them out. As we watched the local television station helicopter also flew in, filming as they hovered like a vulture over the rescue party before landing nearby. As the camera crew hit the beach running, so did the friends of those being rescued, with a full and quick confrontation taking place. The cameraman and camera went down, a pushing match ensued and the media beat a retreat. Sue and I looked at each other and quietly sailed on. Just another one of those things you see in the middle of nowhere while cruising around Australia!

Meandering through the mangroves we eventually found a tired campsite on North Stradbroke Island. Being so close to Brisbane's 1.5 million people and being such a beautiful spot I guess the state of it was understandable. The next morning our launch required us to drag *Tom* through low tide and our first introduction to mangrove mud. It left us and *Tom* covered in a thick black slime.

"People pay lots of money to be covered in mud like this," I tried to convince Sue.

"Yeah, well I'll keep my wrinkles," she responded while cleaning both herself and *Tom* as we sailed along.

Sailing and motoring in the calm conditions we found our way to the south-eastern shores of Moreton Bay and the outer Brisbane suburb of Manly. The Royal Queensland Yacht Club and yet another marina welcomed us. At least we had a safe parking space for *Tom* as we headed off to the luxury of floor space at our friend Maree's home in suburban Brisbane. Her traditional weatherboard Queensland home sat on tall stilts to let the air circulate underneath, presumably to keep the house cooler and less moldy in the humidity. This type of dwelling, not the high-rise of Southport and the Gold Coast, represented the north of Australia to me.

We spent four happy days lounging at Maree's in a real house with running water, a washing machine, a fridge and a cake shop just down the road. Heaven! We took advantage of the lay-off by having our trampoline fixed with new grommets and a few lines of stitching. I don't think it was meant to take all our weight on a daily basis. We had grown confident of *Tom's* durability with this being our only major maintenance since we departed. We wrote stories for sailing magazines and letters to our sponsors, still in search of major cash support. Then, out of the blue, came a letter from my American mom, Jo Hopkins in Cleveland, who had been my sister's mom on an exchange program. It contained something she had saved for me and thought would help us now — $1,600. Yet again, it was a friend coming to our help. At least we would make it to Darwin now. I didn't hold out much hope of any major sponsorship until we sailed into Perth. A few calls around to the Brisbane media led to one radio station interview, a short newspaper article, and, after much frustration, a television interview. "You should have called us before you came in," was the usual remark.

After much hassling we didn't really care whether the television crew was there or not. However when we saw them waiting for us at the Royal Queensland Yacht Club I volunteered Sue to answer their questions while I got *Tom* ready for departure. As I stood up I was introduced to the reporter. "Didn't we play basketball together?" he asked me. Bob was a fellow student from university days six years earlier and we recalled stories until it was time for us to leave. Eventually we set sail. A helicopter hovering over us added to the already strong winds gusting at over twenty knots. The things you do for publicity! With Sue and I yelling at each other, the sail madly flapping, and the helicopter hovering, it was chaos, and definitely not the scene we needed to convince others of our sanity.

We waved a thankful farewell to Bob and his crew and were soon screaming across Moreton Bay with 20 to 25 knots of wind pushing us along. Thank goodness it was high tide as I constantly looked down to see no more than a couple of feet of water below us. Water streamed over the bow with sheets of spray covering us and the full length of *Tom*. The leeward hull continued to bury itself in each passing swell, but it was just wind swell and not the full force of the Pacific. Now this was sailing! It certainly woke us up and put back the crust of salt it had taken four days of fresh water showers to remove.

A large sand island and now mostly national park, Moreton Island lies directly east of Brisbane across the large expanse of Moreton Bay. Huge sand dunes are its sculptured heart, surrounded by low-lying sandy shores. We spent an extra day camped at a special grove of casuarina trees on the shore, exploring some of the island, fiddling with *Tom* and generally enjoying the solitude. We weren't completely alone though, with soldier crabs providing a low tide symphony, turtles feeding nearby, and crows demolishing all our breakfast food. Late one night we both woke to strange sounds.

"What is it? What's that noise?" Sue whispered.

"I don't know, but it sure is big!"

Cane Fields and Beaches

"Well aren't you going to find out?" she challenged.

"Uh... OK," laughter followed as I rolled back into the tent to tell Sue it was only horses nuzzling our tent.

The next day our planned sail to Mooloolaba took a short detour to the southern end of Bribie Island as the wind got stronger from the north. We pulled into a section of sand on the point very near about 30 fishermen with beach rods. Once again our attempt at an inconspicuous landing came undone as a four wheel drive truck with several fellows hanging off the back came hurtling down the beach toward us. "What the hell took you guys so long?" came the yell. Startled, we recognized the fishermen who had helped us off the beach at Charlotte Head in New South Wales, what seemed a lifetime ago. We exchanged fishing and sailing stories while sharing a beer. "We knew you'd make it! We've been looking for you for weeks." Cynical comments had been replaced by words of encouragement and we had reached a milestone of credibility.

For the next few days we cruised with full sail in sunshine and calm winds up the Sunshine Coast, past Mooloolaba, to Noosa Heads. This area is much more low key than the Gold Coast with smaller beach towns dotting the coast between the sand dunes and backed by the impressive 1500-foot escarpment of the Blackall Ranges only a few miles inland. With a national park on its headland and beautiful rocky coves one after the other, Noosa was the best preserved and prettiest stretch of coastline we had seen in a while. I don't know who got the bigger surprise as we eventually surfed onto the local beach, us or the wealthy holiday-makers exposing bare breasts and sunburned flesh.

We walked over the beach dune to see an endless array of shops and cafes rivaling Double Bay, an upper-class suburb of Sydney, often referred to as "Double Pay." Noosa certainly fit that image with the Gucci-and-gold-set strolling the streets among Mercedes and BMW's. We retreated to the beach for the night and chatted to the occasional interested evening-beach wanderer, pleased with ourselves that we had the cheapest accommodation in town.

The next morning a German fellow filmed our departure on the latest high tech video. It was already 11 A.M. as we made a calm and slow motor-sail in windless conditions north past The Colored Sands to Double Island Point.

Keeping Australia on the Left

This long, flat expanse of beach, backed by colorful sandhills, is the focus of fourwheel drive tours headed north to Fraser Island. The wreck of the *Cherry Venture*, a well-known local landmark, lies in the shorebreak at the northern end of the beach. The 1600-ton ship *Cherry Venture* was washed ashore by an unseasonable cyclone in July 1973. Despite efforts at refloating, it remains as the noted shipwreck on the tourist circuit. The seemingly isolated Wide Bay behind Double Island Point proved to be a major crossroads. A steady procession of four-wheel drives, small private vehicles and giant air-conditioned tourist buses, along with a variety of yachts, on day trips and long camping holidays daily pass by this beautiful stretch of coast.

With a wet and windy day expected to follow, I hitchhiked the six miles from Double Island Point into the next town of Rainbow Beach for supplies. Catching a lift on a local dunebuggy, I was educated about the area by my tour guide. "You think it's busy now! You wouldn't believe how much I turn over in the summer season with all the campers. The beach is like a used car lot, although they are hardly used." With a large fiberglass coated cooler bolted into the back, this dune buggy was the local mobile supermarket, taking campers' orders along the 60 miles of wilderness, and delivering the next day. This service ensured that people could "rough it" in comfort.

As I staggered back to camp rather bedraggled from the rain and the lack of lifts home, I was enthusiastically approached by a couple from my home town on holiday and taking a four-wheel-drive bus tour. I recovered from my shock to pose for a photograph with them, then turned to see Sue giving an interview for the local radio. Sue smiled behind slightly clenched teeth. I found out that on such a wet and rather drab tour day, *Tom Thumb* and Sue had been discovered and through the two-way radio network quickly became an extra sight on most of the tours that day. This was the tenth bus group, along with numerous individual four-wheel drives for which Sue had provided commentaries and interviews.

The entry to the quiet waters behind Fraser Island meant crossing yet another bar with a dangerous reputation. Wide Bay Bar required yachts to venture a couple of miles further out to sea to line up leads that directed them through the narrow passage. Our chats with shore travelers, especially fishermen and women, had given us the inside scoop that in calm conditions we could probably squeeze through close to shore. In anxious anticipation we cruised the 15 miles Wide Bay searching for our passage in a misty rain. At one point the fog was so thick that we lost sight of the shore and steered on with compass and dead reckoning. The tide was in the right direction, and the wind and swell low. When finally spotted, the bar still seemed to take forever to come closer. The sight of boats entering through a scattering of white breakers did not help calm our nerves. As we got closer, our passage was obvious — just clear of the breakers further out and not too close to the shore. A slightly bluer line of deep water showed us the way. We battened down the hatches and strapped on lifejackets. We were clear of the whitewater but the swells were sharp and up to six feet high. With a heavy grip on the tiller, we held our breath as *Tom* was tossed about like a cork. We kept the outboard running for safety and it screamed madly as it was buried in water one minute and in midair the next. In a few tense minutes we were into the calmer waters of the inlet. All we had to do now was miss the car ferry on one of its regular trips across the 50-yard wide channel.

We waved at the surprised operator and his ferry full of four-wheel drive adventurers off to explore Fraser Island. In the end, our passage was no worse than a sloppy departure from a surf beach. It was with a sense of accomplishment and pleasure that we noticed a yacht, which had anchored with us at Double Island Point overnight and had left an hour before us, still a half-mile out to sea weaving its way through the leads. Soon after, we sailed into the calm waters of Tin Can Bay and turned north up the narrow waterways between island and mainland.

Fraser Island is the largest sand island in the world with about 60 miles of surf beach surrounding sand dunes and beautiful fresh water lagoons set in coastal forest. It is separated from the mainland by mangrove-lined passages in the south and the large expanse of Harvey Bay opening out to the north. Only a decade earlier Fraser Island had been the site of sand mining and timber interests before conservationists won a long battle to have most of it registered as national park and later as a World Heritage area. We celebrated its beauty and munched our breakfast while sailing through the calm waters of the mangrove passages, watching turtles feed around us. What was recommended as a good anchorage for larger yachts was once again not suitable for us because of high sand walls and nowhere to get ashore. We motored on in the increasingly narrow passages searching for a comfortable campsite. It was a shock to see that the best locations were occupied by privately owned houses with Keep Out signs. We eventually settled for a muddy cove, with the remains of an old sand mining operation, its disused sheds and empty 44-gallon drums lay scattered in the bush. As dusk settled we retreated to the haven of our tent pursued by plagues of mosquitoes and sandflies. Sue was not impressed. "Welcome to the largest Sand Island in the world and the biggest collection of sandflies and mosquitoes!" I joked.

The next morning we pushed on to find a more comfortable campsite. We were happy to call it a day after only two hours sail when we came on a unique beach which had a clear high tide mark and was not built on or being used as a parking lot. Among dingo tracks and neglected camp sites we found a nice patch next to a token palm tree that gave a desert-island look if you closed one eye and let the imagination take over. We spent the afternoon fishing off the boat and watching turtles schooling small fish then gasping at the surface for a breath of air. Our pathetic efforts at fishing with a piece of cheese for bait contrasted dramatically with these professionals. A dugong and its calf surfaced to say hello. We could see many stingrays and other marine life from the beach while a multitude of colorful birds called from the bush. After a relaxing afternoon of drying clothes and enjoying the first sunshine in many days, we baked damper and washed it down with a large pot of tea. At sunset fruit bats yelled in the trees behind our tent, in a strange harmony with the howl of dingoes. Sue was uncertain whether this was a privileged Australian experience.

We headed out across Harvey Bay early the next morning with gray skies and drizzling rain to cut behind Woody Island and had a great sail past the long jetty at Urungan. We caught one glimpse of our destination, Burnett Heads, in the distance before suddenly losing visibility in rain and mist and having to follow compass bearings alone. The wind was rising and we'd have to find a safe landing soon. We were welcomed at the mouth of Burnam River by a sign saying "No Camping," so we went a mile farther and found a lonely tree near the shore surrounded by sandhills which offered us some protection from the wind and rain. In record time we were in the tent cooking dinner with *Tom* unpacked and tied up for the night.

I grimaced when I saw what Sue pulled out for our dinner — Chinese Nutalene, a rather poor excuse for protein that looked and smelled like dog food, but was at least slightly disguised by a sauce. The price you pay to stay healthy! It was a clear indication that we were getting low on supplies and close to our next supply stop. As we had not packed lunch for the day because we didn't expect to go far, we were starving and both managed to eat every bit.

When the new day dawned, it was less dismal, but with strong wind warnings forecast on the radio for most of the coast we decided to stay put. We were totally bored with the tent and each other by mid-morning and ventured out in the rain to the nearby holiday community of Woodgate. This quaint town had wooden bathing pools scattered along the beach stranded by the low tide. It was a strange sight for an Australian ocean front and I almost expected to see colorful European bathing sheds and a fun pier. Sue saw her first wild kangaroos grazing on the Woodgate Lawn Bowling Club greens. Arriving back at our campsite, we saw a fresh four wheel drive track going right up to the tent door. We were eating our lunch and wondering who our recently departed visitor had been, when a National Parks vehicle came around the corner. After our initial hellos, we offered a cup of tea to the solitary ranger. "No thanks. You can't camp here, you know!" he replied stoutly. We explained that we hadn't planned to camp here but we had run out of options with the strong wind warning. "I don't care," he said. "You have an hour to get off the beach or I can fine you $1,000."

When we attempted to ask for suggestions as to where to go, he hopped back in his vehicle. "I'll be back in an hour and I don't want to see you here!" With that he disappeared in flying sand. Sue and I were both trained in parks and recreation management, and were not impressed by this standard of customer service. "What the hell, I didn't want to stay here anyway," I said. As quickly as we had arrived, we packed up and headed off. The wind wasn't as strong as predicted and the rain was warm as we sailed off to our original destination of Burnett Heads on the mouth of the Bundaberg River, birthplace of my grandmother and Bundaberg Rum. It was also our next mail drop — only twenty more to go!

With the headland in sight, I saw a beautiful beach with a tent and what looked like catamarans. It was the mooring of our dreams. On a grassy bank, under the shade of a casuarina tree we pitched our tent and sat looking down on the small sandy cove with *Tom* barely twelve feet from us. It was part of a caravan park with hot showers, washing facilities, and a general store, and all this for seven dollars a night. What more could we ask? The only problem was signing in.

"Yes, I know you are here to sail, but what is the registration number of your car?" asked the woman in the park's office.

"We sailed in," we stated again.

"Yes, I know" she said getting frustrated with us, "But what is the registration number of your car?" "We do not own a car," I said slowly and clearly. "Our boat is on your beach" She looked at her assistant and back at us.

"You really sailed? Right up onto the beach? Oh my goodness!"

We eventually had to lead the two English women to *Tom* to convince them that we had actually sailed from our home address in Sydney. It was a first for their books.

Later we chatted with my parents on the caravan park telephone and described our new home for the night. "Oh yes," they said, "that is at Mon Repos where the turtles nest." They had camped here on their way around Australia in a campervan two years earlier. Sure enough, at the northern end of the cove was a protected stretch of beach that becomes a nesting site for turtles when they lay their eggs in the sand between November and February. In such a beautiful place it was hard to be motivated to push on the next morning despite our sense that time was slipping away, so we enjoyed the first sun and warmth for a week and dried all our gear out. In the comfort of Mon Repos we wrote the next article for *Multihulls* sailing magazine and sent it on to my parents to proof, type and forward. It had been great to see our first article about *Tom Thumb* in print.

Both of us were having trouble with constantly wet hands and feet. Mine were peeling continuously in layers, with the many cuts covered in bandages taking longer to heal. Our joints were tender and stiff from hours spent sitting at odd angles. Sue was still recovering from the bites of the sand flies on Fraser Island and looked as if she had a good case of the measles. We still had our moments of frustration with each other and ourselves, but had settled into a travel and lifestyle routine. Sue was gaining confidence in *Tom* and sailing in general. She even talked of borrowing the remaining funds from her parents when we got to Perth to finish the trip. It showed forward thinking far beyond my own. We didn't talk much about the rest of the trip. It was too overwhelming. Some days were just brilliant. On others we wished the miles of beach away as quickly as possible in anticipation of a dry, warm night's sleep, as the sailing became simply the means to an end.

We said goodbye to all our newfound friends in the caravan park and headed off into the first clear sunshine in weeks. It was lovely to be skimming along at a brisk pace again on a broadreach. Just as it all seemed too easy, the wind changed and we found ourselves about five miles out with a steady 15-knot breeze west-by-northwest off the shore. Two very wet, sloppy, close-hauled hours later we got in near the shore and pulled in for a very late lunch, exhausted and despondent. We had not given enough consideration to the distance, wind, or weather patterns. It served us right and at least it was a forgiving lesson.

In the following few days we continued to creep along slowly, battling solid headwinds. The coast was beautiful, with rugged rocky headlands fringed with pandanus palms and casuarinas sheltering sandy beaches in scattered coves. All of this was miles from anywhere and inaccessible except, unfortunately, to four-wheel drives. The headlands, the coves, the casuarina groves, even the beaches themselves all showed signs of some of the worst use and abuse by four-wheel drives we had yet seen on the coast — trails cut freely throughout the bush, the scars of fires and scattering of rubbish. While we may dislike the rules and regulations of national parks at times, if they are necessary to prevent this, they are worth it. A sign put on a tree by the local four-wheel drive club actually asked people to take their rubbish home, but it was obvious they had lost the contest.

Despite all this, we enjoyed the solitude and celebrated having just picked up our latest food supply. Macaroni and cheese with a glass of wine certainly beat canned meat substitutes. The cask of wine had long since replaced our excess clothing as an essential item, and a regular glass of wine with dinner as the sun set became our way of relaxing at the end of each day. Our supply box contained the usual dried foods, vitamins, sunscreen and new charts for the next section of coast. Food essentials consisted of muesli or weetbix with powdered milk, and tea for breakfast; bread or cracker biscuits with cheese and salami or sardines for lunch, and snack food of nuts and raisins followed by pasta or rice stew for dinner. We also had a small grill plate on which we prepared the fresh fish caught along the way.

After many frustrating days of slow, wet sailing into headwinds, as well as days of waiting on the beach for better weather, we eventually rounded the small rocky Round Hill Head and turned into the inlet of the town of Seventeen Seventy. "What kind of name for a town is that?" I asked. The official looking monument on the headland proudly proclaimed this as the first landing site of Captain Cook in Queensland in 1770. The town, on the northern face of the grassy headland, was a rustic collection of fibro holiday and fishing shacks reminiscent of the 1940s or 1950s.

After packing a few fresh food supplies we caught up with some of the cruising fraternity who were pulling up their dinghies on the beach. By this stage of our trip people had heard of us. Newspaper stories or occasional television coverage had supplemented the gossip lines of the cruising group, to the point we were welcomed as long lost friends by complete strangers. We had the chance to meet the crew of *Seventh Heaven*, a yacht we had seen tied up at Crowdy Heads in New South Wales. However I was keen to get some miles behind us on what finally seemed like a favorable day so I persuaded Sue to refuse the offers of coffee aboard a number of yachts.

Now something besides the weather took over. As we motored out of the inlet, the outboard spun in mid air over a swell and the propeller stopped as the engine roared on. Shit! I tried all the options I knew and we floated in circles in the light breeze still trying to get clear of the inlet. With limited knowledge of outboards we now thought we were destined not to make it past the east coast of Australia. We returned to Seventeen Seventy with me swearing in frustration and Sue at least comforted at the thought of being able to take up those offers of coffee.

The crew of *Martine,* a large steel-hulled ketch, was surprised to see us back so soon, and came across in the dinghy to pick us up from the beach. Jeff, a laconic Queenslander, taught us a lot about the cruising frame of mind.

"How long are you going to cruise?" we asked.

"Y..e...p," came the reply.

"Where are you planning on going?"

"Y...e...p," came the even longer considered response.

Jeff and Julie had sold everything to buy *Martine* and just go with their two young children. It appeared to agree with the entire family and they planned to enjoy life afloat. With pride, Jeff gave us the guided tour of their home, a very sturdy steel-hulled boat with twin diesels and an engine room that would put many powered vessels to shame. The children were proud to show us their bedrooms and their school work. Their lessons were by correspondence and Julie kept them on track with a daily schedule. "They learn more out here than they would in any school," insisted Jeff and Julie. Watching the kids and listening to their knowledge of birds, marine life, winds, weather, and geography we had to agree.

After dinner and a hot shower aboard *Martine* we sat and watched their home videos and talked into the night, then accepted the offer of a bunk for the night. Cruising hospitality at its best! Sue and I were blissfully rocked to sleep in our warm bunks. "Are you sure we can't finish the trip in a boat this size?" Sue asked the next morning. Jeff and I went over to look at 'Oscar', the outboard on *Tom*. We fixed it in only a few minutes — a broken shearpin. I didn't even know we had one, let alone how to fix it! As it was a cool overcast day, we thought we'd stay on anyway and shared a day consisting of a Queensland style breakfast of avocado and freshly fried fish served on the deck, followed by a canasta card game challenge with the neighboring yachties. We drew strength and refreshed ourselves from meeting such fellow travelers, sharing tales and encouraging each other. It was also a chance for Sue and I to interact with other people and relax with each other and the idea of what we were doing. Given all the time we spent together it was important to be in the company of other people. I think both of us had realized that we were travelers more than sailing enthusiasts, the sea and boat being merely our chosen way of travel.

We headed out of Seventeen Seventy the next afternoon in gloom and drizzle, with Jeff and Julie filming our departure for a new home video. We cruised across Bustard Bay, keen to explore the Bustard Head lighthouse. We pulled into the sandy inlet at the northern end and wandered up to say a quick hello to the lighthouse keepers, a young couple who were surprised to see us.

The view from the lighthouse of isolated beaches stretching off into the distance and the untouched mangrove inlets of Jenny Lind and Pancake Creek on either side of the headland was spectacular. We left the lighthouse keepers to their work and strolled down to our beautiful solitary campsite. It was good to be back on the "road" and charting our own course again with renewed enthusiasm.

The following day we made it to Gladstone, on the shores of Port Curtis, named by Matthew Flinders. This was the largest town we had seen since Noosa. Gladstone is a major shipping port for coal and aluminum and its industrial port facilities with a 15-foot tidal change over muddy mangrove beaches, were not inviting. After a quick visit to town for essentials and take-out fish and chips we sheltered in a small cove. The following day's passage marked another significant stage of our progress. We had to catch the tide flow through The Narrows, a mangrove-lined passage behind the large Curtis Island, which would save us from going back out to sea. The only difficulty was that you had to catch the 15-foot tide in for 12 miles, cross over the narrows at high tide, then catch the tide a further 12 miles.

To ensure our early getaway the next morning we turned down the offer of a hot shower and a coffee from the wharf security guard. We shivered through a damp and uncomfortable night with *Tom* tied to a disused pier, brightly lit by the nearby coal-loading wharf. A shock awaited me at first light, as I had to stare up at the pier trying to find our mooring lines. Because of the huge tides we were now many feet below the pier that we were level with the previous evening. It took some early morning gymnastics up the mast to release them. The passage, however, was uneventful. Although Sue, in full thermals including a balaclava, grumbled about Queensland's lack of warmth until we thawed out. Cattleyards mark the midway point of the narrows. When Curtis Island was used for pasture, stock were herded back and forth across to the island at low tide. We went with the flow out the other side, cutting the engine to take in the beauty of the morning and the bird life. Kingfishers, small swallows, finches and the usual cormorants all provided plenty of entertainment.

After a morning of passing mangroves on both sides we finally popped out into the mouth of the Fitzroy River and the wide expanse of Keppel Bay. The Fitzroy leads up to the inland town of Rockhampton, the original beef

Cane Fields and Beaches

capital of Queensland. Large inland cattle stations supplied the meatworks in Rockhampton, a place whose smell I remembered from many years earlier. We weren't tempted to visit, and after the mangroves of Gladstone, the crystal clear, blue waters of Keppel Bay shone brightly in the sunshine. It really felt like we had arrived at the Barrier Reef and tropical north Queensland. The Great Barrier Reef stretches some 1,200 miles along the northeastern coast from Fraser Island in the south to the northern tip of Cape York. World renowned among divers and sailors, it is claimed to be the largest structure on earth created by living creatures. It is not actually one long barrier but a broken maze of individual coral reefs and shoals on the outer edge, with some 2,600 individual coral reefs and cays as well as many islands which lay close to the mainland. At Fraser Island the outer edge of the reef was still some 180 miles to our east. When we rounded the northern tip of Cape York we would almost be able to see the outer edge as it plunged away into the depths. This whole unique region was all part of the Great Barrier Reef Marine Park with a federally funded authority to manage and care for its preservation. We were excited as to the potential shelter it would provide us for the next thousand miles, but also by its natural wonders we were keen to explore.

After a short sail the next morning we pulled ashore on a beach off the main street of Yeppoon. This small coastal town has wide Queenslander-style buildings all furnished with awnings. It was the most welcoming town we had visited. It felt relaxed and friendly. From the comfort of the main hotel, with a beer in hand, we could keep an eye on *Tom* across the road on the beach. Even the local press was amenable, being quite well-informed on sailing and offering words of encouragement. We scribbled a few postcards and took a walking tour of downtown around two blocks of well preserved public buildings. Many of the towns we had previously passed had lost their history by creating new multi-story government offices in colored concrete and glass, with the practical wide awnings replaced by air-conditioning.

We moved down to the local caravan park for the evening and parked our tent and gear next to the numerous groups of travelers, with whom we shared cups of tea and stories. It was wonderful that our experience could be shared by people using such a range of travelling styles, from yachties to caravaners, bikers and hitchhikers. Our next door neighbors were an older couple, Jim and Sally, from South Australia. "We always come up this way for winter," explained Sally over a second cup of tea. They gave us their address for when we made it down their way. We didn't dare think about how far that was away from us now, either in miles or days. We were still on the East Coast and had only made a small dent on the map of Queensland at this stage.

Our departure from Yeppoon was watched by 30 people from the local caravan park, many of whom had been following us around Australia on a similar time schedule, or had seen us on the local TV news. We were stunned and humbled by a young boy and girl coming up and asking for our autographs. After hastily scrawling our names on the back of an envelope, we waved farewell to the gathering crowd, taking strength from their encouragement and good wishes. "See you in South Australia," came the call from Jim and Sally.

Over the next few days to Mackay we saw an amazing stretch of coast, with access only to four-wheel-drive vehicles or boats. The predominantly flat sand dune coast was broken by the occasional rocky outcrop harboring beautiful coves of blue and green waters. Ironically its isolation is guaranteed by its use as a military training ground. The name Shoalwater Bay brings shivers to many Vietnam veterans who, as young men, used this site to prepare for fighting in the Asian jungles. Pearl Bay and Indian Head, north of Port Clinton, provided some of our best fishing in totally unspoiled surroundings. For many nights to follow, as we sailed on up the coast, each beach disappeared into the distance with not a soul in sight.

The last stretch to Mackay required negotiating Broad and Shoalwater Sounds, where 20-foot tides produce currents between the off shore islands that flow at up to four to six knots. These result in overflows and eddies which made it feel like rafting on a river, with the waves quickly doubling in size with the wind against the tide. This was all good preparation for the Northern and North West Kimberly coasts, which were renowned for the biggest and most dangerous tidal changes. Our guiding landmark through the sounds was Pier Head, which stood between the two large bodies of water. It was the only observation point shared by Matthew Flinders and Captain Cook on the Australian coast. With Pier Head in sight we island-hopped well out from the sounds.

First we cruised across to Marble Island, to what looked like a well-maintained farm with fences and cattle. Although we were trying to be inconspicuous, a Coast Guard boat followed us right up onto the beach.

Cane Fields and Beaches

Prepared for an inquisition and the order to move on, we found instead the jolly faces of the local census collectors excited about finding some unaccounted-for bodies. I couldn't believe it! There is a census once every four years in Australia and we had been found here in the most out of the way place. I admired their commitment and we shared a cup of coffee and sailing stories with them. Instead of the private island where we were now parked, they suggested a quieter cove around the corner.

The next day our sail was only twelve miles across to Poynter Island, half way across the Sounds and the most direct route to the mainland where Mackay would be our next major port of call. Poynter Island was, as the name suggested, was pointed, with red and yellow-hued sharp peaks covered in natural bush and dark green rainforest. As it became more defined, we lined up a passage between it and the neighboring island on our compass bearing. We had timed our passage to go with the outgoing tide and it was certainly still outgoing. Here was Poynter Island a good six miles from the sounds and any land, with foaming tide-races! I couldn't believe it! The swirling, frothing water was like a fast flowing river, surging between the rocky island points, producing eddies and whirlpools. We prayed that the wind would hold, positioned ourselves in the middle of the 500-yard channel and prepared to be shot out the other end. It was strange to have two forces of nature pushing and playing with *Tom*. We hung on, and before we knew it were able to haul in the sails and have *Tom* shudder and slide out of the current into the calmer swirling eddies of a rocky bay.

It was strange to be on an island by ourselves with the mainland in sight. Our beach was a small tidal section of sand backed by a paving of well-worn, rounded rocks. It was a test for us and the now sadly worn airbags to get *Tom* above high tide without scraping off his few coats of fiberglass. We explored the rockpools and sat watching the remaining tide-race before it turned back toward us. As the sunset lit the rugged rocks in spectacular ochre colors, our gaze drifted toward the mainland and the lights of the city of Mackay. We would be there tomorrow with the promise of new supplies and friends to visit.

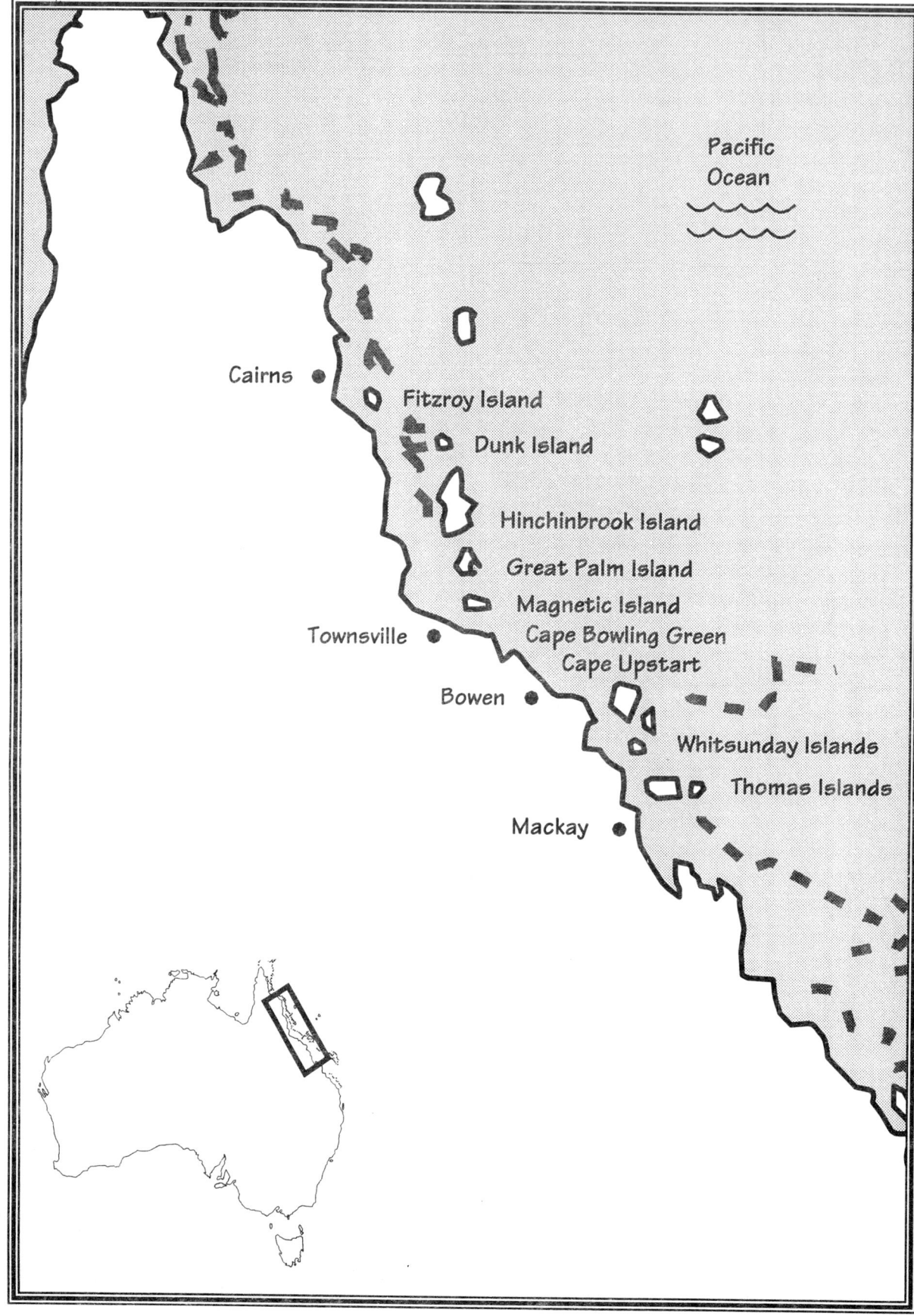

Chapter 4

Cruising the Islands
Mackay to Cairns

The port of Mackay was a welcome sight. It had taken us two months to get there and marked the middle of Queensland with the promise of more favorable conditions ahead. The Whitsunday Island group extends north and is the beginning of the true tropics with steadier southeasterly trade winds to push us on our way. This was to be the more enjoyable, relaxed part of our journey. Or so we thought.

Mackay harbor, the "sugar port of Australia" is backed by bulk sugar sheds and molasses tanks and is enclosed in stone break walls over a mile long. *Tom Thumb* was dwarfed as we passed the main shipping docks to pull ashore on the harbor beach. We were welcomed by local yacht club members and an assortment of cruising yachties, who had met us at various points up the coast. Familiar boats and faces made us feel we were part of a bigger family. Even if *Tom* was smaller than most, sharing a mode of travel was an instant bond. While the yacht club was not an imposing structure, it had Her Majesty's blessing by being a "Royal" club, and was the friendliest we had visited.

For the next few days we stayed with Bruce and Margaret Parr, friends of our boat builder Peter Pool. After camping on cold, lumpy sand we appreciated a comfortable bed. Bruce ran rock climbing and abseiling tours for groups of tourists at the nearby resort of Hamilton Island. We settled in, anxious not to appear to be taking over their house with our supplies. In an effort to clean and dry things we emptied all our belongings at each port of call. More than once we found an item had been lost since our last stop. Bruce amazed us by offering to lend us his waterproof Nikonos camera for the remainder of our trip. It was to give us some great photos long after our smaller cameras succumbed to the sea and salt air.

Keeping Australia on the Left

We had our dependable outboard, Oscar, serviced for the first time and did some minor repairs to *Tom*. A special package of Tekna diving face masks and snorkels arrived from my friend Mark Bensen in North Carolina whose girlfriend worked for the company. It was just what we would need for the Barrier Reef. We did an interview for local television, something that was now becoming easier and part of our commitment to sponsors. We survived yet another press interview with the local paper, whose journalist and photographer were both very polite and knowledgeable. This was a pleasant surprise after some of the journalists sent down to our previous ports of call who knew nothing about sailing. They mentioned they covered an average of eight stories a year about unusual craft visiting Mackay while travelling the coast of Australia. "You guys are the best equipped I've ever seen," came the commendation. God, if only he knew that it had taken us two months to get to this stage! The local yacht club commodore however later reinforced this after grilling us with questions about our equipment. "What are you carrying on board? Carrying any flares? What about charts? "What about repairs? How do you go for food and water?" He concluded with, "You guys are better equipped than most bloody yachts I've seen go through here! Have a good trip!"

On our departure from the Parrs' house, the taxi driver hesitantly asked if we would autograph her local paper. After seeing all our gear she had realized who we were because, there, on the front page, was the article and a not-too-flattering photo. Battling with pens that didn't work in the back of a bouncing taxi we sheepishly scrawled our names across the front page. Fame, however, did not translate to a free ride.

Ready to move on again and find our own space, we quickly packed *Tom* and motored out of Mackay harbor headed for the Whitsundays — a cruiser's paradise.

Well known for their island resorts, the Whitsundays provide a winter haven for southerners and international tourists wishing to soak up the sun and beauty of the Great Barrier Reef. Geographically the islands are a drowned mountain range off the coast, rising steep and green from the sea, fringed by sparkling sandy beaches and coral reefs. They are part of the larger Cumberland group of islands, named by Captain Cook after the Duke of Cumberland on Whit Sunday in 1770. Cruising through them you could mistakenly think you were on a bus tour of the English Lakes District with many islands such as Brampton, Carlisle and Keswick carrying the original names of towns from Cumbria. The group consists of approximately fifty islands stretching 50 miles north of Mackay. Initially providing safe grazing areas and timber supplies for local settlers in the late 1800s, today the islands are a mix of national parks and international resorts.

Our first stop, Brampton Island, was an established family resort with its own airstrip, swimming pools, beach volleyball, kids' activities and a variety of scheduled alternatives. "Snorkeling at 8.30 A.M., Sailing at 11:30 A.M. and this evening's performance at 7.30 P.M." said the "What's On" sign. I felt we had docked next to the *Love Boat*! The resort nestled in a northeastern bay, fringed with coconut palms, facing the rugged and rocky Carlisle Islands, which were only a sand bar and a 50-yard channel away. After a quick tour of Brampton we happily sailed over to a beach on Carlisle, without the bar, umbrellas and in-ground pool. Our arrival was witnessed by a single horse galloping through the shallows. I shook my head in disbelief. Where on earth did it come from? We found later that the original owners of Brampton had bred horses for the Indian Army and a few were left roaming the island.

We had our own coral bay and comfortable tent site. It was great to be out by ourselves and sailing again, well inside the Great Barrier Reef. We reasoned that, due to the large change in tide, if we wanted to depart the following morning we would have to tie *Tom* at anchor or we wouldn't get off the rock and reef until lunchtime. So for the first time we anchored *Tom* offshore for the evening. With two anchors and a line to shore we anxiously went to sleep dreaming of islands to come and, hopefully, a boat still there in the morning.

At dawn Sue peered out of the tent, smiling back, "*Tom*'s still with us." He was actually floating freely in six feet of water, requiring a bracing morning swim. With a fresh southeast tradewind blowing we sailed off through the channel between Goldsmith and Linne Island, past the prominent landform of Finger and Thumb. The water was a glorious clear blue and scattered green, wooded islands were fringed with tempting coves and bays. We pulled into the southeastern end of the smaller Thomas Island, negotiating a manageable passage up onto a beautiful sandy beach. Backed by Norfolk Pines and a hard red rocky mount, we couldn't believe our eyes. On a grassed area sat a picnic table and decrepit (but useable) pit toilet, all courtesy of National Parks, and what's more, not a person around! We celebrated with a cup of tea and an afternoon of fishing on the leeward side of the island, basking in the sun. We didn't catch anything but enjoyed watching the turtles show us how, as two of them sounded the cove.

We cursed that our trusty air bags had both split from the excess weight. We were due to pick up new ones in Mackay but couldn't wait and felt we could manage without them until we reached Airlie Beach at the northern end of the Whitsundays. Emptying *Tom* of as much gear as possible we dragged him up past the high water mark and tied the anchor line off to a tree. Then we settled back to enjoy our dinner with a glass of wine at the picnic table, under the casuarina trees and stars. Now this was the cruising life!

"Mark, Mark, wake up," followed by a dig in the ribs. "Mark, it sounds like *Tom* is moving," urged Sue.

"It's just the wind." I muttered turning over in my sleeping bag.

"We (meaning me) should check." She persisted, digging me again.

"OK, OK."

Wanting to prove her wrong and then return to warm slumber, I stuck my head outside feeling cold rain pelting my face. A strong wind whipped the tent. Was that the sound of surf? It woke me up instantly and my feeble torch showed *Tom* surrounded by shore break!

Our friendly southeaster of the previous day was now blowing at 30 knots and there was *Tom* sideways, totally awash in the shore break. "Shit!" I yelled. We dashed from the tent trying to hold the torch and *Tom* while waves broke around us. We couldn't move him, he was full of water! We both knelt in the waves and water and desperately pumped the hand bilge pumps as fast as we could.

"Where's the spray covers and gear?" yelled Sue through the noise of wind and surf.

"Forget about that now," I said, "just keep pumping,"

We finally hopped between the bows, grabbed the trampoline and hauled with each swell. *Tom* turned up the beach and moved a couple of feet. I jumped out and kept pumping, we hauled again and little by little we moved *Tom* up to safety.

"What about the gear?" asked Sue wondering if anything had been swept out to sea.

"Forget it," I said, "we'll find out in the morning."

I tied two lines from *Tom* to the trees just to be sure. Both of us naked and shivering after almost an hour in the surf and rain we collapsed back into the tent like two drowned rats. I cursed my own stupidity at having misjudged the weather and tried to get some sleep despite the anxiety of what the morning might reveal.

When morning came with clear, sunny skies it was as if the evening had been a bad dream. We tentatively assessed the damage inside *Tom*. The bottom of the hulls were covered with a solid layer of sand and seaweed but luckily we found all our gear, including the cockpit spray skirt washed way up inside the bow. Anxiously digging out cereal bowls full of sand and seaweed, I felt sick as a large crack began to appear, extending 18 inches along the keel. What would we do? We didn't have much choice. For the first time since Peter Pool's workshop in Sydney we would have to pull *Tom* to pieces and do some repairs. I just hoped that if we could get him apart, we could put him together again. It was a good day's paddle in a kayak to any help on the mainland.

With gentle persuasion we jiggled the hulls in different directions and the trampoline popped off. We were left with two kayaks. After dismantling the hulls and trampoline we were relieved to find that the boats foam sandwich construction had absorbed all the shock and the outside had barely a scratch. A solid repair job with fiberglass and a strip of aluminum solved the problem. We now had a solid cross brace built into the hull. During our repairs a yacht sailed into the small cove. The couple aboard must have felt they were coming to our rescue when they saw the dismantled boat taking up most of the beach. We waved and they anchored on the beach and began to have breakfast. Eventually a relaxed fellow wandered over.

"Do you need any help?" offered Peter from Mackay as he introduced himself. "I have some silicon gel onboard if you like."

I replied that it was just a crack and I was fiberglassing in a reinforcing strip.

"Oh, It looks like you're well prepared then," he stepped back.

Watching me work he sheepishly asked what other tools we had. After finishing *Tom*'s repairs and further conversation we eventually wandered over to Peter's boat with *our* hand riveter to fix up some rigging problems on *their* yacht!

Peter and Michelle were sailing up the coast in their 18-foot trailer-sailer, *The Itch*, with a dingy called *Scratch*, and were excited to find someone with a mast smaller than theirs, if only by a navigation light. That evening we shared dinner and wine around our picnic table with a seaside view. We finally felt comfortable, or had drunk enough, to admit to our naked follies the previous evening and how we came to be fixing *Tom*. After much laughter and jovial ribbing, Peter and Michelle admitted they had almost sunk *The Itch* the day before in Mackay harbor after launching it without putting in the bung. They had only just started talking to each other again when they pulled into Thomas Island. Our kind of sailors! Definitely no pretentiousness here afloat in the Pacific.

Sue suffered badly all that night from what she claimed was the food, but was probably the red wine. We stayed put that next morning as *The Itch* and crew beat a hasty exit feeling somewhat responsible for her condition. Sue and I put *Tom* back together, surprised at how well everything seemed to fit and how solid it all appeared. We had a casual day of fishing and snorkeling, as Sue slowly recovered. With a calm night, *Tom* farther up the beach, and no parties beckoning, we both slept well.

The next morning steady trade winds blew us north. The mainland added an impressive backdrop to the islands, being only six to twelve miles away with steep green hills, some 1,500 feet high, dropping sharply to the ocean. Each island rises from the ocean with emerald water lapping golden, sandy coves. They were much higher and larger than I had imagined. Whitsunday Island itself is twelve miles long. Both so intent on taking in the scenery we misread the charts and almost crashed into the slightly submerged Platypus Rock at the southern end of Shaw Island. Part of the national park, Shaw looked tempting with beautiful beaches stretching north. Then we passed Lindeman Island with its long-established family resort. As it is a low, flatter island, Lindeman was used as a sheep property from the early 1900s and still has large open paddocks. After our extended stopover at Thomas we had set our sights further north, nearer Hamilton Island, one of the best known resorts in the area. Coming into Dent Passage we passed close by the Australian Himalayan Expedition tour group's square rigged sailing ship with its full complement of sails unfurled and a waving crew.

As Hamilton Island came into view we stared in disbelief at a large quarry face in a hillside adjoining an airstrip which jutted out into the passage. This was a jetport capable of handling flights direct from the southern capitals of Sydney and Melbourne. The area behind this high-rise accommodation against the skyline resembled council flats of inner Sydney. We pulled into the newly completed artificial harbor on the western side and found a berth in the large floating marina. As we motored in, the berths just kept going and going, each five to six times the length of *Tom*. The surrounding multistory decks of our neighboring vessels seemed to look down at us disdainfully. We hadn't felt like this since Southport or at the Royal Cruising Yacht Club in Sydney. The dock was full of beer-gutted sports fishermen and a sour group of yachties. Perhaps they were all just having a bad holiday! A ten-year-old child on the 50-meter yacht next to us proceeded to tell us all the things they had on their boat that we obviously didn't. "So there!"

After berthing we wandered off along the paved roads. Before I had a chance to wonder why there was so much paving a horn sounded and I turned in time to dodge a speeding golf cart. This was the local transport for those who were not keen to walk the few hundred yards from bar to harbor to beach. While recovering from this, I started to take in the many restaurants and imported palm trees. Polynesian-style villas nestled on the far side of the island around a central building with dolphins swimming in a small pool next to the bar. The beach was at low tide and, despite all the imported sand we had been told about, shallowed out to gray reef and mud flats.

Keeping Australia on the Left

We had heard stories of Keith Williams, the creator of Hamilton Island Resort, as we came up the coast. He rivaled the Queensland Premier, Joh Bjelke-Peterson, for notoriety. People either loved him or detested him. Some Queenslanders saw him as the savior of the coast by providing jobs with his resort, while others thought he was destroying Queensland for his own profits. Years later Keith Williams is still at it, now building a controversial resort further north near Hinchinbrook Island.

On our way back to the marina we were surprised to see Peter and Michelle from *The Itch* appear from a phone booth. They offered us dinner at a local restaurant and a night sleeping on their deck. For two of the smallest boats in the harbor that night, both sharing the one berth, we certainly made our share of noise, having drinks on deck as we could not all fit below. Early the next morning, despite a strong breeze and a short five-foot swell, the two smallest boats headed out across the channel to the neighboring island. We had decided to get away early. It had nothing to do with the fact that the marina manager hadn't yet called around for berthing fees! People stood incredulous on the breakaways to the harbor as we sailed off to Dent Island, a half-mile away.

We went ashore for breakfast and to explore Coral Art, a small shop and gallery, for 101 things you can do with coral and shells. The couple who ran it were the original residents of Hamilton Island, and now lived across the water in their own tourist paradise. It was obviously very popular and on the circuit for local tour groups. We had much fun watching the visitors arrive in yachts, glass bottom boats and Maori war canoes complete with engine. The wind and tide were not in our favor to sail, so we pulled beers from the cooler to enjoy our wait. The owners of the gallery were not very impressed, but a lost tourist appreciated our presence. He stood forlornly on the dock in his walk socks and sandals watching his wife motor off across the passage onboard a tourist boat without him and he gratefully accepted our offer of a cold beer!

Late that afternoon we sailed into Airlie Beach, the mainland township and principle access point to the Whitsundays. We rushed in to the post office and picked up a supply package. Then we went up to the yacht club to meet the locals, including Norm who invited us to stay in the annex of his caravan on the shores of the bay. We also met Ian, the "bloody crazy idiot"

Cruising the Islands

people had told us about who had come up the coast from Sydney in a twelve-foot aluminum dinghy with outboard. A down-to-earth Australian Huck Finn, he just loved the sea, whether it was surfing or fishing, and had set off to have an adventure. We could relate to this, and after we heard about his 2,000-mile journey we realized he was as well planned and realistic as anyone. He had built extra flotation into the dinghy and carried a spare engine, oars, flares, charts and, as a final backup, his surfboard to paddle ashore. He also had the advantage of only travelling a couple of hours each day and only put to sea in good weather. The three of us enjoyed sharing our spirit of adventure and small boat stories of the east coast.

We spent the next day touring the area with Peter and Michelle. In their bright pink VW convertible rental car, we cruised to the nearby town of Proserpine to do some shopping and see the surrounding countryside. The holiday and resort image of Airlie beach quickly faded to the more natural surrounds of sugar cane fields from which the area originally grew. Walking into Proserpine was like going back fifty years in time. Progress may have come to the Queensland coast, but the rural communities still had their own identity. Shop fronts with wide galvanized-iron awnings lined the street in a wonderful collection of classic Queensland architecture. You could guess the types of shops before you saw them — the great cake shop with classic meat pies, the newsagency where everybody met for local news and the hardware shop that sold everything and anything. We went to the rural supply shop for new overalls and were attended to by the entire family, grandparents to grandchildren, as the dust was blown off my pair which were buried on the top shelf. The entire family waved us farewell from the front door of the shop as our conspicuous car turned back to Airlie. I couldn't help wondering how they felt about the development on the coast that was so removed from the country life they knew. Somewhere between the canefields and the coast there seemed to be a time line that separated the past and present in community and family values.

Sue had become much more confident in managing *Tom*. She now rigged the boat by herself and at Airlie Beach actually swam out to set anchor lines at midnight so we could get away on the early morning low tide. Over the next few days we made great progress past the port of Bowen and on towards the landmark of Cape Upstart. This coastline was a contrast to the

Whitsundays. Stark, dry, sandy scrub rose out of low rocky headlands and from the sea it resembled one long, low non-descript sand dune. Cape Upstart, named by Captain Cook for its prominence, loomed impressively in our sights as the sunset colored its rocky outcrops a dark red. Early the next morning a calm, clear sail towards the Cape allowed us to take in this impressive landmark, its steep slopes strewn with large boulders. Our enjoyment in sightseeing would not have been so complete had we known of the sudden turn of events that would soon threaten our boat and our lives.

With the end of the Cape in sight the wind rose suddenly along with a steep, sharp swell. In a few minutes the wind was bulleting in sharp 20-to 30-knot gusts, kicking up short whitecap waves. We were letting out sail fast and leaning out as far as we could. Suddenly, from what had been a moment for taking photos, we were now hanging on for all we were worth and looking for the protection of the bay just inside the Cape.

"Furl that jib and hang on," I yelled to Sue.

"Let's drop the main," she cried.

"We're nearly there, just close that gear bag and get your feet under the straps."

For ten long minutes we hung on, covered in wild spray with the mainsail fully out and *Tom* groaning with the strain. We were out of control and something was going to break soon. As we came down off one swell, both my arms struggling to control the tiller, *Tom* started to dig into the preceding swell. The lee hull went into it and continued to dive down as I tried to pull it out and turn us into the wind. The water was now over the front hatch and *Tom* lurched drunkenly with the strain. As we surged through the next swell both hulls were buried in water up to the mast. Sue and I scrambled to the stern trying to stop *Tom* from cartwheeling. Slowly the bow came back up to the top like a submarine. Suddenly free of the weight of the water he swung into the wind and jibed. This was our chance and we both moved fast, dropping the sail and starting the outboard in a flash.

My heart was still pounding as we turned *Tom* slowly back around to run with the swell and the wind. Within two hundred metres we were in the lee of the bay and motoring through absolute calm.

My heart was still pounding as we turned *Tom* slowly back around to run with the swell and the wind. Within two hundred metres we were in the lee of the bay and motoring through absolute calm.

"Mark, that was bloody scary," Sue exclaimed.

I tried to make light of it but she glared at me.

"OK, sorry. We'll get the sail down straight away next time," I said.

It was our closest experience to a total nosedive and could have tipped the boat. We had never practiced tipping Tom back over fully loaded. It could have been the end of the trip and us. We were both shaken by the experience.

We took the afternoon off to recover and find some space from each other. There were other tensions surfacing which we were both still working out. Spending 24 hours a day, every day for what was now weeks inevitably highlighted some differences in the way we liked to do things, and this afternoon was one of those. Sue took her usual afternoon solar shower while I went off to climb Cape Upstart and enjoy the firmness of the ground and the sunlit boulders. I was intent on seeing as much of what was around us as possible whereas Sue would happily stay at the campsite reading and relaxing in her own way. However, she felt that we didn't stay anywhere long enough to see things and that I was constantly pushing us along with little time for relaxing, which was true. Somewhere between we found a compromise between my need to explore and keep us moving, and Sue's need for comforts, which admittedly I also enjoyed.

After recovering from our near capsize we slowly continued north, past the brown-stained mouth of the Burdekin River and Cape Bowling Green, which was definitely flat but hardly green. For a Cape I was expecting something more substantial than a 50-yard wide sand spit with several low trees and a navigation light. We finally rounded Cape Cleveland, the last headland before Townsville and pulled into a sandy bay to be welcomed by the sandflies and mosquitoes. It was strange to sit having dinner by the campfire looking out on the flickering lights of a city. Townsville, often considered the capital of the north, is Queensland's second largest city after Brisbane. Originally a port for cattle and sugar cane it also became the exit point for mining exports primarily from Mount Isa, 1000 miles directly west. I had worked at the mines around Mount Isa many years earlier and Townsville was considered the nearest coastal weekend retreat. It was only ten hours and one carton of beer (drunk on the way) away by car on a Friday night at an average speed of 100 miles an hour!

In Townsville we both felt we had finally arrived in Queensland, perhaps because of the warm evening air or the fact that we were now so far away from Brisbane and a very long way from Sydney. Basking in our success and the warming morning sun we made our departure much too casually the next morning and paid for it as the tide quickly departed exposing a muddy expanse. We cursed and slipped and slid *Tom* out through a hundred yards of shallows, eventually finding the sea but with the boat and us covered in black slimy mud.

The majestic Magnetic Island was our destination, with its house-sized granite boulders protecting beautiful sandy bays. Once again it was named by Captain Cook due to the strange effect the island had on his ship's compasses. It lies just five miles off the coast from Townsville so some locals who live here commute daily to Townsville to work. We passed a number of small resorts before pulling into the easternmost beach of Horseshoe Bay. Anchoring *Tom* slightly offshore we caught the tourist bus over the island to the small town of Acardia for outboard fuel and mail. Then we hitched a ride back in a local mini-moke, the popular cheap rental car that a friend of mine often compared to a sardine tin powered by a lawnmower engine. After our shopping excursion we went swimming — our first voluntary swim after a day's sailing since we had departed from Sydney. Maybe things were getting just a bit warmer 1,500 miles to the north!

While swimming we met a young couple from Sydney, Brian and Cindy, sailing a rental catamaran around in the bay. They owned the yacht *Breezin* that was anchored nearby and had passed us many miles back when we came out of the town of Seventeen Seventy. Having followed our travels in local newspapers at each port along the coast they were glad to finally catch up with us. An official looking powerboat also came to visit as we were cooking dinner. Certain that it would be another officious Queensland ranger telling us to move on, we were pleasantly surprised by two friendly fishing inspectors who had also heard about us and were interested in sharing stories.

Cruising the Islands

Up and off early the next day, we sailed in the wake of *Breezin* and headed for Palm Island, 30 miles to the north and some 12 miles offshore. The beautiful bays of Magnetic stretched off to the northwest tempting us to explore this larger northern section that is predominantly national park. The huge granite hills shrouded the sandy bays and blue water. Now this was sailing! We lost sight of Magnetic and were swallowed by the heat haze, or sea mist, barely able to see the mast of *Breezin* 600 feet ahead. Cruising on a light southeasterly we were enjoying reading and sunbathing, easily keeping up with *Breezin* under full spinnaker. The mist cleared a couple of hours later and we could see our destination of Great Palm Island.

This large, impressive island with rich vegetation rises steeply out of the ocean, and is central to a collection of smaller islands making up the Palm group. We cruised into a beautiful northeastern facing bay with a sandy beach backed by casuarinas and a green forest and bush. As we cruised in past *Breezin,* Cindy's brown bare chest greeted us as she proudly held aloft two large fish, their day's catch while sailing. Sue and I were stunned. We were not quite sure if it was the uniqueness of the greeting or the fact that Sue had never dreamed of exposing her breasts to the elements aboard *Tom* without the fear of freezing them off, until now.

We pulled into the beach and I swam out to *Breezin* to invite them in for dinner ashore. Over a few beers we learned they had left Sydney two weeks after us, also headed for Perth, but had changed their minds, as they realized they didn't have the time or money. *Breezin* was an 8-meter *Endeavour* designed sloop that was part of a fleet of hire boats from the Hawkesbury River near Sydney. Apparently she had been purchased with the money from a divorce settlement. Cindy was a surfer girl who worked to support her travelling habit. We shared dinner by the campfire and introduced them to our slightly different version of travelling under sail. It was a brilliant starry night as we sat next to the glowing embers with only the sound of the gentle lapping of waves on the shore.

We were off well before *Breezin* the next morning and skimmed the swells with a beautiful run past Orpheus and Pelorus and other islands in the Palm group. As the last small island was left in our wake we could see dark swirling clouds streaming from the mountain peaks in the distant dark. The sheer magnitude of Hinchinbrook Island with the rugged, rocky 4,000-foot peak of Mount Bowen towering in its center and emerald green rain forests falling to the sea, was a truly spectacular sight.

It is the world's largest island national park, separated from the mainland coast by a mangrove-lined channel. Its steep mountains and some of the highest rainfalls in Australia ensures that its rainforest is some of the best-preserved in Australia. Public access is by a small ferry from the coastal town of Cardwell. A small resort nestles on its northern tip but the majority of visitors are hikers who are prepared to walk a day or two along the eastern coast to find their tropical paradise. As with many other parts of Queensland we had passed, a contrast to the natural beauty of Hinchinbrook also caught our eye. Near the southern end, the long Lucinda wharf extends miles out from the coast to make it easier for the loading of international sugar ships. It appeared an abrupt boundary had been drawn across the landscape between functional coast and national park.

We headed for the southern Zoe Bay with its golden beach wrapped with coconut palms and green rainforest. Sailing and hiking friends had waxed lyrical about this bay as one of their most memorable places in Australia. As we came in closer, two figures were walking purposefully along the beach towards us. They turned out to be another couple sailing a catamaran, who had been parked in the back lagoon of Zoe Bay and had explored Hinchinbrook for two weeks! With a draft usually less than three feet, catamarans have an advantage in getting into small, protected lagoons or rivers. Meanwhile *Breezin* and crew spent a very uncomfortable night at anchor in the bay.

We shared yet another lovely night on the beach barbecuing fish and baking potatoes before the mosquitoes drove us to bed. In the morning we waved *Breezin* off as we were keen to stay and explore the swimming hole at a nearby waterfall. We basked in the enjoyment of freshwater swimming and cleaned the encrusted salt off our clothes. Both of us had rashes from the constant rubbing of sea-salt crusted on our skin. Our hands and feet were also soft from being constantly soaked, and cut or bruised easily. It was often difficult to find time to care for ourselves after long days of sailing. We wrote postcards and articles all afternoon in preparation for our last major port for a while — Cairns. If all went well we should be there within the week. We went to bed with a full moon shining across the bay, throwing shadows along the beach.

The next morning Hinchinbrook was even more impressive as we continued to sail north past some of its longer beaches. We continued to look back at the impressive sight of the island slowly diminishing in the distance. The sun shone as we cruised past the luxury resorts of Bedarra and the Family Islands, the best in the northern islands. Tiny islands of no more than 10 to 20 acres, they provide a private retreat for the very wealthy.

Inspired by our recent fresh fish meals, Sue now had a spinner regularly trailing behind *Tom*. She regularly chatted with other sailors, fishermen and women, to pick up their hints for the best lure and bait. Cruising past Bedarra Island at a fresh six knots, spinner trailing, we almost came to a dead stop. Reeling in the line we found the spinner had three of its four hooks straightened out almost flat! Something bigger than I dared to think about had been on the line, but Sue was very possessive about her spinners and reluctant to cut any of them loose. I had images of a shark or marlin towing *Tom* and crew out to sea.

Life on the ocean wave was beginning to become more than familiar. We could tell a change in the wind direction on our face, and *Tom*'s subtle roll told of a different swell. We almost didn't notice this gradual learning, as our reactions were becoming automatic. Lifejackets were compulsory when the wind reached anything over 15 knots. We were also quick to change our sail selection, furling the jib or being prepared to drop the main. Even with the small size of our mainsail I was still considering having reef points put in it to allow us to make it smaller, yet continue sailing and have control. It was a new idea for catamarans of this size as they were usually built for speed, not long distance cruising. *Tom* and our equipment were holding up well, with any major mishaps occurring because of our own carelessness.

Approaching Dunk Island we were surprised to see *Breezin* who had made a slight detour. We did a quick walk around this family resort island with hotel style bungalows, children's holiday programs, swimming pools and beer that cost more per can than a meal in some Sydney restaurants. We took the opportunity of making a few phone calls to friends and the press to coordinate our arrival in Cairns in a few days. It was hard to believe we were almost there after such a long month. There were no deserted beaches in sight so we tied *Tom* up behind *Breezin* for the night and slept in their cockpit on deck. Being over six feet tall, I didn't fit comfortably below in many boats. It was quite a change to be rocked to sleep on the water, although we had to remember where we were and not do our usual walk off down the beach when nature called in the night.

Brian and Cindy had left behind the chart for the Cairns area and were considering turning home at this point. We happily loaned them ours knowing we could cope better over any unexposed reefs with *Tom's* draft of six inches. *Breezin* and *Tom* met up in the lee of Fitzroy Island after a beautiful morning of sunshine sailing in 15 knots of following breeze. With an afternoon to spare, we decided to walk up to the lighthouse above the small resort. There was a strong sense of deja vu for me as I climbed the steep trail to the small but prominent lighthouse. It was on this spot that I had the inspiration for this trip four years earlier. I had visited the island while on a cruising trip with friends and looking south down this gorgeous blue and green coastline I knew I would be coming back. I could see and feel myself sailing up this coast.

We spent the afternoon on the local nudist beach trying to focus on scrubbing up *Tom* in preparation for meeting the press the next day as people were finally starting to take our trip seriously. The following morning we took our time zig zagging around the long leads into Cairns which lies around the corner from Fitzroy Island. The impressive hinterland drops away to short coastal plains that merge with the shore. Cairns is actually quite a big port for the fishing and tourist fleets plying the Great Barrier Reef. With an international airport and a large amount of foreign, mostly Japanese, investment, it has grown to a major center. The yacht club is up the river slightly and seeing no one ashore at the harbor entrance, we had almost given up on the thought of the press meeting us.

Suddenly we heard yells from a little runabout with a photographer aboard. "We didn't expect you this early. Could you go back out, put your sail up and come back in again?" Sue and I smiled politely and negotiated an action shot of us pulling down the sail rather than going all the way back out into the breeze. We heard a yell from the docks and saw a collection of familiar faces as "Operation Raleigh" people and other sailing friends appeared. We stepped ashore at the yacht club to be welcomed by the commodore and interviewed by newspaper, television and radio while trying to say hello to many friends. With the formalities over, the commodore granted us permission to store our boat under the yacht club during our stay. We then stunned observers by having *Tom* totally dismantled and stored under the club and all our gear in the back of a utility truck in 15 minutes.

Sitting in the back of the truck with a couple of friends, Sue and I breathed a sigh of relief. We had arrived and could relax for a well-earned couple of weeks off. We had made it to the far north of Queensland. Our "cruising days," however, were over. No more island resorts and help just around the corner. The far north of Cape York was our next test with 600 miles of unpopulated coastline.

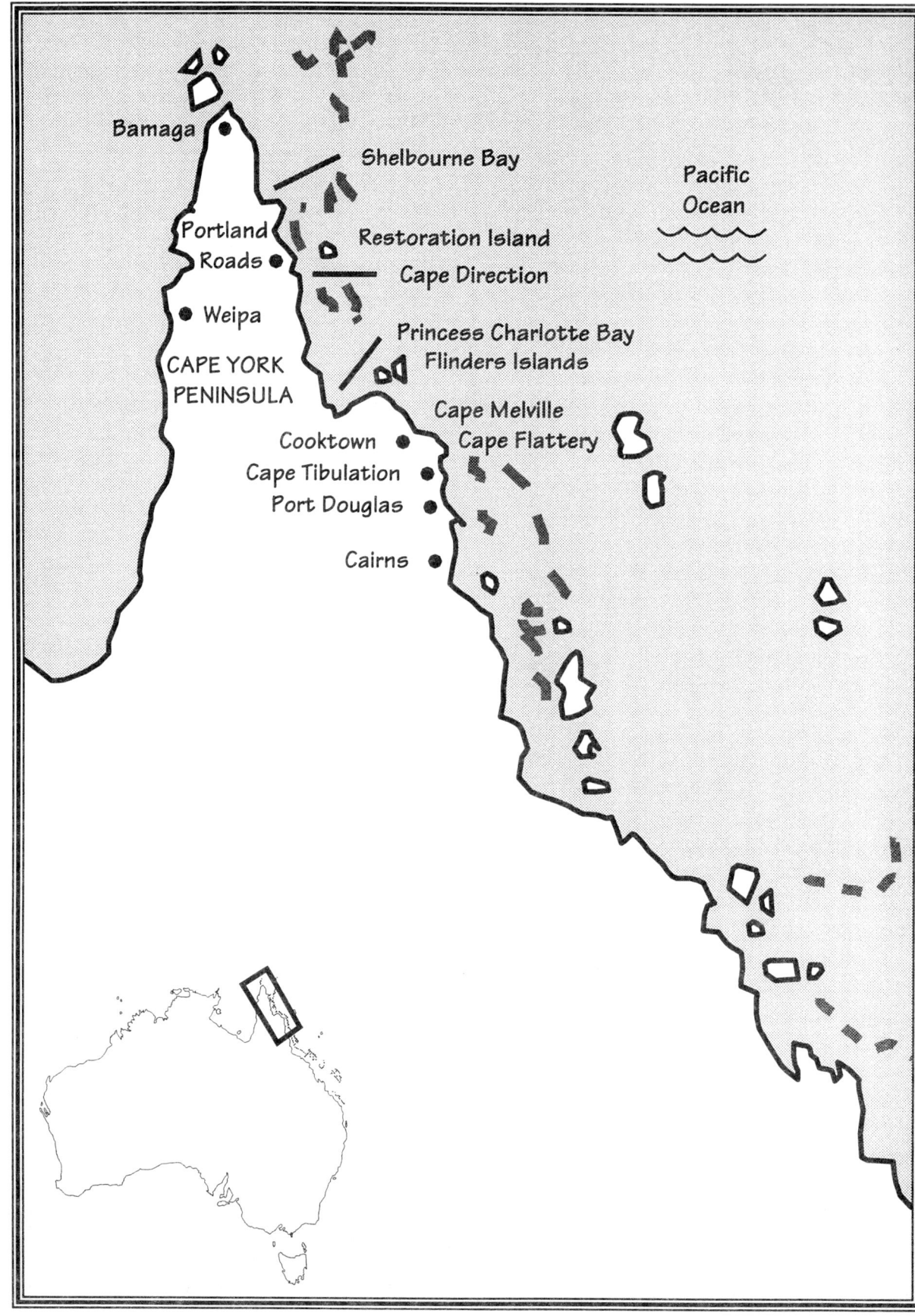

Chapter 5

Cape York and Beyond
Cairns to Weipa

We stayed for two weeks in Cairns, catching up with youth participants from the USA whom Sue and I had selected for the Operation Raleigh program the year before. Their enthusiastic tales of sailing the square-rigger *Zebu* across the Pacific and working with communities in Cape York were exciting. We could see the change in them from such powerful experiences. It was also an opportunity for us to catch up on some sleep and for *Tom* to have some minor repairs. We also completed further press and sponsor commitments, and Ann Tweady from Operation Raleigh interviewed us for the next book about the program, which made us feel quite proud.

When we were ready to head north to Port Douglas and beyond, our friends from Operation Raleigh joined us for a day jaunt from Cairns to Port Douglas in their Avon inflatable dinghy. We tossed frisbees back and forth between the boats and drank a few beers before camping on the beach beneath the shadows of the $300 per night Mirage Resort. It was with mixed feelings that we waved farewell to our friends at the end of the day. We would miss their friendship and the two weeks of comparative luxury we had shared in Cairns, with hot showers and an endless selection of food. We were only too well aware that this marked the beginning of Cape York, the northern frontier of Australia. Cairns would be the last major city before Darwin, nearly 1,800 miles away, with only a few small mining and fishing towns between. *Tom* groaned slightly under the extra weight of three weeks food and ten days water. From here on we were on our own. After three months of relative comfort and security on the well-inhabited section of the east coast, the next 600 miles north and the coast beyond would be lonely. Or so we believed.

As we sailed along the vibrant green, rainforest-clad coast of the World Heritage area from the Daintree River area up to Cape Tribulation, we warmed to the new adventures that lay before us and enjoyed being on our own once more.

"Mark, is that a log moving over there?" asked Sue as we cruised past a creek inlet.

"I'm not going to check, but I think we just saw our first crocodile," I replied steering us a little further out to sea.

That night we made sure our campsite was well away from any creek. Warmed by the flickering fire of our campfire on a secluded sandy cove, I enjoyed the fresh, familiar smell of salt air and the sound of waves caressing the shore.

Cape Tribulation is the last well-known and frequently visited section of the coast - the end of the road. A few small isolated cabins and holiday retreats are slowly being replaced by backpackers' resorts with bars and restaurants in the middle of the rainforest. The next day, as the rainforest gave way to low sand dune and scrub, we pulled into the small community of Cooktown. When Captain Cook had explored a route north through the Barrier Reef, the river inlet, at what is now Cooktown, had provided a much-needed port. In the 1800s it became one of the largest towns in northern Queensland and a hub for the inland goldfields. Although its heyday may have passed, Cooktown, in its own unique way, has remained a frontier town for the north, welcoming tourists and fishermen exploring the Cape. The scattering of faded weatherboard shops and houses that lined the potholed main street, spoke of history and proud moments. The locals, when they heard where we had come from and where we were going, didn't begin the usual lengthy tale of woe and warning, as had their urban cousins. Instead, it was usually a case of "Good on ya, you'll be right, have a good trip." The only word of caution was, "Ya carryin' a gun with ya?"

"We've got a 12-gauge powerhead for any sharks or crocs," I suggested.

"Shit, you don't have to worry about them, it's the bloody people up there that you have to worry about," he replied! He didn't return my smile, and I sensed he wasn't kidding.

Cape York and Beyond

We negotiated camping near the public boat ramp to ensure an early departure. The local town museum, housed in an old Victorian, two story house with many photos of the grand old days, was well worth the visit. We signed the yacht register at the museum and felt we had entered the annals of history. To generate some form of income while sailing we had been lucky enough to secure payment for regular articles for the American sailing magazine *Multihulls*. I hastily completed the second, hand-scrawled article that would then go to my parents who typed it up on computer, added a few photos, which we had taken but never actually seen, and mailed it off to Massachusetts. We also called in the latest 2GO Radio station update, knowing it would be a long while before I had a chance to do either of these again.

It was strange sailing out the next morning knowing that we were headed into the unknown. The "top end" of the East Coast, as it is known, was the graveyard of many early explorers' vessels as they sought the passage through the Barrier Reef northwards and onto Asia. Captain Cook, Flinders and many others had become frustrated with the narrow maze of the reef that closed to within six to twelve miles of the coast. We were grateful to have charts that showed the coral reefs and narrow passages ahead, even if *Tom's* shallow draft could skim over most areas. It was only on the odd occasion that we were slightly off, having misjudged the tide, or finding the reef had a few high points. *Tom's* rudders would kick up and we would gasp at the razor sharp coral heads flashing past inches below our fiberglass hulls.

In fact, with such a featureless coastline, it was often safer for us to be six to eight miles offshore in the narrow shipping lanes. At least we could then chart our progress by the marker and light buoys. The reliable southeast trade winds now blew strongly on most days and we did a rough calculation of our course each day, planning sights and the most direct route. Mile upon unpopulated mile stretched off as far as the eye could see. Scattered rainforest, long rolling sandhills, isolated tabletop mountains and low boulder-strewn headlands alternated along this wild and beautiful coastline. Gazing through the ever present haze, a feeling of emptiness pervaded, as we were absorbed into the shimmering seascape. We would now be relying on our own initiative, with no expectations of anyone coming to our rescue. The umbilical cord had been cut.

The large flat-topped hills of Cape Bedford and higher rocky headlands quickly gave way to flat, non-descript sandhills with a scrubby interior stretching inland. Cape Flattery was our first camp in the lee of the headland on a beach. It showed signs of the sand mining camp that was marked on the map as just over the next hill. Empty 44-gallon diesel drums and decaying timbers lay scattered among the casuarinas. Recent four wheel drive tracks showed that either someone was still mining, or this was a favored fishing spot. We stayed in the afternoon shade, as what had been appreciated as winter warmth in Cairns was now spring heat. Layers of warm clothing had now been replaced by loose fitting shirts and plenty of sunscreen, and we began to feel the effects of the heat on top of the effects of sailing and packing and unpacking the boat each day.

A few days later Cape Melville loomed large and dignified out of a flat and undefined coast. It rose out of the low sand hills and lines of green mangroves, resembling a pyramid as if of human construction, formed from large car-sized granite boulders. The Cape and its bay actually provided a haven from the south easterly trade winds. In March 1899 a pearling fleet thought so too, only to be set upon by a fierce cyclone that wrecked over 50 boats. Skeletons have since been found at various times exposed in the sand throughout the area. Wandering behind the scrubby shoreline we found the memorial stone listing the names of nine dead white seamen. In an indirect way it also recorded the sadder perspective of Australian history by casually concluding that "over 300 colored men (had also) drowned." As regular crew of the pearlers, the colored men did not rate a mention by name or country. Their omission told of how little value was placed on their souls in working for pearling bosses. We would learn more of the grimmer side of Australia's pearling history on the Western Australian coast.

Our passage to Flinders Islands (named after Matthew) across Bathurst Bay was in calm conditions, and Sue was in fishing heaven. Not content with landing a fighting seven-pound Spanish Mackerel, she tossed her lure in again. After a couple of minutes we both stared at the thing that jumped from the water on the end of her hook. It was still 100 feet from the boat and fighting like mad. After half an hour of battling she eventually pulled the fish onto *Tom* with the help of a following swell. I stuck my hands down its gills and sat on it while we continued to sail. A 13-pound tuna puts up a hell of a struggle! Sue was as proud as punch.

As we turned into the passage between the rocky bluffs of Flinders and Stanley Islands we had cause to shake our heads in disbelief. After a week of solitude, here was a floating marina! Anchored around a fuel barge were a collection of fishing boats and seven yachts. With our tuna as currency, we went off to negotiate making a radio call to home and getting some fresh water. Eventually the skipper aboard the 30-meter steel hull yacht, *Sea Eagle*, took pity on us, invited us aboard for a cup of tea and placed our call for us. Sitting in the large stateroom with air-conditioning, plush lounges and porthole windows covered with curtains, I wondered what this kind of sailing was all about. We swapped fish for fresh water and enjoyed a second cup of tea in the air-conditioning.

On our way back to a campsite on Flinders Island we dropped by to visit the oil barge, which was anchored as a floating supermarket for trawler fleets during the fishing season. It was apparently towed in and out of Cairns every year to provide not only a re-supply point for food, fuel, water and beer but also a post office and social center for the trawlers which returned from fishing every two weeks to wait for the mothership to collect their catch. The season had not been good this year and many boats had gone west to the Kimberley coast hoping for better luck. A young, muscle-bound skipper in a sweaty grey T-shirt and black underpants, who mass-produced crab pots on Flinders Island, assured us that things were fine in the crabbing business. He and his brother negotiated to fly crabs out live by seaplane to Cairns and on to Hawaii for $25 or more per crab. Soon he would be off north again where he had made about $140,000 the previous season! Big money comes and goes on this frontier as adventurers seek their modern-day goldrush.

The next day we motored across the wide, calm expanse of Princess Charlotte Bay, surrounded by a heat haze and needing a compass bearing to find the other side 12 miles away. At one stage a fishing trawler came out of the haze and offered us a tow, but we politely refused, still determined to make it by ourselves. Once the haze had cleared, large sand dunes shimmered around the bay — an impressive sight but as we were barely half way to the top of Cape York, we didn't stay to explore. After finding a landing on the other side of the bay we did a quick scout each way along the beach. Not

300 feet from where we had landed I found some marks leading up the beach. Anxiously following them up over the sand ridge I saw where they disappeared into a large lagoon directly behind the beach. The tracks were about a three feet wide, which made this crocodile the biggest one we hoped we never saw. "Sue, come and have a look at this," I yelled. She didn't complain when I suggested we go just a bit further that day.

Crossing Lloyd Bay towards the one and only area of settlement on the east coast of Cape York, we saw Lockhart Mission and knew that Portland Roads community lay just over the headland. Our solitude was broken by the presence of another yacht in the bay. It wasn't until we took a closer look that we realized that it wasn't actually anchored and had quite a list, having run aground on the only reef marked in the bay! We pulled in for lunch to a sandy spit of beach on Restoration Island, a small island approximately half a square mile in size, only a small but deep 100-yard channel separating it from the mainland. The eastern side has a high rocky ridge, which then flattens out to a sandy coral strip covered in low scrub. Having noticed a number of cabins, boats and a radio antenna around the small football field-sized clearing off the beach, I decided to see if anyone would mind us having lunch on their island, before getting shot as trespassers. I knocked on the door of what looked to be the main house, distinguished by its clothesline in the back yard, and woke Ron and Elaine from their afternoon nap. They gave their approval to this strange request, rather shocked at my appearance and brief explanation. I beat a hasty retreat back to the beach. Midway through lunch Ron appeared in his stubby shorts, T-shirt and thongs. "Sorry if I was a bit rude before," he said, "We were asleep and aren't used to having visitors! You're welcome to stay if you like. How does a hot shower and a bed sound?"

Sue glanced at me over her cheese and dry biscuit. I took the hint.

"That sounds great if you're sure it's all right," I replied.

"Move yourselves in and come on over for a beer," suggested Ron. Wasn't this the "frontier" coast where we were due to face hardship or certain death? Ron and Elaine were from Victoria and had answered a newspaper advertisement to caretaker an island on the Barrier Reef. They didn't know exactly where it was, but for the past six months they had been lord and lady of Restoration Island. The island was privately owned by a group from Melbourne who flew in for fishing expeditions during winter retreats. They had invested some money in establishing three prefabricated fiberglass cabins for accommodation for tourists but so far they were not exactly being inundated with visitors. Ron and Elaine introduced us to the good life of fresh seafood such as barbecued lobster tails and fresh oysters picked from the rocks that afternoon. We stayed for two nights and felt they were as happy to have our company as we were to have theirs.

In order to keep our family informed of where we were and assure them of our safety Ron allowed us to place a radio telephone call to my parents.

"Hello Mum, it's Mark calling from Restoration Island. Over."

"Oh. Are you alright? came the concerned reply.

"Yes, we are fine. Over."

"Yes, over... Um, ah...where are you again?

"We are at Restoration Island and Portland Roads. Over"

"Oh. Where is that? Are you sure you are all right?"

"You need to say over when you've finished talking Mum. We are fine. We'll be at the top in a week and we'll call you from Weipa. Good-bye, Over."

"Oh, yes over, good-bye, over. Lots of love. Talk to you soon!"

Poor Mum. She got the strangest calls from us and messages passed on from people she had never met from all over Australia. She was our link though, and passed on to Peter Pool and various sponsors the latest updates on our progress. Sue's parents received regular letters and updates in California, but due to the distance it was often two weeks or more after the event. They admitted it was best that way as they couldn't worry about where we were exactly.

Ron took us over to Portland Roads the next morning. Once a center for over 100,000 Australian and American troops during World War II, it was now a sleepy junkyard and home for a small number of people escaping the outside world for whatever reason. The few shacks and a half-constructed yacht that looked like it had been wrecked on the shore before ever setting sail was all there was of the town. In a galvanized iron shed sat an unfinished fiberglass yacht gathering dusty cobwebs, which was being used as a visitors' book for passing travelers who had emblazoned their own and their yachts' names over the hull. The dogs had barely enough energy to get up, let alone bark as you walked by. We were told, however, that the remnants of the airstrip and many others in the Cape area were still very active. Night flights landed regularly with illegal loads of people and drugs. "You don't ask questions, and I've certainly given up counting passing night flights," Ron said. We dropped in to the local oil barge managed by Marge and Keith and stocked up on a few essential supplies such as chocolates. They were an entertaining couple, taking a break from cruising while their yacht was in Cairns, and having a different experience on the coast for a season. They insisted we drop by on our way past the next day.

It felt good to be having a holiday from our trip on a resort that we hadn't even known was there. Perhaps it was history repeating itself as we restored ourselves. A small plaque at Ron and Elaine's cabin highlighted the fact that Restoration Island was Captain Bligh's first landfall in Australia on his epic voyage following the mutiny on the *Bounty*. After miraculously surviving many days afloat in their small lifeboat and crossing thousands of miles of open sea, as well as finding their way through the Barrier Reef, they stumbled ashore here to restore themselves before sailing on to Indonesia. They had sailed in a vessel the size of *Tom Thumb* across half the Pacific Ocean! We shared with Bligh a sense of restoration on this lovely island as Ron and Elaine bestowed on us their hospitality and gave us fresh food for the trip north. We sailed off feeling renewed from fresh-water showers and a comfortable bed, with a dozen fresh eggs aboard. Marge and Keith waved hello and good-bye as they admired *Tom* from the barge. We were ready to finish sailing Australia's east coast and head west for a change.

We didn't get far. Landing at Fair Cape for the evening we should have been suspicious of the name. We spent most of the night running around naked in a sand storm trying to stop our tent from ripping to pieces. The strong to gale force winds blew for the next three days as we sat frustrated and sand blasted on the shore. We were now getting behind schedule if we were to get favorable seasonal winds across Australia's northern coast and I was becoming anxious and impatient. It was equally frustrating passing beautiful places yet feeling we couldn't stay. Sue and I satisfied ourselves by developing a list of places we most wanted to come back to after the trip was finished.

The Coastwatch observation plane provided a contact with the outside world every now and then as it looped past, waggling its wings to say hello. Part of a contracted service by the Australian Customs Service, these small, twin-prop planes are based in Cairns and fly a regular route to Thursday Island at the top of the Cape, keeping an eye on Australia's northern coast. Locals laughed at the suggestion that Coastwatch was an effective deterrent for illegal importers, claiming the only time the Cape was quiet was when Coastwatch flew by. We had called them in Cairns and told them about our trip. Occasionally *Tom* and crew would become the focus of their interest as they doubled back and flew down low over us out at sea, or on a beach. It was comforting to see the regular waggle of the wings. More than once, however, as we celebrated the solitude and natural beauty together, we were almost caught out by the familiar plane diving low over a headland and circling round us. Likewise we were surprised a couple of times by container or transport ships silently cruising up in the shipping lane behind us with waving crew members on deck only a few hundred yards away.

The weeks became longer and the top end seemed further away as we spent numerous days sitting impatiently ashore eating sand and watching 30-knot winds and a rolling swell. However, we enjoyed some good solitary beachcombing, finding glass fishing floats and some amazing shells. Fresh coconuts also became a welcome part of our menu, with good coconut palms now a requirement for our campsite. There was just us, the amazing wilderness of Cape York and the rich Barrier Reef. One of the most spectacular sights we had yet seen was the huge sheer sided, untouched white sand dunes of Shelbourne Bay. It was like the Sahara and rainforest meeting the Barrier Reef, as high desert-like dunes rolled in patterns around dark green lines of bush and mangrove, down to the sapphire blue sea. We stared in silence at this surreal picture shimmering in a mirage of heat and salt sea haze.

The long awaited Albany Passage, gateway to the northern coast of Australia at the tip of Cape York, finally came into sight as we ran in 15-knot winds with six-foot following seas. I was anxiously lining up between the exposed reef and wondering how fast the tide was running in this narrow channel when our trolling line hooked what I thought was a single lump of seaweed.

"No, I'm not going to cut my lure off," insisted Sue.

"Well you pull the bloody thing in," I yelled, with both hands on the tiller knowing that in the tidal race we were now entering there was only one direction we could go.

"Jesus Christ," I heard Sue yell. In a quick glance I saw a long flash of silver as her fish continued the fight.

"Just pull it in when the next swell comes over the back of the boat," I instructed impatiently.

"Here we go," came the call, and without much of a glance I sat on top of the fish and held it with one hand while holding the tiller in the other. Not until we shot in behind the first island and the wind calmed did I look down to check my grip on the fish now struggling in its death throes. A long razor sharp set of teeth glinted up at me, along with an angry glazed eye. "Bloody hell, Sue," I exclaimed at her prize six-foot long barracuda, while quickly counting my fingers and reasserting my grip.

In the calm of the passage we took in the view of an area that had, in the 1800s, been hailed as a future northern port — the Singapore of Australia. Plans for it faded with the abandoning of any hope of taming this wilderness and its tropical hazards. Suddenly the vista of deep green rainforest and dark sandy beach was broken by brightly colored sails of catamarans dotted on the sand. Shaking my head once again I remembered that there was a resort somewhere near. I hoped they told their guests about the tidal currents before they set them loose for a day sail. You could easily imagine them coming out of the bay and finding themselves swept to New Guinea, only a few hundred miles to the north.

Cape York and Beyond

Tom glided through the passage as we gladly left behind the east coast swells. We were now rounding the northernmost tip of Australia, about to enter the Gulf of Carpentaria. Small groups of adventurous travelers who had braved the rough four-wheel-drive road to the Cape were scattered on the shore. We waved as we passed. As *Tom* was spat through the 75-yard gap between the tip of the Cape and the outlying islands, we headed due west for the first time. On the beach we joined a group of road-weary trail-bike riders covered from head to toe in red dust, having arrived a very different way on a commercial travel holiday. They shared a can of cold beer with us to celebrate our arrival at the top of Australia. "The best I've had in Australia," declared Sue. The bikers were quite happy to trade a few beers for the bulk of our fish. It was certainly a change from their baked bean diet. We were in a different world as we sailed off into the sunset, the water as still as a lake on this leeward side. No more anxious finger indentations on the trampoline frame for a while.

The following day we arrived at Bamaga and New Mapoon, communities of Torres Strait Islanders and Aborigines. Its camping area and beach at Red Island Point was a dry, dusty paddock crammed with four-wheel drives, holding everything that opened and closed. Some people come to see the Cape, while others are into "been there, done that," or "got the T-shirt" type trips, usually carrying more beer than fuel to help numb the body and settle the dust. We were looking forward to returning to lonely, untouched beaches. Perhaps we had been spoiled by the past three months.

We hitch-hiked the six miles into the community of Bamaga on the back of a truck to get some more outboard fuel and food. On our way back down the dirt track main street, we saw a leather clad biker with full face helmet covered in red dust swaggering down the middle of the road. As the visor opened and the helmet was torn off in a cloud of dust, we were surprised to see an Operation Raleigh friend, Nick Horn. He had ridden up the Cape for a holiday, arriving at Cape York tip an hour behind us and had since been trying to track us down. We celebrated with a beer in the local pub of Bamaga, where the concrete seats and tables were bolted to the floor. Nick told us of his butt-numbing adventure through the red, bull dust and the corrugated, rutted roads of the north. "It's been an adventure, but I'd catch a train back if there was one," he declared. Apparently, soon after arriving back in Cairns he abandoned his plans to continue riding the bike cross-country through Asia, India and the Middle East back to his home in London. It took him two weeks before he could walk without bowed legs. We spent a memorable evening with Nick at Red Point camped out under the stars before we each headed our separate ways.

We were now heading across the top of Cape York. The coastline was low, flat and non-descript, the beginnings of real "croc" country, as mangrove-lined river mouths mixed with dry, sandy scrub country. Rivers that criss-cross large sections of the Cape, such as the Jardine and Wenlock, produced gaping mouths which encouraged you to enter and explore. As always, we could have spent months in this area, as indeed had two salty catamaran couples we met on an isolated sandy beach. It had taken them two years to get there from Brisbane! It was a relief to be on the lee shore of the trade winds. The further north we had gone, the stronger they had become, to the point where we were battling steep choppy swells and hanging on in 15- to 25-knot winds every day. In contrast, passing the Jardine River we were happily running with just the jib over flat water and taking turns to sunbathe and read a book.

Our passage to the town of Weipa once again became a battle, as trusty southeast trade winds now became headwinds as we turned to sail south down the west coast of Cape York. As practice for what we knew was to come, we ventured off on a night trip in somewhat calmer conditions than the regular 30-knot afternoon breeze. The rudders suffered a pounding as jellyfish one to three feet in diameter appeared, and our navigation technique consisted of checking off the rivers as we ran into their sandbars, one by one. Ever conscious of the possibility of crocodiles, we both nearly fell overboard when, close to shore, for 150 feet around us the sea exploded in a frenzy of foam and phosphorescence. Too shocked to go looking we assumed we had come across a school of prawns, but headed a little further out to sea just to be safe.

Around midnight we anchored for two hours, content to wait for the moon to provide some guidance. The shoreline was low and scrubby, which meant that the only means of accurate navigation was checking off the river inlets one by one again. We pushed on in the dim moonlight, motor sailing to make some distance. The slight wind favored us in the hazy morning sunrise and we kept on going, knowing this was good training for the three day Gulf crossing we were planning. Very tired, but much relieved, we were finally blown ashore by a southwest wind at 3:00 P.M. the next day.

Weipa, a bauxite mining town of 3,000 people marked the end of the Cape and Queensland. After three months and over 2,000 miles, we had finally completed our first full state of Australia. We were exhausted and hot, yet happy. Mark and Annette Dodge, who were friends of friends, opened their home and workshop to us. Mark was a fitter by trade with Comalco, the mining company, and his tools and advice were greatly appreciated. *Tom* was in need of repair after the toll the jellyfish had taken on our rudders and the coral of the Barrier Reef on our fiberglass hulls. The rudder brackets were single castings and never quite strong enough to cope with the extra stress of carrying heavy loads. Pulled completely apart for the first time since Thomas Island in the Whitsundays, *Tom* lay in various stages of repair across the backyard. It was then that the local newspaper, The Bauxite Bulletin, called to get photos and a story. I'm sure the locals were convinced we were slightly insane after the front page photo of us in the midst of what appeared to be a wrecked boat.

During our stay we had a full tour of Weipa and its surrounding areas in all its complexity. I had worked in an inland mine in Queensland before, so the mining process, and the concept of a company town, were not new. Sue could not get over the facilities for such a relatively small town, including cinema, swimming pool, tennis courts and primary school, "in the middle of bloody nowhere," as she put it. Of interest to us both was their flora regeneration program. Native plants were replanted by hand and aircraft seed-scattering techniques throughout previously mined areas. A number of forestry research projects were also being conducted. The regenerated areas and stands of timber put some of the deserted, empty open mining pits I had seen in other parts of Queensland to shame.

We also visited South Weipa, the nearby Aboriginal community of about 600 people. The relationship between Aboriginal communities and mining projects has always been fraught with difficulties, especially when reported by sensationalizing city media trying to promote a story. With the ideological differences there may never be an easy answer to the debates about the value of land as a sacred and spiritual entity or as a valuable commodity.

In Weipa it appeared, however, that some balance had been achieved in recognizing the rights and values of this indigenous group of Australians. Sacred sites were identified and preserved in the mining process. The community was given the opportunity to train aboriginal youth to work in the mine. Funds and assistance had been made available for the community to build facilities including a school and community hall, and access to medical facilities was now immediately available. But at what price? Traditional Aboriginal community and family values conflicted with those of the new town of people just down the road. Broken beer bottles scattered around the community hall suggested unresolved issues. As much as Sue continued to ask questions about Aboriginal issues, I struggled uneasily as an Australian to provide any convincing reply or solutions. This was an issue that would continue to present itself in many ways in many places around Australia.

During this break both of us were quietly preparing ourselves physically and psychologically for the next stage, the Gulf of Carpentaria. We had considered sailing down into the Gulf and along the coast, but the extra distance, and reports of light winds, crocodiles and miles of inhospitable tidal mud flats outweighed a few days of anxiety on the more direct route — straight across. Three days and three nights of sailing across 350 miles of lonely sea. In many ways the last four months had been training for just this event.

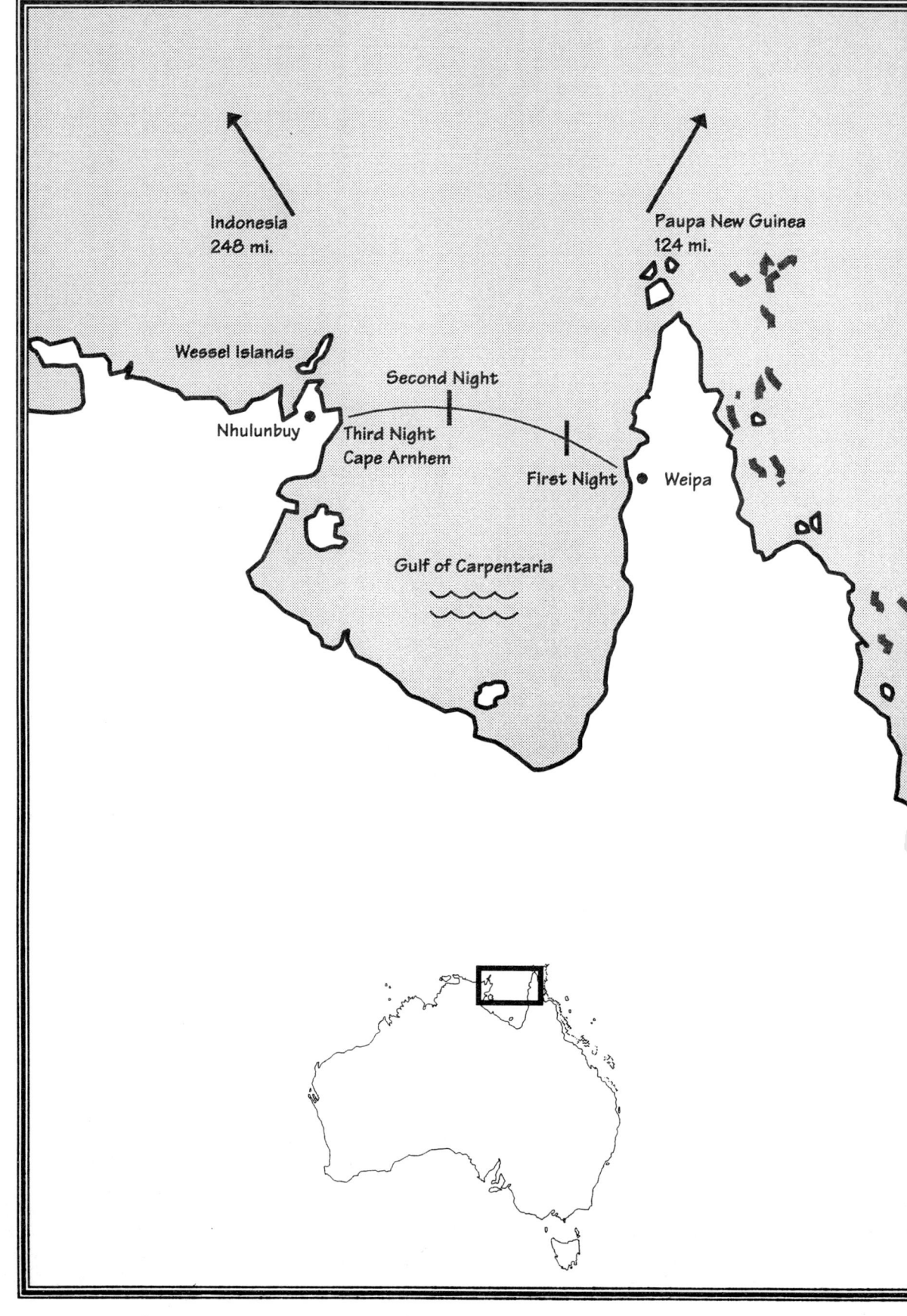

Chapter 6

Into the Never-Never
The Gulf of Carpentaria

I wasn't quite sure why I looked down at that moment. Packing *Tom* had required quite a few trips back and forth to the shore at Rocky Point. Through the murky water my eyes focused on what I had been anxiously looking out for over the past three months. I slowly and carefully moved my foot away from the small but deadly sea wasp box jellyfish. It wasn't yet the summer season when these jellyfish make the waterways of northern Australia dangerous for swimming. A sting could have killed me within a few minutes. I pointed it out to Sue. We finished packing and pushed off, both more worried about our next few days ahead than the deadly jellyfish.

In silence we sailed out of Weipa and across Albatross Bay, quickly covering the 25 miles to Dufkyen Point and the open sea. The tide and wind were in our favor as we cruised past the points that we had battled around to make our landing last week. A red-dust heat haze settled on the water and calm sandy shore as we anxiously glanced back. Our compass bearing was set. We would not see the next shore for three nights and 360 miles of lonely ocean sailing across the Gulf of Carpentaria. Sue was anxious and quiet. My heart was in my mouth and my stomach was in absolute knots.

When the Dutch navigator William Jansz made the first recorded European landing in Australia at Weipa in 1606, in his vessel the *Duyfken,* he was unimpressed by the "miserableness" of the coast. The yachting guide for the region states, "the coast remains uninhabited and dreary in the extreme, the eastern coast being low scrubland fronted by miles of unbroken beaches which fade into mangrove swamps towards the south." Rather than face a long hard battle around the base of the gulf in similar conditions, and an extra two to three weeks of travel, we had agreed on sailing a direct passage from Weipa to the mining town of Nhulunbuy, on the northeast tip of Arnhem Land. Large tidal mudflats, unfavorable winds, minimal habitation and reports of "bloody plenty of big crocs down there, mate." had made this direct option more acceptable, or so we had convinced ourselves.

We also had the feeling that we were now past the point of no return. In many ways the east coast was still a familiar shore for me and we were that much closer to help and home. On the other side of the Gulf we would suddenly be in the Northern Territory, a long way from anywhere with the only way being forward. From there even greater challenges lay ahead. We were now ready to move beyond the familiar and test the skills that we had learned over the past months. We would certainly need them on the more powerful Indian and Southern Oceans still ahead of us. All these thoughts combined to twist me into tighter knots.

So far we hadn't said much to each other. As the low flat shoreline quickly disappeared into the sunset behind us, Sue burst into tears,

"I'm scared." What could I say? I was anxiously coping with my own uncertainties. If anything I wanted someone to reassure me that sailing off across the Gulf of Carpentaria in a sixteen foot catamaran, on a Tuesday in August, with a large high weather system coming across the center of Australia was the right thing to be doing. I ran through all the things we had been through so many times before that had led us to this decision.

"It will only be three nights. Isn't that better than two to three weeks in the Gulf? We can do it. We've come this far. The weather conditions are perfect."

In many ways I was trying to reassure myself as well. I reached out to clumsily offer a hug. "Come on, we can't go back now," I said uneasily. Sue said nothing and we kept on heading west.

Our small four horsepower outboard would be important for our safety on this section. Prepared for the worst, a demasting or blown out sail, we carried enough fuel for approximately half the distance. A small but comforting consolation. As the land disappeared from view and a large Weipa-bound ore-carrier headed our way, a light onshore breeze blew up. We would end up sailing backward at this rate! "No worries." said Sue feeling a little better, "Let's start the outboard to make some distance and lose some weight in fuel!"

She was wrong, we did have worries! The outboard kept cutting out and we glanced back nervously at each other and then behind to where the land had been. It was too late to go back unless we wanted to do some fancy nighttime sailing in flukey winds through Weipa harbor. Why now? Why, for the first time, did the outboard have to give us trouble? How many weeks had we planned to be out here? In the dimming light I started stripping down the carburetor, the potential source of our problem. Our log read "Stripped carby as Sue sailed us SW at two knots for two hours," Slopping into the headwind trying to keep the spray off the bits and pieces of carburetor spread across the trampoline, I blew out whatever dirt I could find. In a state of nausea, from anxiety, petrol fumes and fiddly work on a rocking boat, we threw in a new spark plug for good luck, reset the engine and crossed our fingers. It spluttered and coughed but kept going, and much relieved we headed off into the sunset for the first long lonely night at sea.

As protection from the cool 59°F night ahead we took turns resting perched on the trampoline. I snuggled in a ball on top of the waterproof bag, we sat behind a loosely rigged spray cover. It wasn't the low temperature that made us cold as much as the continual seaspray and breeze. All our layers of clothing made us look like slow moving, soggy koala bears, but at least kept us a little warm. First came the Damart thermal clothing, balaclavas and gloves, followed by full length O'Neil wetsuits and booties, then the spray jacket and life jacket, all tied together with our life lines. Despite all this the occasional wave still fell down on us and went in our ears, or splashed up through the trampoline and freshly soaked our wetsuits. But the main problem arose when nature called and you had to quickly peel it all off and put it back on again before a wave slopped over you.

Food was important to keep us going, but with no chance of cooking on an open deck all we could eat was sandwiches and snack food. We had prepared plenty of orange flavored Tang in advance. We munched on muesli bars and fruit during the day, supplemented by lunches of salami and cheese on hopefully dry crackers. Still suffering from nausea, food was the last thing on my mind during our first evening as I focused on setting our course and making distance.

Our route was far enough north in the Gulf that any tide flow or currents were negligible so we set our sights directly for the far shore, almost due west. Planning on averaging five knots as a comfortable speed we couldn't see any way that we could make it in less than three nights unless we wanted to be looking for landfall in the dark. With this in mind we had planned to set out from the eastern shore at midday on the 5th of September and hopefully see land early on the morning of the 8th. Neither Sue nor I had taken a nautical navigation course, so we could not accurately plot our progress with a sextant. Handheld Global Positioning Systems, or GPSs that automatically plot your position from satellites were far too expensive. We had a deck mounted compass and two luminous handheld, sight bearing compasses. To chart our progress we regularly kept a log indicating the wind, our direction and estimated speed. Using this dead reckoning system our target was Cape Arnhem, 18 miles south of the small mining town of Nhulunbuy, one of the few points of habitation in the Gulf. We chose this spot knowing that if we went too far north we could end up in the Arafura Sea heading for Indonesia. I would just be glad to see land at some time on that third day and step ashore.

We had waited for five days at Weipa to get the best weather conditions. I had the Australian weather map imprinted on my brain with a huge high pressure system slowly moving over central Australia at our departure. This is what we had been waiting for. As the previous high had moved on, the first few days of the following system usually produced lighter winds and calmer seas. Everyone from the harbor masters at Gove and Weipa, the Coastwatch base on Thursday Island and of course my parents knew our schedule. We insisted they wait two days beyond our planned arrival date to sound any alarms, as we could take longer than expected. If we were still floating around the sea by then we promised to activate our Emergency Radio Beacon. If there was no sign of that, it would be more likely that we were wrecked on the shore somewhere to the south. My parents wished us well and made a special attendance at church that week. Sue decided she would call her folks from Nhulunbuy. "They are better off not knowing," she suggested.

We settled into a routine of two hours on, two hours off at the tiller as we found that was the limit of our concentration trying to focus on the dark swirling sea and the night sky. You couldn't actually call what we had in between "sleep," as we dozed in a damp state with the occasional wave reminding us just where we were. Unfortunately, our crossing was out of phase with the moon, which meant there was only dim starlight to see our way. However we soon discovered the advantages of traveling almost due west, when we picked out a star in line with our mast and followed its approximate path until its glimmer had disappeared into the black horizon. Near midnight, after hours of listening to the drone of the outboard in relatively calm seas, the wind finally swung around behind us at 15 knots and we sailed on into the night with just the mainsail set. Sue didn't feel comfortable taking the tiller, so she slept as I sailed on, rewarding myself with a butterscotch for each half-hour I stayed awake. Our wake streamed out behind us in a phosphorescent glow as we averaged five to six knots. It was wild sailing *Tom* off into the blackness. Over 2,000 miles of experience was paying off as I steered by the wind on my face and the roll of the swells as they passed under and disappeared into the night. I sang and yelled to myself, sailing on adrenalin, occasionally splashing water in my face to help keep my concentration. The night was peaceful as we blew with the breeze out into the middle of the Gulf, further and further from land.

Bang!

I shook my head and opened my eyes in time to stop the boom from hitting me again. Blood was running off my nose as I bent my glasses back into shape and tried to see into the darkness.

"Sue," I yelled. She forced herself awake and grabbed the boom.

I'd fallen asleep and we had slowly gybed coming off a black unseen swell. Luckily, apart from a headache and a small cut I was OK. It certainly woke me up! Sue helped tie out the boom and ran a line back through a cleat. I cursed that we hadn't thought of it before.

I was never so glad to see the dawn. Both somewhat groggy, we warmed to the rising sun and peeled off the restricting layers. The following wind had built up a sizable six-to-nine-foot swell and we changed to a jib for most of the day, continuing to average three knots. We had been out of sight of land before but this was another feeling, knowing we were on the ocean. We still had another 48 hours before we would see land again. We had a sense of freedom in one respect being totally out there and going with the flow, at the whim and mercy of the sea. Our feeling for the sea was now acute. We felt the slightest change in wind or swell. We were growing in confidence as the morning progressed. Sue managed a smile and I lost enough knots in my stomach to feel hungry.

We had a new found respect for the Indonesian and Malaysian fishermen who ventured to this coast in their small wooden sailing vessels long before European sailors. They had a strong affinity for the sea, steering by stars and currents in their small frail vessels. They came for the *beche de mere*, or sea slug, a delicacy in abundance in the gulf waters. Remnants of their fishing settlements have been found on isolated beaches throughout Australia's north. Matthew Flinders even met a number of them in the *Investigator* in 1802.

We had seen the occasional flying fish before, but now revelled in their efforts to see which could fly the furthest as they skimmed across the surface at much the same height as *Tom*. As they were only eight to twelve inches long and silver in color, we often mistook them for birds. Our winner that day flew about 50 yards. A group of dolphins joined us for play early that morning and we were in fine spirits as they splashed us. The day was warm and cloudless and we relaxed a little as we pushed on to the middle of the Gulf.

A light headwind sprang up in the late afternoon requiring us to motor into the night rather than be blown backwards. Our only reassuring thought as we climbed into damp thermals and wetsuits again was, "Well, only one more night of this!"

We knew that the next day we would be well into the Northern Territory. At sunset we were joined by a school of twenty dolphins that followed us into the night, rising in pairs so close to the boat we could have touched them. They enjoyed playing with us, glancing sideways as they leapt in unison, turned sideways, and splashed us as they landed. Their phosphorescent shapes darted back and forth under the boat. It was as if they were guiding and encouraging us on to the other side of the Gulf.

Our eyelids were heavy, and the stars shone like familiar friends. The sea was calmer as the wind died at dusk and was still throughout the night.

At times it was as though we were on a lake. Little Oscar the outboard droned away only stopping to top off the fuel tank around midnight. In the evening calm Sue was happy to take turns skippering. My two-hour watches seemed to take forever as I would bribe myself with butterscotch candy (what had become my staple diet for the past few days) just to focus for a little longer. In our soggy sleepiness we would often hear each other singing loudly or talking to the sea and stars to help stay awake. It was a relief to see the faint glimmer of morning light. Our second night was over and we would soon be warm again.

The third day provided our best day's sailing with 10- to-15-knot southeasterlies continuing to push us along at four to five knots in comfortable conditions. The high-pressure system was finally coming through the gulf giving more consistent winds, leaving us confident at the thought of only one more night on the sea. We saw a few sea birds flying high overhead but very few at sea level. Our greatest surprise was what appeared to be a large area of thin reeds sticking about 18 inches into the air. At first I thought I was tired and imagining things and then thought it was a strange seaweed scape. When we finally got to them I could hardly believe my eyes and grabbed Sue. They were sea snakes, hundreds of them, all periscoping up out of the water in a 150-foot radius. We stared in amazement at all their different brightly colored bands. We realized that we didn't want to take any of them on board and quickly sailed out of them. As quickly as they had appeared, they disappeared behind us and we were staring at the empty sea.

From our dead reckoning and compass work we expected to sight land in the morning, at least some section of the Northern Territory coast and not New Guinea or Indonesia. We headed into the blackness and cold of our third night at sea. What if we were wrong? What if we had to spend another night at sea, not knowing where land was? Even if we found land, how far would we be from our destination, Nhulunbuy. I was too tired to think. Sunrise would answer my questions. The calm three-foot swells slid under Tom as we cut through the dark under full sail. Our eyelids hung heavy and we were beginning to feel cramped and salt encrusted. We both had large red, irritating rashes from the constant rubbing of wet clothes and salt water. Light snacks and cold water were beginning to lose their appeal for want of a good hot drink and a cooked meal.

Keeping Australia On the Left

At 1:30 A.M. Sue awoke me from my wet slumber to inform me that there were lights ahead. Since they appeared to be moving, we assumed they were trawlers and slowly made our way forward, strobe and flashlights handy to prevent any possible collision. They would be trawling the eastern shores of the gulf, so we must be close! I held back my excitement as we both sat alert and focused on the darkness ahead. We passed between the distant lights and moved on toward the land that I calculated would perhaps be another 12 miles, and three to four hours away. We furled the jib and with a mixture of anxiety and relief I steered on into the night, just the outboard ticking over. Half an hour later, with thoughts of dry, warm land running through my mind, my eyes struggled to focus on the blackness. I rubbed them and splashed myself with water. Was I tired and imagining things, or was that a black shape to starboard moving differently to the swells. I splashed myself yet again and stared intently into the dark. The black, three-foot high horizon was not moving, it was solid. "It's land!" I yelled, none too sure at what we had found.

Just as I turned *Tom*, he rose on a swell that foamed away beneath us to break on rocks that must have been only a few yards away. We were closer than I thought. Sue was wide-awake and flashed our torch ashore to confirm the presence of a dark jagged rock. We'd made it! We hadn't a clue where we were, so we went back out to sea, passing a large solitary rock that we had luckily missed on the way in. A faint glimmer of light appeared off in the distance to our north. Floating around bleary eyed we realized that the only place with lights on the coast was Nhulunbuy, our destination. We couldn't be so lucky! During the three hours remaining before sunrise we floated back and forth under a jib, about 500 yards offshore. A trawler passed within a half-mile and we prepared torches and strobe to flash in case we faced the rotten luck of making it across the gulf only to be run over and sunk.

As the first light glowed over the ocean, the most beautiful view opened up, a rugged rocky headland wrapped around to a sandy beach and bay, backed by trees and grass and plants. It was land and it looked and smelled beautiful! The sea birds welcomed us as we set sail and headed northwards up the coast, wanting to find out where we were exactly. We closely checked the chart for all the possibilities 30 miles up or down the coast from our target of Cape Arnhem. Nothing seemed to match! The shoreline features of low flat scrub, broken by small rocky points offered little as identification. Finally after two hours a large bay appeared, a prominent headland, a small collection of buildings and then another headland and taller buildings. It was Nhulunbuy, and the point we had almost run into after three days and 350 miles of sailing was none other than Cape Arnhem, our exact destination.

Rounding the final point we saw the town beach and decided to pull in near what was marked on our guidebook as the surf club. Four burly fellows taking in the morning with a can of beer eyed us from the club verandah. One of the more inquisitive strolled down to see us pull in.

"G'day. Where have you fellas blown in from?"

"Weipa" responded Sue more brightly than she felt.

"Shit," came the reply.

"Get off your arse and get down here," he motioned to the other fellows.

In no time the four of them had pulled *Tom* up clear of the high water mark, carried most of our gear over to the clubhouse, given us towels, pointed out the showers and offered us a beer. A steady stream of questions flowed, mixed with the usual exclamations, "You've gotta be joking", "Bloody hell", "Shit, you can have that to yourselves." "Good on ya."

Our legs were unsteady, aching, and stiff but welcomed solid ground as we washed off the crusty layers of salt that hid large rashes and chaffs on our unexposed skin. We felt like new people, not only clean but incredibly relieved. We hurried to a telephone to call the various harbormasters, Coastwatch, our friends in Weipa and my parents. We picked up our mail and poured over letters from far off friends.

As we devoured hamburgers and slurped thick shakes we gradually took in the sights of Nhulunbuy. Although it was another bauxite mining town, it had the feel of a tropical resort. Its shops and town square were modern and well equipped and acted as a center for the mining community and government for the Arnhem Land region. With 3,000 people it was the largest town we had seen since Cairns.

Despite the excitement, our fatigue was catching up with us. We went off to find Margaret, our boat builder's sister who had been a good friend to Sue in Sydney. She was now working here as a nurse and had offered us accommodations. Margaret gasped when we strolled into the hospital.

"God, I didn't expect you for ages."

It was comforting to meet someone we knew so far from home. She quickly led us to the nurses' quarters to sleep while she finished work.

Air-conditioning and clean sheets! It was almost too good to believe. My mind was already off around the next headland to Darwin, but my body was only just beginning to arrive from Weipa. I closed my eyes and woke up six hours later still rocking to the motion of the Gulf. Then it dawned on me. We had done it! We had crossed over the boundary of the Gulf and entered the Never-Never.

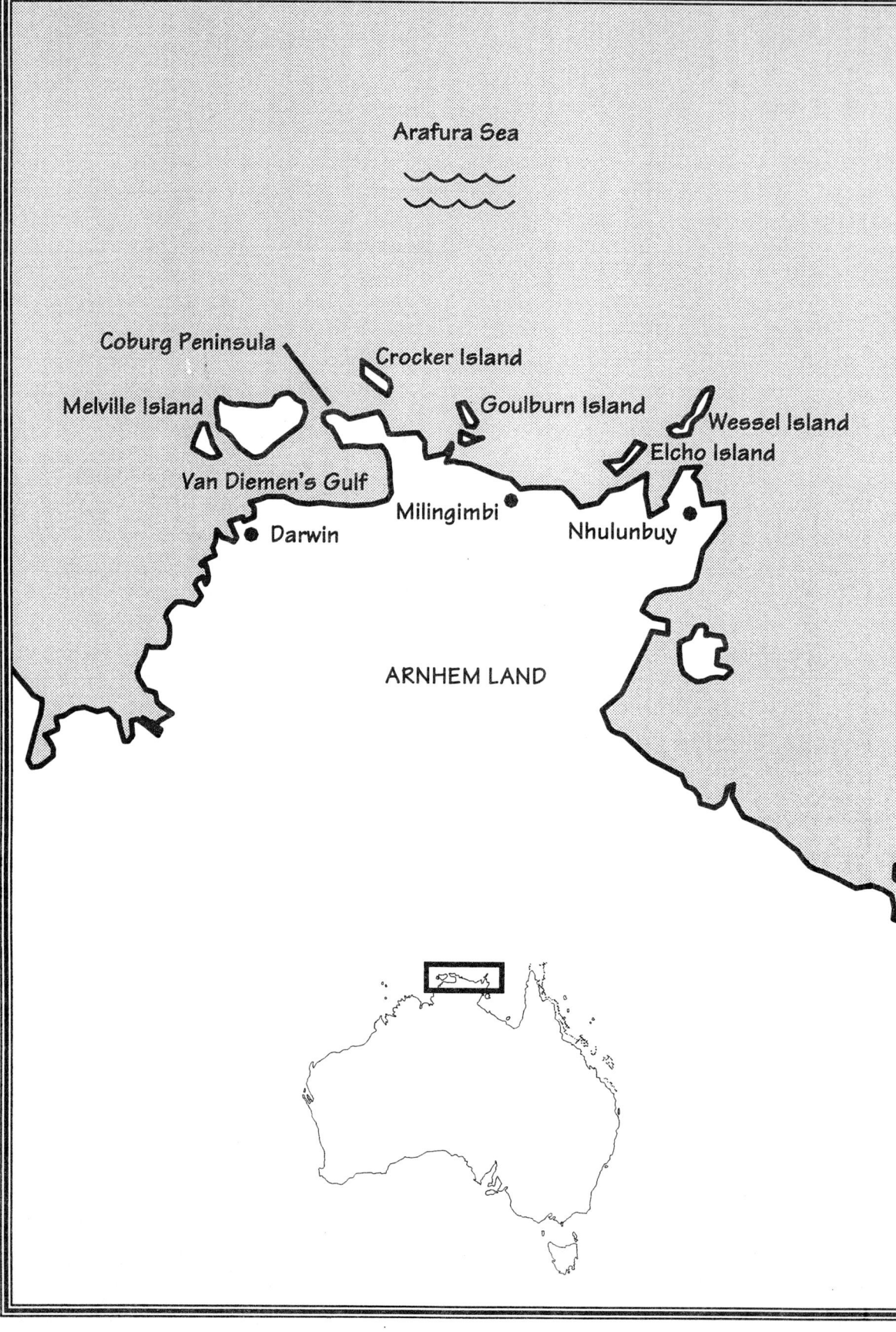

Chapter 7

Arnhem Land
Gove to Darwin

In the early 1900s the Australian novel *We of the Never Never* was written by Aeneas Gunn. The "Never Never" refers to the hundreds of thousands of square miles that stretch away from any isolated settlement in Australia. For European Australians the expression became synonymous with the awesome and often frightening vastness of the arid and inhospitable interior and western shores of the continent. It also recognized something of the spiritual quality of the land and its unique relationship to the indigenous aboriginal Australians' life and heritage. It is a 'timeless land,' unchanged for centuries as Europeans and Asians encroached and retreated, beaten back by a harsh, unrelenting, apparently empty landscape that threatened to swallow up any intruder. To many early explorers it did just that, without a trace.

After four months of sailing up the East coast of Australia we were now on the edge of the Never Never, in Arnhem Land, a 60,000 square mile section of northeastern Australia in the Northern Territory. Much of the area remains Aboriginal land — the only white settlements of Nhulunbuy and Groote Eylandt being leased mining interests. Access is generally by sea or air — the alternative being a rough ride of two to three days over four-wheel drive tracks from Darwin. Nhulunbuy is the service center to this region, a modern town that brings together the Nabalco bauxite mining operation and the Aboriginal administration and service provision for Arnhem Land. It is located on Gove Peninsula, which extends northeast into the Gulf of Carpentaria and provides protection for Melville Bay, "The best natural harbor in the Gulf of Carpentaria" according to Matthew Flinders. It can comfortably accommodate the bauxite ore carriers as they ship their cargo off to aluminum smelters elsewhere in Australia and the world. Green parks and playing fields, a shopping square, motel and offices, not to mention the yacht club and surf club made Nhulunbuy an oasis of the north.

We stayed for five days replenishing ourselves with food, drinks and sleep. After four months of travel and three days of little sleep we were exhausted. What luxury to slide between clean sheets in an air-conditioned room. It was ironic that the only bed available was a waterbed! It was a couple of nights before I could wake up without thinking I was not still somewhere in the middle of the Gulf. We went to a number of local parties, taking in the small town gossip. I'm sure many people thought we were quite rude and strange as we excused ourselves by 9.00 p.m. both nodding off to sleep. We took Margaret on a short day sail from the surf club round the point to the yacht club, to extol the virtues of her brother's boat. *Tom* appeared more at home among some dinghies and catamarans than at the surf club. We also felt more comfortable given that someone had apparently been attacked by a large saltwater crocodile recently, near where *Tom* had been parked.

Darwin was only 420 miles, and hopefully two weeks, away, but as the regular 86°F, spring September days testified, it was not going to get any cooler. The season was changing and we were now a month behind schedule getting through this northern stretch of coast where wind patterns can be fickle. "Many yachts that cruise the East Coast get over here and turn back after stuffing around with wind and shoals," came the learned comment from a local yachty. Would we actually make it to Perth in four months?

Permits are required from the Aboriginal Lands Council to travel through Arnhem Land and visit aboriginal communities, which was necessary to ensure our supply of water and outboard fuel. Numerous phone calls and certified mail packages from Sydney to Darwin, eight months earlier, had resulted in nothing. We visited the local Nhulunbuy Lands Council office daily for a week with no response. In the end we decided to head off and do as many locals recommended, to contact the communities upon arrival and get their approval.

Extending in a northeast direction from Nhulunbuy is the Wessel Islands chain. A long narrow strip of islands only 150 feet high, they are dry and desolate with a low covering of rock and scrub. Sandy beaches and great fishing areas make them popular as one of the few accessible island groups in the north. The highlight for "shortcutters" is the Hole in the Wall, a deep but narrow gap between two islands that tends to spit a boat through on a

Arnhem Land

foaming eight-to-ten-knot tidal current. We avoided the excitement and opted for a more sedate passage behind The English Company Islands. The sun glowed off the red and orange-ochre cliffs as our eyes scanned for crocodiles through the mangroves. I felt like we were being slowly baked as the heat shimmered off the surface of a slick, calm ocean. *Tom*'s hulls cut through the glassy water like knives through butter.

There are approximately ten to fifteen Aboriginal communities scattered through this northern coast each with a population of between 200 to 800. Many were originally established missions but have since become communities, the hand of God being replaced by the hand of government. Many poorly directed programs were initially introduced to provide them with instant civilization. The ruined remains of buildings and signs are all that remain of many well-intentioned ventures. On our second day out we pulled into Elcho Island at the town boat ramp, amidst a scattering of small fishing boats and a small yacht at anchor. From the beach it was a pretty looking place with an orderly green patch of trees leading down to clear blue water. As we walked along dusty streets winding between tired palm trees the town revealed a collection of broken and battered houses, a weed-covered basketball court and a vandalized and deserted fishing co-op.

The people, however, were friendly and interested in helping us as we tried to track down Frank, "The man you have to talk to," about sailing through the area. "Yeah, he'll be up at the Post Office." It was closed and we waited at the beach where two sweaty figures in public service uniform of black street shoes, black dress trousers, a short sleeve shirt and tie with briefcase in hand, joined us in the minimal shade and hot sea breeze. They had flown in from Darwin to talk to a local member of the community council about making a video to teach the Aboriginals about voting and signing up on the electoral roll, which is compulsory for every Australian. After half an hour, someone wandered down to inform them that the person they had come to see was actually in a Darwin hospital and had been for the past week. Adding wages to the cost of a charter plane flight and considering the potential value of such a video — I wondered if any lessons had been learned in terms of the prioritization and effective use of money for indigenous programs.

An hour later we were told, "Sorry, Frank is sick and won't be in today. Someone else will be there soon." After another hour we had given up and wandered back to *Tom* when someone came running down the track, "Sorry, sorry. Frank actually left and flew to Gove this morning, but the Town Clerk will see you."

"Let's just get out of here," pleaded Sue, with a splitting headache from the heat. We politely said thanks and sailed off, figuring we would work it out along the way.

The small yacht we had seen belonged to a young skipper, apparently also destined for Perth. He had run aground six weeks earlier, luckily making the beach before sinking, and was still carrying out repairs. Most yachts avoid the coastal area, staying well out in the Arafura Sea on a direct passage to Darwin. A large amount of the area is shoaled with reef and sandbars extending five to ten miles out from the mangrove-lined river mouths. Many times we were thankful for our shallow draft as we rode the nine to twelve-foot tides. This was ideal crocodile territory and the Coastwatch air patrol had warned us of regular sightings on the beaches and some of the local islands. With the recent attack and death of a local fisherman in the Gulf, our 12-gauge buckshot powerhead remained loaded and handy.

As Sue finished her solar shower that evening on the deserted beach, six dark figures popped out of the sand dunes and wandered down the beach towards us surrounded by ten young children. Somewhat shocked, Sue tossed on her sarong as Joe and Billy, the two older aboriginal men introduced themselves with wide toothless smiles. Their black curls tipped in white poked out from under their woolen beanies. "One of our blokes seen ya from the Toyota up there," motioned Billy to the nearest headland, "and gave us a call to come see if ya was all right." We nodded our thanks. It appeared they had a number of four wheel drives equipped with radios, and with good bush manners they were looking out for each other and us. We were to become familiar with this bush telegraph as we met more groups at different stops. Joe and Billy explained that many aborigines head bush, in family groups, referred to as outstations, during the dry season of June to October. Living off the land, they travel back to the communities only when supplies are needed, or before the onset of the monsoon season when travel by land becomes almost impossible. "Better for the kids away from the communities. Keeps everyone busy and off the grog," claimed Joe. They and about six to seven other families, "about sixty of us all together," explained Billy, were camped a couple of miles away. Joe and Billy were impressed that we had come all they way from Sydney in *Tom*. In local language they tried to explain to the children. "No worries. Have a good stay. See ya later. If you've got any problems just come and see us," they said with wide smiles as they departed. The north wasn't so lonely and isolated after all.

We gained strength from these exchanges with locals, drawing on their encouragement and enthusiasm for what we were doing. It had been a long four months and the next few months down the West Australian coast were likely to be even tougher. As the heat settled with the sun, Sue and I talked of the trip and how we looked forward to Darwin and then Broome. "What if we take winter off in South Australia," Sue suggested, contemplating accepting an offer from our friends Jim and Sally. Winter seemed a strange concept to me at that moment as I tried to imagine feeling cool.

The log read:

Friday the 19th. Heat Heat Heat, The temperature is baking by 9:00 A.M. and you cannot stand on the hot sand in bare feet. We sleep in a sweat, unable to read as the candle gives out too much heat and even writing is difficult as you drip all over the pages making them soggy. I can just imagine what it was like for Matthew Flinders below deck on a leaking old vessel. We both hang out for an afternoon salt water shower. Although the water is tepid after a days sailing it feels like the salt spray and sunscreen are baked on in multiple crusted layers. Today, one flat hot monotony.

We peered through the misty haze on an oily flat sea trying to identify non-descript islands, motoring most of the way. Both of us were still positive about getting to Darwin and across the top, but after the luxuries of Nhulunbuy it was taking us a while to get back into stride.

Waiting out yet another day of fresh westerly by northwesterly winds near Skirmish Point, we saw a group of people walking down the beach toward us. This was supposed to be the middle of nowhere — no airstrips, no roads for hundreds of miles! "G'day," said the tall, gaunt, terry-towel hatted white fellow, as though he ran into catamarans like this on the beach every day. "Just getting the guys out for a walk," he motioned to the surrounding group of aboriginal boys. It turned out that Derek was the recreational officer of Milingimbi community, on the Liverpool River, just around the corner. As we shared the same profession, Sue and I wanted to hear of his experiences. The greatest challenge he said was motivation, but inter-community and statewide sports were developing a sense of pride and self-confidence among the younger people. Meanwhile his six teenage charges were splashing through the clean blue shallows chasing some fish with spears they had made.

"Well, must be off," Derek declared after half an hour. "Got to get back to watch the footy," he said casually.

"What footy?" I inquired.

"Oh, it's AFL semi's on this arvo," he yelled as he rounded up the troops. I was speechless.

"What's he mean?" Sue innocently asked. I explained they were going back to watch the Australian Rules football semi-finals live on television from Melbourne! I could have fallen over to think that these care-free souls were running back to plug into a different world over 4,000 miles away.

Now most of our days were long, hot and calm. By 8:30 A.M. the flies and the heat had driven us off the beach as we motored over the mirror surface that seemed to glue to our hulls, making progress painfully slow. We sought every inch of shade our limp sails could provide, at times going onto a shady tack, even if it wasn't the best direction. We'd been forewarned of these calms and were prepared with extra fuel, but the incessant drone of the outboard was stretching our sanity. Afternoons were particularly exhausting as we were baked and parched from the salt spray. It was difficult to quench our thirst with warm water. Our fresh water supply was limited to six to eight liters a day between us, as there were limited sources through the region. We tried to avoid going ashore before 5:30 in the afternoon as the sand was too hot to stand on and the flies came in droves. A number of times this problem was solved for us when the low tides meant we waited for up to three hours, 500 to 600 yards offshore from the high tide mark.

We often felt a sense of isolation despite meeting the occasional group of people where we least expected. The only radio stations we could pick up were Indonesian. It's a shame I couldn't understand the language, as their weather reports would probably have been quite handy and more accurate than the local ones we occasionally received. Sue took to reading or listening to her small collection of tapes on the waterproof Walkman. Tracy Chapman and Aretha Franklin were beginning to sound as tired and waterlogged as we were.

A week out from Nhulunbuy, tired and thirsty, we arrived at South Goulburn Island aboriginal community to replenish our water supply and, hopefully, our fuel. Its large coral bay and scattered palms made it initially more appealing than Elcho. However, a deserted fish co-op, and houses of broken fibro and shattered glass shimmering in the dusty heat gave it a greater sense of despondency. From out of the shade of a tree appeared a figure with bright, multi-colored hair, oversized earrings, a loose-fitting batik dress and cheerful California accent. After greeting us as long lost friends, Marsha introduced herself as the local nurse. She and Sue exchanged some west-coast USA camaraderie and informed us that she has been here three years. "You aren't seriously ever going back (to the USA), are you?" questioned Marsha. Sue was stunned and politely replied that she had thought about it.

While offering a critique of the American political and social system, Marsha directed us to the local shop for fuel, insisting we drop around for a drink later on. We topped up on twenty liters of fuel and water, for what we hoped would only be seven more days to Darwin. Drinks at Marsha's turned to dinner, and we met her Australian husband, Kevin. Originally the island's school principal, Kevin had resigned to take over the bilingual teaching program at the school. He now taught the community kids their original aboriginal language, specific to this area which had a current population of 200. I was impressed by his commitment. We also toured the prized vegetable garden and were loaded up with fresh homegrown pawpaws and sweet potatoes from the Californian/Australian garden. "I don't miss much, but I fantasize about fresh fruit and vegetables," laughed Marsha.

Camped on a low, swampy, singularly unattractive shore, surrounded by hordes of mosquitoes, we were awakened early next morning by a voice outside our tent.

"Good morning and bless you."

I rose with sleep filled-eyes trying to focus on the dawn. A bright, dark face with a broad white smile greeted me through the tent's mosquito netting. Charlie introduced himself as a local church minister and was delightedly reading a Bible passage and asking probing questions of our faith. Without waiting for replies, which our morning stupor prevented anyway, he continued with further readings. After the fourth one both Sue and I had finally woken up. At that point Kevin came to our rescue, "Just makin' sure you guys get away early," he smiled. We took our opportunity to politely say thank you to Charlie, cover our nakedness and leap out of the tent. *Tom* was quickly loaded with helping hands and we headed off across the bay, waving farewell to a memorable island and its people.

A long morning of motoring, followed by a ghosting afternoon sail, meant we needed to be well placed for the next day. A dot on the chart in the middle of the bay was our chance — Cowlard Island.

"What the heck," I said to Sue. "At least we won't have as many mosquitoes and no one will wake us up in the morning."

As we got closer to this 20-foot high blob of rock capped in low, scattered bush, it appeared less promising. It was six miles to anything else and the sun was low. Finally, as its western side came into view we spied a small section of sand above oyster-strewn rock. The tide was coming in.

We crept over the reefy bottom, did a quick measure of the ground and threw the anchor out. Our wetsuit boots slipped and slid over the rocky bottom as we unloaded *Tom* 30 feet from the shoreline. The tent was up against the bushes and rock with the high water mark on our guy ropes. We prayed for a windless night! A glimmering silver road shone across the bay to our front door as the moon rose. We sat on our private rocky island enjoying the peace and cool seabreeze. Just at dark we floated *Tom* onto the patch of sand we had cleared, tied him to a stout bush and put out two stern anchors. He would be afloat at high tide. We could well imagine the waves just about breaking over this little rocky outcrop in a big blow.

We slept well in a slightly cooler and quieter campsite than our previous night. Or perhaps it was the extra glass of sherry we had to celebrate our private island. As my eyes adjusted to first light and my mind struggled to remember where we were I heard the lapping of water. "Shit," I undid the fly screen and found the tide teasing the edge of our tent. "I think we'd better get up Sue." It was my birthday, but breakfast-in-bed was hastily postponed as we sailed off Cowlard Island, before we were washed off.

After ten miles of a lovely northeasterly winds we were convinced the wind must change soon, but it stayed with us providing the best birthday present I could have asked for — a 50-mile sail that day! We reveled in the fresh, cool breeze under full sail with an almost forgotten spray of water glistening off the bows. As we cut up the protected waters of Bowen Strait between Crocker Island and the mainland Sue pulled out her trolling line to trail along behind in the sapphire blue water. In a fresh 15 knots we shot by Danger Point in the early afternoon and onto Smith Point where a six-foot high, white phallic monument stands to mark the establishment of European civilization in 1845. Smith Point is the northern-most end of the Coburg Peninsula, now part of the Coburg National Park — a joint Aboriginal and Federal Government management venture. It harbors Port Essendon and the original settlement of Victoria, another northern outpost of colonial Australia. With fanfare and enthusiastic support the colonial fathers had attempted to sell the new settlement of Victoria as a town that would eventually rival Singapore and become a great city. They attempted to entice public servants to this forgotten outpost as an exciting adventure and an opportunity to serve the empire. Some would say it still appears that way today in Darwin some 150 years later.

As we rounded the point a yacht sailed past with the crew waving greetings to us. In a state of shock at seeing company we nearly ran over the reef! We pulled *Tom* onto a calm, sandy beach under the welcome shade of a grove of casuarina trees. We had heard that there was a tourist resort on the point and wandered off to explore. It wasn't quite the international type of hotel with a pool by the water, but a much more appropriate, low-key collection of wilderness huts, with small balconies and a very impressive solar power and water reticulation system. No one was around as we gave a few yells and poked our noses in a few open windows. The tented kitchen area showed recent signs of life with damp patches from water run off. Some character had put up a crocodile warning sign in the showers. We wandered back to our beach.

As we sat in the shade listing to Indonesian radio I had a strange sensation of being somewhere other than Australia. The heat, the tropical water, the twanging Asian music. I knew that I could walk south from here and not see a person, town, or even major road for months, if I survived. It was like hanging on the edge of this vast continent, its wide-open space overpowering, threatening to cast us adrift from its shores. For the first time in my life I felt the space and size of my country and was in awe of it. Arhnem Land was said to have a mystical place in aboriginal dreaming — perhaps its spell was working on us.

Waking next morning under the shade of a casuarina tree, which was a luxury because the sand didn't burn your feet before breakfast, and looking across a glittering, bright blue bay, we couldn't resist taking a day off, our first in two weeks. We took advantage of the early morning cool to explore Black Point, a mile down the peninsula. Enjoying the sound of birds, wandering amid sparse, low scrub, shaded by small gums and paper bark trees, we stumbled onto an open clearing. Stubbled with grasses, I took it to be a natural open area farmed by the local kangaroos. Then I spied a strange collection of white spindly trees at each end. "I can't believe it," I said out loud. The sacred ceremonial site of an Australian Rules football field! At the far end a young National Park ranger, making new park signs in a large well equipped ranger station, welcomed us and gave us the local story.

Opened in 1975, Coburg (incorporating Geriag Marine Park) is set up with an Aboriginal Commission that consists of members of tribes in that area. Only ten vehicles are allowed into the park at any one time and then only in a certain spot. You must apply for a permit in Darwin, then face a ten hour drive over a road that is rough even by Northern Territory standards. The resort area we had seen the day before on Smith Point was a separate concession run by a safari company that flew in visitors and supplies, paying a percentage to a local Aboriginal Commission. The

Arnhem Land

Coburg rangers were well equipped with two fast aluminum shark cat boats, and a collection of smaller working dinghies. They provided a presence on this isolated section of the coast as well as servicing the national park.

We returned to our camp and lay in the water fully-clothed, only our hats afloat, to ward off the heat of the day. With one eye scanning for sharks and crocodiles we floated through to the cool of the afternoon. We talked of the food we would eat in Darwin, and what we would do first.

"A shower and a bed, with cool white sheets," dreamed Sue.

"A jug full of ice cold water, followed by beer," was my request.

Our water supply had held out well over the past few weeks, but no matter how much we drank our throats felt parched and ached for cooling, soaking liquid. I was worried how we would cope with the increasing heat as we raced across the remaining half of northern Australia, and down the west coast. Perth and the America's Cup seemed a distant dream, fading like a mirage in the heat haze. Would someone find *Tom* and these two empty hats floating aimlessly off Coburg Peninsula many years from now?

Darwin lay just two days around the corner of Cape Don, across the expanse of Van Diemen's Gulf. A large body of water 60 by 50 miles, the Gulf is bordered by Melville Island to the north and a mangrove lined coast to the east and south. With up to twelve to fifteen foot tides across that expanse, tidal currents through the 20-mile wide Dundas Strait between Melville Island and Cape Don can be up to three or four knots, creating turbulent overfalls.

To coincide our crossing of Dundas Strait with neap tides and, hopefully, reasonable weather, we pulled into the protection of Alcaro Bay beneath the final headland, Cape Don. The bay was typical of all the beauty of this area with a wide sandy beach backed by a strip of tall casuarinas, giving way to a scrubby sand flats which, in turn, gave way to a rich mangrove maze — three dominant vegetation forms, all clearly defined within 100 yards. A sudden rapid movement, followed by the splash of a disappearing three-foot tail beneath the mangroves discouraged any further exploration. "Jesus," exclaimed Sue, "I didn't know crocodiles could move that fast".

Keeping Australia On the Left

We retreated to the shady beach and listened to the VFL grandfinal between Hawthorn and Carlton — Hawthorn by 42 points — wish I was down there drinking beer with them at the moment, read my sweaty journal scribe. It was that crazy time of year down south where football finals were on. "It's kind of like the Superbowl mixed with an evangelist gathering," I tried to explain to Sue.

Anxious but excited at the prospect of at least seeing the lights of Darwin that night, we edged our way out next morning and set a compass line through the 20 miles of haze for Melville Island. We were spurred on by the sight of a sports fishing boat, an increasing business in the region, obviously out for a day trip from Darwin. *Tom* bounced around in the overflows and we dodged the occasional swirl of water that resembled a large sinkhole. The dim, low outline of Melville reassuringly appeared out of the haze after half an hour. Our passage turned out to be a relatively smooth ride with the occupants of one more fishing boat giving us odd looks. Melville Island is the largest aboriginal owned island in Australia, being over 4,000 square miles and lying 30 miles off Darwin. The main aboriginal community lives on the farthest northwestern end, so we didn't plan to visit. We passed long sections of narrow, scrub-backed beaches broken by the occasional red and orange rocky point. As the afternoon easterly wind calmed we coasted along past Cape Keith listening to the Sydney Rugby League grandfinal, "Parramatta won four to two over Canterbury." Sue was not enthused and slept. We pulled into a small beach marked by a distinctive giant orange headland resembling a termite mound, aptly named Ant Cliffs. As we settled into our camp late in the afternoon it was with relief we tuned into Darwin radio. Tomorrow, after over two weeks of sailing from Nhulunbuy, we would be there!

Determined to make it, we were up at 5.30 A.M. and away by 7:00 A.M. Billowing out of the south as we pushed off were large black threatening clouds. "Better keep an eye on them," I pointed to Sue. An hour later it was darker as the clouds rolled in, now coal black, and a morning tropical storm engulfed us with rain. At the first flash of lightening we scurried back to shore to wait it out. So close yet so far as the 25-to-30-knot winds whipped maddening white caps out of the bay! Two hours later we tried once again. It was a full day of struggle, dodging around small islands and markers

A Small Boat
In A Big Ocean,
Leaving Terrigal,
New South Wales

Campsite At
Broughton Island,
New South Wales Coast

Broughton Island
Looking Back To The
Main Land Of Myall
Lakes And Barrington
Mountain's Tops, Coast
Of New South Wales

Dinner And Breakfast,
A Good Days Catch

Campsite At
Fraser Island,
Queensland

Tom Thumb
Under Repair
With "The Itch" At
Anchor, Thomas Island

Sunset — Night Two Crossing
The Gulf Of Carpentaria,
185 Miles From Land

The Crocodile's Slide Marks That
Encouraged Us To Move Camp,
Cape York Penninsula (*left*)

Tom At Anchor With
Brumey, Carlisle Island,
Whitsunday Islands (*below*)

The Great Sandy Desert Meets
The Indian Ocean, Eight Mile

A Safe Harbor, Mandurah,
Western Australia (*right*)

Author With Dead Sea Snake,
Eight Mile Beach, Western
Australia (*below*)

Sand Dunes, Coast Of Western Australia

Admiring The Repair Job With Steve At The Slipway, Geraldton (*left*)

Tide's Out, Coast Of Western Australia (*below*)

Australia
Warming Up For The
Last Race Of The
America's Cup, Perth

The Great Australian
Bight — The Nullabor
Plains Meet The Great
Southern Ocean

Crossing The
Nullabor Plains,
Western Australia

Author In Victor Harbor, South Australia

The Murray River Locks

Different Company — A Murray River Paddle Steamer

The Boom Tent Set Up

Campsite Friends,
New South Wales

A Dolphin Escort

Arnhem Land

against tides and slight headwinds. The most prominent landform since the relatively small loading towers of Weipa came into view — Darwin Hospital. As the afternoon settled with Darwin in our sights the Coastwatch plane flew low over us waggling its wings. Sue and I smiled at each other. It was our familiar friends welcoming us in. We had made Darwin and almost completed the Northern Territory. It was a great feeling. We staggered ashore at the Fannie Bay Darwin Yacht Club just on dark. The members were quite polite about the two bedraggled figures who strolled barefooted and salt-encrusted to sign in and head for the showers. "We do scrub up okay," we assured the manager, his mouth still open in shock as we listed our homeport as Sydney.

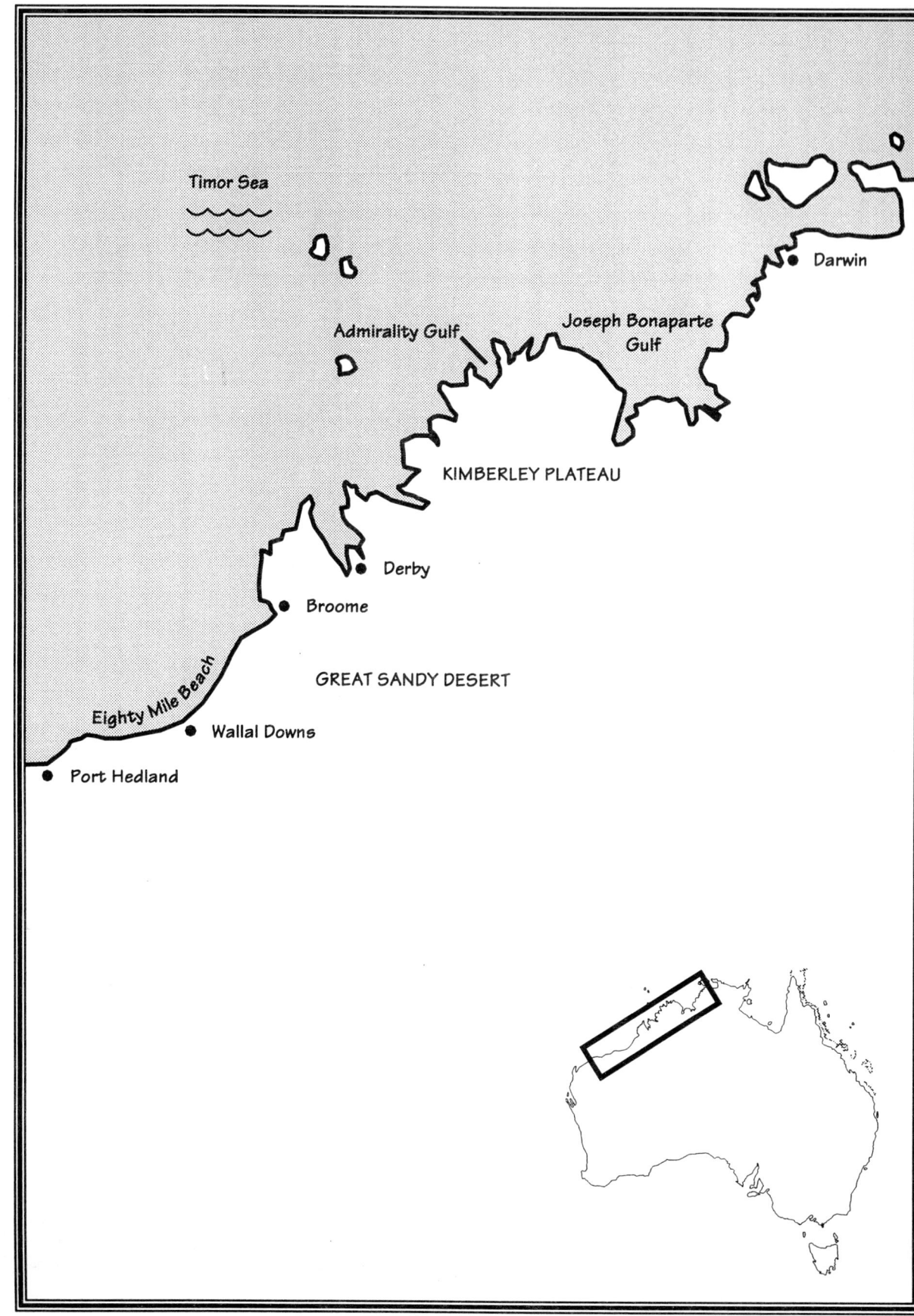

Chapter 8

Pearls and Great Sandy Deserts
Darwin To Port Hedland

I woke to the sound of traffic. Was I still dreaming? Quick, up and pack, lets get moving. I sat up and rubbed my eyes, slowly taking in the sights of boats on slips or bobbing at moorings and people walking past us along the beach. Darwin, Australia's most northern city with a population of 60,000 people, was our largest port of call since Cairns, over 1,200 miles and two months ago. I returned a few smiles and waves from my sleeping bag perched on *Tom's* trampoline. We had made it and it was nice to be here, but my biggest problem right now was where to go to the toilet!

Sue arose and while attempting to have a leisurely breakfast on our very public trampoline bed we were inundated by the local press. Feeling rather disheveled, we nevertheless smiled for the television crew, who luckily did not insist on us setting sail and re-arriving. We also tried to respond intelligently to radio interview questions, while still trying to make a morning cup of coffee. Amidst all this an army truck arrived to transfer our gear to Larrakeah Barracks. Through our contacts and letter of introduction from the Admiral of the Australian Navy to the Naval Patrol Base, the local military had offered assistance. Besides providing us with accommodation, they also had excellent information concerning the next section of our trip through the Kimberleys. Norforce, an independent section of the army, patrolled sections of this isolated coast in inflatable Zodiacs and therefore had a wealth of knowledge concerning landing points and fresh water sources.

An informal cup of tea with the commanding officer of the base, Colonel Bruce Kemp, a keen sailor, resulted in being immediately installed in the VIP flat at the Officers' Mess. We were wonderfully spoiled thereafter. We were returned to gather our last possessions from the yacht club and make sure *Tom* was secure in the locked boat yard. We dropped off our outboard and trampoline at the naval base to be serviced and repaired, and also arranged some sponsorship for a new handheld VHF radio to replace the 27 Mega Hertz (MgHz) one we had rarely used. The 27 MgHz band is only commonly used on the east coast and monitored in major fishing areas for general communication. Even though the range of the VHF was less it has a full-time emergency channel.

Darwin is a colorful city. Sue considered that in some ways it is to Australia what the West Coast has become to America, the place you go to escape all else and find yourself. When you get there you can't remember why you came, but you stay anyway. "There are a lot of people up here who don't want to be found, so don't ask personal questions. It's a rule in Darwin," advised a local. There were also many public servants who had come to do their tour of duty, or for a brief change, but had stayed. "You get to love it and the freedom, as long as you can put up with the troppo (tropical cyclone) season," suggested a woman and her two young sons who were now almost considered as locals after 15 years. The wide, palm-lined streets with houses set on stilts and the business dress of shorts, long socks and short-sleeved, open necked shirts epitomized Darwin's tropical, casual nature.

The history of Darwin, apart from the Japanese bombings in World War II, is defined as "before or after Tracey" — the cyclone that flattened her on Christmas Eve, 1974. For some people it was the end of life in Darwin, but for those who stayed, it marked the beginning of a new life in a rebuilt city. "I lay over my two kids and wife against our bathtub for six hours that night, as the house was destroyed around us," a friend had recounted to me many years earlier. "The roof was gone, most of the walls were gone. The wind was howling and the rain was pelting down. I didn't know if we would survive. In the morning when the rescue crews found us they thought my wife was dead, as there was a lot of blood from a cut in her head. Luckily we all walked away, but we lost everything." He had left and never been back. It was a defining point in Australia's consciousness. As the extent of the devastation in this major city was realized, the hearts of people across the entire country went out to Darwin.

During its reconstruction, Darwin had added many new buildings, including a Casino to attract people to the north. Judging from the number of tourists wandering the streets, the strategy appeared to be working. It had become a watering hole and rest stop for those who traveled overland from any direction, and was the main access point to some of Australia's wild northern country. Nearby Kakadu National Park, a large World Heritage listed wetlands with crocodiles, buffaloes, and an amazing abundance of bird-life, was the setting for the film *Crocodile Dundee*.

The unbelievable luxury of a bed, in air-conditioned comfort, slowly revived our bodies and spirits. Colonel Kemp wanted to ensure that we experience sailing Darwin-style so we set a date for the Yacht Club's Wednesday Twilight Sailing Competition. How strange it was to be aboard an eleven-meter yacht. It felt more like we were on a ship after *Tom*. It took us a full leg of the race to adjust to a monohull's tilt and not spill our beers. This race series gave a fair indication of the spirit and fun of the Darwin Yacht Club. It was open to all boats, from dinghies and 14-foot catamarans, to 20- to 30-meter racers and cruisers. The fleet of 30 boats raced around a short course, dodging moorings and each other for one to two hours. No handicapping systems, no protests — you just had to finish. The winner was decided back at the club, after more drinks and a barbecue dinner when contestants spun a chocolate wheel which determines the points scored for that race. The lucky winner of the series, a woman and her two young sons in their four meter dinghy, were presented with the first prize — a week's yacht charter holiday for six people in the Whitsunday Islands!

During our social sailing we met the owners of Paspaley Pearling, one of the largest pearling operations in Australia, and were invited down to their store to be shown how things were done these days and obviously to see some pearls. They still take the shells from the coast near Broome, a couple of thousand miles further around the coast, culture them, artificially creating a pearl, and transporting them back around the coast to grow them in the protected waters of Arnhem Land. It obviously is worth the investment. The staff explained that their main market was Asia and that the company was expanding all the time, including a recent investment in another lugger. Their skipper, Toph, was intrigued with the story of our trip. "Are you sure you don't need a lift through the Kimberleys," he proffered. "You've got your work cut out for you there." I smiled and declined. We didn't need reminding.

We were physically and mentally gearing up for sailing the Kimberleys, a thousand mile section of wild, unpopulated, and in some places uncharted, section of the coast. We were also tackling it at the beginning of what are known as the "suicide months" of October and November. Apparently because of the oppressive heat and humidity just before the onset of the wet season, the suicide rate rises noticeably! The information from Norforce's staff and Ian Gibson of Coastwatch, an ex-Navy patrol-boat skipper, all seemed ominous. There were limited re-supply spots, dangerous rip tides, lots of crocodiles and we were about a month behind our schedule to get favorable winds. It was also ironically the stretch of Australia's coastline I most longed to explore. Images of deep red gorges cutting into the rugged desert, with waterfalls dropping into the sea, were part of what had inspired this trip in the first place. It could be done — of that we were sure — but with the changing season bringing west to northwest headwinds, it wasn't going to be easy.

After ten days respite we headed back to *Tom* with our truckload of supplies and mixed feelings. We slowly packed, shadowed by Steve Coates who was writing a story on our trip for *Modern Boating*, an Australian sailing magazine. *Looked at from the beach, Tom Thumb, a CatCan, resembles any other small catamaran, but as she draws closer, or rather waddles because of the load of stores on board, her lines are very different,* wrote Steve. With three weeks of supplies on board and ten days of water, we indeed felt we were waddling. We waved a reluctant farewell to more new friends and set sail across the bay, keen to make some distance while the wind was with us. With full sail *Tom* cut westward across Fannie Bay, as we kept a look out for the regular traffic of various ships, fishing boats and yachts coming in and out of the harbor. We sat back in comfort on our newly reinforced trampoline while the breeze freshened behind us. Even with his heavy load *Tom* planed across the water and we trimmed the sails to get maximum speed. As Darwin disappeared behind us the wind turned to the west northwest as a headwind, and built in strength. We couldn't risk stressing *Tom* by pounding through swells in his overloaded state and as both of us soon became saturated by the spray we headed ashore.

Early next morning we pushed off to make some distance in the calm of the dawn. With not a breath of wind we started the outboard to clear the shore and reefs. It coughed and died! No amount of persuasion, mechanical fiddling or cursing would change its mind.

Pearls and Great Sandy Deserts

What were we doing here? Frustration at our lack of progress and the prospect of a month of hard slog ahead had brought us to the point of assessing who and what this trip was all about. As one of our sailing friends had said, "You seemed to be headed off on an 80-mile march with full pack, rather than as keen sailors." He was right. We weren't out to set any records. We were facing a tough decision. If we didn't make it to Perth in time for the America's Cup, sometime between November and January, we would not satisfy our sponsors and the rest of our trip was likely to be in jeopardy because of lack of funding. But what if we had not sailed the whole way by ourselves? We were behind schedule and at this rate the odds were against us making it anyway. Sue and I uneasily battled to an agreement and retreated back to Darwin. The reality now was that we needed to find a quicker way to cover some of the distance around to Perth. The Kimberleys would stay there, the timeless land that it is, and we would return some day when the conditions were more in tune.

Eager to continue by sea if possible, we quickly sought out our pearler friends who had casually offered us a lift to Broome in their lugger the week before. Toph, the skipper, immediately assured us that the offer was still good. We breathed a sigh of relief at the prospect of finding ourselves almost 600 miles further round the coast in just four days, at Koolan Island in the middle of the Kimberleys. Our transport was a modern 118-foot pearling ship, *Paspaley II,* of fiberglass construction, modeled after a Japanese fishing boat. It was a unique boat to Australian waters, being specially constructed to enable *Paspaley Pearling* to transfer the shells from the beds off Broome, 1,200 miles north, to the calmer waters of bays near Darwin. Six large holding tanks in the center of the boat held this precious living cargo, keeping a continuous flow of water over them during the trip. With a new five-million-dollar ship on order, it appeared to be a profitable technique.

With our outboard rebuilt we once again departed Darwin, this time on the comfortable dry deck of *Paspaley* II, with *Tom* happily bobbing in our wake. What we thought would be a relaxing cruise soon proved otherwise as we encountered their roughest trip of the season. *Tom*'s happy bobbing soon looked more like he was sinking, and it became obvious the place we should have put him was on deck. As the sun set over the rough ocean, we took advantage of *Paspaley's* wide davits and made *Tom* ready to sling off the stern. Akere, a Torres Strait Islander crew member, jumped overboard and swam over to help me out. His black smiling face came through the water and aboard in a flash, deftly tying the thick, tarred rope into slings. Looking at his hulking frame, you would swear he was their winch, capable of plucking *Tom* out of the water and delicately placing him aboard. Bouncing around in the chop and avoiding rising in and against the stern of *Paspaley* we managed to lift *Tom* up just at dark, with the only casualty being me collecting a black eye from a swinging block.

Sunset merged with the disappearing flashing light on Charles Point as we headed off into the dark. A bright red and orange sky contrasted against the black spiraling storm clouds, presenting a stunning picture. We pounded on into the rising swell and I gave up anxiously watching the stern rise and fall, almost dipping our only worldly possession into its foaming wake. It was like some form of ancient torture, daring the sea to rip *Tom* off the lashing, or smash him to pieces on the stern. I quickly retired to the crew's quarters, uncertain whether the onset of nausea was brought on by *Tom*'s precarious position or the new motion of the ship resembling a multi-cycle washing machine. It was strange after our close encounter sailing on *Tom* to be experiencing large seas and winds in this environment which felt not only dry, but detached.

I braced myself sideways across the small bunk and attempted to block out the steady roar of the engines. As *Paspaley II* carved its way through each swell the hull absorbed the tension, building to the climax when a great shiver and shudder ran from bow to stern. We dared not think of *Tom* suspended in the blackness. *Tom,* however, did have a safekeeper in Gise, Akere's uncle — an elderly islander with keen, wise eyes and white-tipped, steel wool hair. He spoke no English, but understood the sea with an uncanny sense. At the isolated culture farm up north, Gise had displayed his talents in carving a traditional islander boat, complete with outrigger and sail. Despite the modern medium of fiberglass, his discerning eye appreciated and valued the craftsmanship of our small vessel.

Very groggy and feeling as though I had been brutally shaken and pummeled black and blue all night, I staggered atop late next morning. Staring into the distance at cool, sweeping whitecaps, my eyes slowly focused on an additional block and tackle. *Tom*'s bouncing had caused one

Pearls and Great Sandy Deserts

of the davits to buckle and extra support had been necessary. After a quick tour of the bridge, where an unattractive weather report was being received, I returned to my rough and tumble bunk pursued by the nauseating odor of breakfast. Even the crew was beginning to feel the strain of this rough trip. I tried to forget where we were and slept fitfully all day.

Sue, a much sturdier traveler, checked on my state of well-being in between reading a novel. A groan was my only response until the ship's bell signaled all on deck at dawn next morning to re-sling *Tom*. With the crews help we took *Tom's* weight off the block and tackle and back onto the davits before tying a series of heavy ropes slings back onto the ships frame. The wind had abated somewhat and the islands of Admiralty Gulf helped provide the calmest conditions we had experienced since dropping our lines at Darwin wharf. First light showed a very relieved group absorbing the calmness and tranquillity of a Kimberley morning.

The red and orange sun rose large and high over similar colored rocky islands, heralding another warm day. Beaches and hedlands poked out of slanting shadows and early morning haze rose from deep, penetrating bays said to be uncharted. My camera clicked as Toph said, "What's this? No taking photos and pretending you sailed all the way." I smiled. "They're for future reference — we'll be back some day." The emptiness of the Kimberleys, even at this extremity, draws you in. A rugged untamed land, it is likely to remain so for many more years. Rocky waterways, descending through spectacular gorges, spill over waterfalls mere feet from safe anchorages. Tales are told of people rinsing their boats and sails under these natural showers. Thirty-foot tides and an increasing population of crocodiles demand a healthy respect but, in many ways, are part of the attraction. Yes, we would be back.

As we crossed one large bay between a scattering of rocky islands, Toph called us up to the bridge.

"Would you like to see how we fish?" Fixing on a compass bearing between the hedlands, he focused the sonar to bring up the image of a single pyramid-shaped reef that rose to within ten meters of the surface. Many small shapes moved around it on the sonar image. Toph gave a yell to the stern and Ackere and Gise tossed out their spinners as Toph began to circle *Paspaley*. Within a minute there was a yell and an assortment of large mackerel and tuna were being hauled on board. Ackere battled to land the largest tuna, a good five feet long. With ten respectably sized fish, it was enough to fill the freezer. Sue was envious of this kind of fishing and noted what spinners the guys were using on the west coast.

The remainder of the trip was slightly more forgiving and I began to enjoy meals prepared by Debbie, the cook. It was just as well, because, knowing that *Tom* had taken some damage and would require some extensive repairs, our drop off at Koolan Island was extended to Broome. Poor Toph had been most apologetic, certain he had destroyed our boat, and had given us numerous contact addresses of people in Broome who might be able to help. Gradually the harsh, ochre colored country of the Kimberleys changed and soon the long golden sands of Cable Beach marked our arrival in Broome. A half-mile offshore from the town in the calm of Roebuck Bay, *Tom* was deposited back into the water and we clambered on board to motor ashore. We must have looked a strange sight with the mast lying on the trampoline piled high with gear, and ourselves perched precariously on top. After a final wave, *Paspaley* turned and headed further south to the shell beds.

Our dazed minds tried to assess the landscape. The dull throb of *Paspaley's* engines continued to echo in our ears, as it would for a number of days. If it had been low tide we would have had to drag *Tom* a mile across the sand, but luck was with us and the tide was in. An oasis appeared before us. There were trees — big shady ones — and green grass. In the chill of the late afternoon air our minds and bodies grappled with the three-quarter hour time change since we had last been ashore. We were not only further west, but also many miles further south. After our previous months of slow, steady assimilation, this rapid change would take some getting used to — we were ship-lagged.

Broome is indeed a coastal oasis, as it lies at the edge of the Great Sandy Desert providing respite for travelers from the harsh, dry conditions surrounding it. Scrub-covered country, cut by deep, rocky gorges, gives way to white, undulating sand hills stretching down to the Indian Ocean. The now sleepy old town was once a thriving pearling center for the world. Tales of mystery and intrigue are plentiful, as men sought the instant wealth provided by the small, shiny balls or "tears of the sea." The risks were great, with primitive diving techniques and thirty-foot tides in a cyclone-prone region. Hundreds of men have perished pearling in these waters.

At the campground overlooking the Bay we were soon befriended by a Dutch couple, Guy and Jacqueline, who were retracing their own mystery with a film crew. Jacqueline's previous husband had been shot down by Japanese Zeros while escaping from the fall of Singapore during World War II. The plane, en route to Broome, had crash-landed in the sea some distance north. A number of the crew had survived, but no one had recovered a mysterious package they had been told to deliver at all costs — a bundle of diamonds. Individual stones began to surface and were used as trade between people in Broome, but despite an inquiry by the Reserve Bank, they were not all recovered and it remains a mystery to this day. Jacqueline was visiting the wreckage of her husband's plane for the first time and was also trying to unravel what had happened to his body after the crash, before it was eventually returned to Indonesia three years later.

The faces in the streets of Broome exhibited the unique features of Australia's multi-cultural community with Malays, Filipinos and Japanese mixed with Europeans and the local Aboriginals. Some of the women bore the striking beauty of such diverse mixes. This cultural mix wasn't always a peaceful one, however, as history recounts vicious clashes between the various racial groups often seeking to control sections of the pearling industry. Broome still has a few cultivated pearl companies but now relies greatly on its romantic history to attracts tourist dollars. Its warm sunny winters attract travelers, holiday-makers and alternate lifestylers. Unfortunately, it is also the alcohol supply center for a number of nearby Aboriginal communities with a regular group living between the public bar and the local park. A number of young travelers also assured us it was the best place to be unemployed since the weather is great, the welfare checks regular, and the chance of finding a job very slim.

Not wishing to be tempted, we hastened the repairs to *Tom* feeling it was time we explored more of the Western Australian coast. What we had thought were major repairs consisted of two small holes in Tom's hull, easily patched with fiberglass. Our departure, timed to catch the tide, was witnessed by a small crowd of well-wishers. It is difficult to explain the tides in an area where the difference between the high and low water mark is up to two miles. Reaching across the gray tidal waters of Roebuck Bay we dodged regular small tidal whirlpools that marked the channels where this massive amount of water exits the sea. As we sailed over the top of some twice the length of Tom, it felt we were sucked to a stop before being spat out the other side. The open expanse of the bay stretched off to the south and the Indian Ocean now in the west. Our only human contact for the day was with people from various cultured pearl companies who waved to us from their floating work-platforms bobbing up and down on their moorings. Packed with diving kit and compressors, along with food and basic accommodation, the 12 by 20 foot platforms up to six miles from land, were a unique workplace. Our passage over the small reefs was measured by the tide charts and eyesight. The swell at three to six feet, although uncomfortable, did indicate areas best avoided even with our six-inch draft.

Off into the haze we sailed, searching for flat, sandy hedlands that might resemble something on our charts. By 2:00 P.M. the afternoon sea breeze whipped up to 20 knots of south, southwest headwind, blowing us ashore, and sending us in search of shade and protection from the stinging sand — a daily pattern with which we were to become familiar. If only we were going the other way. Bossult Creek provided us with our last sheltered hedland before the great expanse of Eighty Mile Beach. This little creek, which dries out at low tide, provided a cyclone shelter for the pearlers fishing off the beach in the past. One could imagine 30 to 40 vessels tied to the mangroves as the cyclone-driven waves pounded the shallow and unprotected beach. At times we almost felt the presence of these past seamen guiding us down the coast.

A small light tower on Bossult Head provided a great view of the endless parade of low, three to six feet sandy, scrubby dunes stretching off into the horizon to the south and marching off into the Great Sandy Desert, hundreds of miles into the Australian interior. There was not a tree in sight, and the small stunted bushes were barely a meter high. With dull gray tidal ocean meeting a dull gray sandy beach it was impossible to pick out the horizon as it blended in the heat haze in the distance. It was an uninviting landing for such a long section of beach. The only human access and habitation we knew of was a caravan park at the far southern end.

Pearls and Great Sandy Deserts

Uncertain of how long it may take us to negotiate Eighty Mile Beach, we decided to take a day off to resupply our water from the neighboring Frazier Downs cattle station. The maps we had didn't mark all the tracks, but we had our compass and a spot as to where the station was located. The sea breeze disappeared a few miles inland and the reality of 95°F temperatures in the sandy dusty tracks scorched our feet. We marked our turning points on various tracks just to make sure we could get back. After two hours and no sign beyond a few recent tire tracks we considered returning. "Just one more hour," I suggested. Sue was unimpressed as the novelty of land travel had long worn off and the heat and flies were now distressing. Another hour-and-a-half later we strolled up to the station house rather exhausted and hoping they wouldn't refuse us water.

The Aboriginal manager, Kas, was stunned to see us appear from the coast, and even more surprised to hear we had walked. "You could have got lost on any of those tracks and never found us," he said shaking his head. We were most grateful for his offer of a lift back out to the Cape, our unexercised sea legs being unfamiliar with such lengthy exploration. The property, originally very run down, was now owned by the local Aboriginal community of La Grange. They had taken over ownership on a deal with the government and Kas and his team were now trying to build it up as a profitable concern. We waved our grateful farewells after a quick 15-minute drive back to *Tom.* That hot, dry ten-mile walk to the station, surrounded by hordes of flies, convinced us that we really were much more comfortable at sea.

Eighty Mile Beach, a misnomer as it is twice that length, started vaguely and kept on going as the days blurred like the landscape. At times you literally had to pinch yourself or put your hand in the water to ensure *Tom Thumb* was still moving. Mile after monotonous mile of scrubby sand hills glided past and when you finally raced ashore and up to the highest point the desert dunes continued to roll inland as far as the eye could see. One expected Lawrence of Arabia to arrive at any moment. Our anxiety concerning any shorebreak was unfounded in these calmer conditions, for the long shallow coast provided a gradual introduction to the sea. A stretch of foot-and-a-half surf almost provided an enjoyable end to the day even if making for the occasional damp morning start. With very little change in the landscape our days of travel were defined by the different displays of natural coral art on the beachline. The reefs and shell beds offshore scattered their debris in colorful banks of sponge, seaweed, coral and shells up to a couple of feet deep on the beach. We admired the variety and quantity of shells, from large balers to multicolored earring-sized scallop shells. Sue's fast increasing collection looked certain to sink poor *Tom*.

The rapidly receding tide often revealed knee-deep mud — a slight problem if we were to get out next morning. On one occasion, after consulting the tide charts, we discovered our last chance to leave for the next two days was 2:30 A.M. Oh boy! We grabbed a few hours sleep by the campfire, huddled in our sailing gear, trying to be enthusiastic. It became a night of motoring by compass, due to lack of wind and great difficulty in judging distance from the shore when the only silhouette is a six-foot high sand hill over a half-mile away. We sailed right through the morning a couple of hundred yards from shore on a rough compass bearing. The most accurate measure as to how close we were to shore was the occasional wave that broke over the boat soaking us, but at least keeping us awake for another half-hour.

Dawn was a dull gray one that took ages in coming, but allowed us to see where we were going. The off shore breeze stayed with us and we kept sailing, while snacking on food. The view stayed the same. If you napped for an hour and looked out at the shore, you could have sworn you had not moved along the coast. With streaming eyes and tired bodies we eventually collapsed ashore at 3:00 P.M. that afternoon. Unfortunately, a change in tides greeted us with a 400-yard haul of boat and gear above a high tide mark. The next job was to scout out a protective sandhill to prevent getting sandblasted and allow for a cooking fire. Our green tarp strung out between paddles and anchors provided the only shade and evening shelter. The heat was a consistent baking temperature and very wearing.

Wallal, an isolated caravan park on the end of a dirt track, marks the only public access to Eighty Mile Beach. On our third day of sailing the beach we scrambled up a dirt track to look down upon the brown stain of road gravel among the white sand hills. It was dotted with a few isolated caravans shimmering in the heat haze. A scruffy, solitary figure walked back and forth from a 44-gallon drum with a bucket, trying to keep a scattering of small trees alive. We introduced ourselves to Russell and his faithful canine companion,

Pearls and Great Sandy Deserts

Trinity, both of whom eyed us skeptically as we told our story. "I'll come an' 'ave a beer with ya after work" he declared. At 4:30 P.M. with his boss, Ken, in tow, Russell arrived with beers in hand to accord *Tom* the dubious honor of being flagship and us inaugural members of the Eighty Mile Beach Yacht Club. Sue was presented with a baseball cap with the club's insignia, previously a joke until our arrival.

We crawled away next morning slightly hung over from the hospitality, but determined to see the end of this beach. Three days later we finally put in a 43-mile run to arrive at Port Hedland. The signs of this industrial iron ore port on the skyline kept taunting us all day as we slowly neared the town. It was an exhausting 12-hour day. We made it ashore just at dark before collapsing into a hot and humid tent at 11:30 P.M., too tired to eat. We were already worn out by the Western Australian coast and there was three quarters of it still to go!

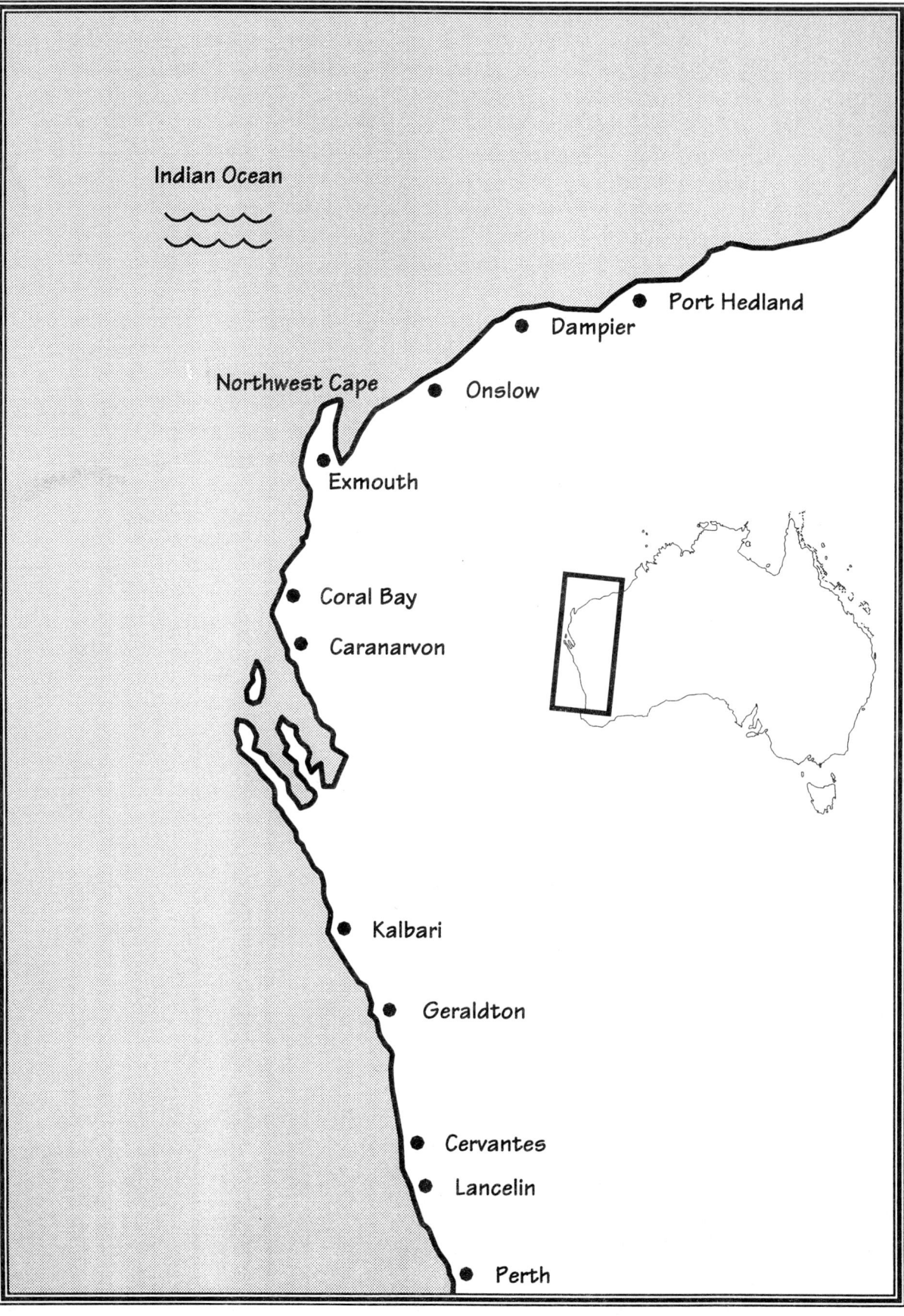

Chapter 9

Mining and Lobsters
Port Hedland to Perth

Dawn crept over Port Hedland. Aching from days of heat and tough sailing, we had sweated the night away through broken sleep and both woke irritable and tired. The town looked like we felt. Matching tired, fibro houses stood in rows along open streets dotted with wispy, stunted trees all covered in a red, grimy iron ore dust. Our clothes stuck to our backs with sweat as we walked a mile or so to the town center. We looked in surprise at the few scattered shops. "Na, most everybody goes out to South Hedland these days. Got a shopping mall," explained a local. With the thought of air-conditioned comfort we happily jumped on a bus to travel the eight miles out to South Hedland and the new mall. New suburbs of bright brick veneer houses stood in stark streets and several large salt piles awaiting export showed a dynamic side to the town. Air conditioning and food! We ate and ate, longing to just collapse and go to sleep on the floor in this sterilized comfort. How we longed for some coolness and white, clean sheets.

Reluctantly we returned to our camp and settled for a cup of tea under the patchy shade of two red-brown casuarinas, while we fended off a few thousand biting black ants. "Aachoo," went Sue with a bad case of hayfever. "That's it." she said in a moment of total frustration. "I don't know if I can go on." Sue started sobbing. Oh, God! I didn't have the energy to deal with this. Without much compassion I tried to point out our limited options. We had made it this far against all odds and I was not going to give Port Hedland the pleasure of seeing us quit and leave town with our tails between our legs, $6,000 in debt. "I'll sail by myself if I have to! Come on Sue, we can make Perth and we'll see what happens from there." We talked about the possibility that, if no sponsorship was forthcoming in Perth, we may well have to call it quits. It was another turning point in the trip, but I was too tired to realize it.

Keeping Australia On the Left

Fatigue seemed to have accumulated over the past months of heat, and despite our assisted respite I still felt I could have slept for a week. We found small cracks in *Tom's* trampoline mounts and I was concerned that we would need to do some major repairs in Perth. Here we were at the halfway mark of our voyage, on the edge of the Sandy Desert, covered in the red iron-ore dust of Port Hedland, just wanting to curl up in a quiet, cool spot and sleep. Our financial difficulties were also mounting and we seriously questioned the remainder of the trip. My parents had put more money in our account. "Go for it. You've got this far, keep going and worry about the money later. Just give us a call," my Dad said. It was a relief but even more we felt a sense of urgency to just put our heads down and make distance south. Perth and the America's Cup remained dangling as the carrot that urged us on. We made some phone calls to Perth and told them we were still coming.

We both slept well that night and were in a better mood in the morning. We went off to explore the yacht club and drop in for a glass of water. Dave, the Commodore on work duty, greeted us in paint-covered overalls. Hours later, after Sue had charmed a group of members with tales of our trip, we were invited to Ann and Brian's place for dinner and had the use of Dave's car for the rest of our stay. Our luck had changed. Brian was the local airtraffic controller and Ann was doing a two-year country stint as a psychiatric nurse. They confided that the sailing club and other social outlets were their way of preserving their sanity in Port Hedland. We washed the salt water and sand out of all our clothes at Dave's and enjoyed dinner with him and his wife, Jean.

We were determined to get to Dampier the next day after stopping at the sailing club for the Melbourne Cup horse race celebrations. Sue tried to understand the enthusiasm of all Australians for this unique horse race by comparing it to the Kentucky Derby and mint juleps. It is difficult to explain why most of the population stops for the race, perhaps have a glass of champagne, and places a bet but can't remember, and don't care, which horse actually wins the race. Unfortunately, the excellent food led to a few too many glasses of champagne, and our departure was delayed. We slept on the floor of the bar in the yacht club, thanks to the hospitality of the caretakers Peter and Dot. Early next morning we thankfully watched Port Hedland disappear behind us as we finally got away. Although sailing into

Mining and Lobsters

headwinds once more, our trip to Dampier was more enjoyable than our previous weeks because of an amazing change in landscape. Low flat sand dunes gave way to high, rocky hedlands, and the islands of the Despatch and Dampier archipelagos. These 500-foot island peaks represented the highest landfall we had seen since lining up on Darwin Hospital. Blowholes sounded amongst the rocky ledges extending from the sandhills as we scooted in fresh morning offshore breezes from island to island. We still spent the occasional day under mosquito netting to escape the flies and a small tarp to avoid the sun, while waiting out a strong headwind in 95°F heat.

We pounded on into the easterly swell and wind to make the protection of Point Samson, anxious that *Tom* was taking on a lot of water even though we continually used the hand pumps. Sue and I alternately acted as a spray screen for each other as *Tom* was covered in a sheet of spray with every second chop. Point Samson is a beach holiday retreat for mining families, with a caravan park and camping area nearly as big as the town itself. We found an excellent fish-and-chip shop for dinner and appreciated the luxury of sitting at a picnic table for dinner. The next morning we finally made it around the long jetty of Cape Lambert, across the northern expanse of Nickol Bay to cut through a shallow boat passage between the rocky end of Burrup Peninsula and Dolphin Islands and pop out at Dampier. We dodged moorings and maneuvered around ships in this major west coast port as we scooted through to the Boat Club beach. Checking into the club, we were put through the usual quiz.

"What's your car registration?"

"We don't have a car."

"Where have you come from?" she tried again.

"Sydney, and we sailed here." I tried to be more specific.

Apparently she had seen *Tom* and wasn't to be swayed. "Yes, I know you've come to sail here, but where is your car?" she persisted.

I politely gave her a detailed outline of the last six months and how we came to be at Dampier.

"Oh, welcome," she mumbled still confused and embarrassed.

The hospitality was not as forthcoming as in other towns and we realized that this was a boat club catering more to fishing and speedboats. The sailing camaraderie was not present. We picked up our large package of mail, including our latest care package, from the Post Office and sat in a coffee shop pouring over each letter. Returning letters and post cards to our fan club under the wonderful shade of large green trees behind the club, we waited out a stiff two-day blow.

Eventually, we met the sailing contingent of Dampier, consisting of Jeff and Gordon, at the bar. They had spent years of working up north for Hammersley Iron, one of the largest mining companies in Australia, and offered to take us on a tour of Dampier. It was a well-established, company town — green lawns and trees everywhere in contrast to the surrounding arid country. Large quantities of natural gas from offshore rigs was now treated at the new gas plant and loaded onto ships directed to overseas ports. Gas was beginning to rival many of Western Australia's other leading exports. We gladly accepted the offer of dinner and a bed and shared sailing stories into the night.

We received new roller bags for *Tom*, which would make the task of hauling him up and down the beach much easier. It had become something we detested at the end of a long day. I also replaced the rubber flanges on our bilge pumps, which had perished after so much sun and salt water. One of our forestay bridles just fell apart in my hands one morning as I adjusted the rigging. It made me appreciate Peter's double side and forward stays which, from this experience, was all that had prevented the mast from falling over long ago. *Tom's bottom is soggy like a wafer as the water separates the foam sandwich and cracks appear. So much work to do — not the time, tools or money*, I noted. Our boat-builder, Peter, was anxious when we spoke to him on the phone, "Is it going to hold up? How are you going?" I assured him we would get to Perth, but we would need to replace almost all the fittings and repair the hull as well as trade in the outboard.

We were resigned to the thought that *Tom* would not make Perth safely unless we got some help. The toughest section to come was the long, rough, overnight passage down the coast from Caranavon to Geraldton. The Zuytdorp

Mining and Lobsters

Cliffs would prevent us from making a landfall for a 100-mile section. We decided we were going to have to hitch this section, and, though disappointed, it was a load off our minds. Perth suddenly became more realistic. After a couple of frustrating wind-blown days in Dampier *Tom* looked much healthier from the attention and we felt slightly refocused and reassured about what we were trying to achieve.

We headed out around the big red piles of iron ore and salt, grateful to be out on our own again and not being on show. Here we didn't worry about where to stay or go to the toilet. The country did show some relief now with 30-to-60-foot high hedlands and even patches of green. A collection of islands and various passages between reefs and mangrove inlets, provided a protected and enjoyable trip. It was a pleasant surprise to see green colors and variety in the landforms again after the dark, flat sand of Ninety-Mile Beach and the red ore dust of Port Hedland. We actually had some brilliant mornings sailing with a clean northeasterly despite some pessimistic comments about the wind at Dampier. "Yeah, just wait 'til January and you'll get great wind — you'll catch the first cyclone all the way to Perth!" The afternoon sea breeze was still our regular frustration as most days a 25- to 35 knot southerly headwind blasted us ashore.

We pulled in between two catamarans on the beach in the small town of Onslow. This quiet, isolated town had recently been taken over by contractors in the exploration for oil at nearby Barrow Island. We were casually welcomed by Alan, the owner/manager of the local Bleedin' Beadon Hotel, the town's one and only. A fellow catamaran sailor, he took an immediate interest in our trip and offered us the air-conditioned comfort of a hotel room. Inspired by our efforts, he took his *Hobie* and girlfriend 12 miles out, around the oil rig and back, the following day. They turned quite a few heads while out there but his crewmember wasn't impressed with the two pitchpoles (frontend cartwheels) on the way home. "That's it. I'm never going out in that thing again," she said, storming up the beach throwing away her lifejacket. "Great day for a sail," he replied.

Meanwhile we toured the remains of the old townsite now lost to the drifting sand dunes and the local race course — its freshly-painted, white, galvanized iron sheds contrasting with the red anthills surrounding it on a lonely plain. Alan, the publican and New Zealander, employed five Kiwi girls as barmaids and was starting to think about early retirement. The pub had been booked out for nine months during the Barrow Island oil development and turns over 1.5 million dollars in sales to the surrounding Aboriginal community each year. I wasn't quite sure if it was an outrageous boast or embarrassing truth. Certainly this pub was the only liquor outlet for a hundred miles. As we reluctantly left our air-conditioned luxury and clean white sheets after two great nights sleep, Alan presented us with Bleedin' Beadon beer holders as a farewell gift. "Best of luck. You've certainly inspired me to get off my bum."

The prominent landmark of North West Cape was just three days away — we hoped! The coast had returned to flat and scrubby sand hills, as we passed yet another 12-mile stretch of beach. Suddenly, we noticed windmills and a familiar sign of civilization on the skyline — a television antenna. We beached *Tom* and walked over the sandhills into a barren looking property with a dusty, weatherboard house to meet Jeff and Rosey, the new managers of Urala, a sheep station carrying 6,000 head "give or take one." After we finally convinced them we had sailed in, the offer of a cup of coffee moved on to a beer and a caravan to sleep in. Together we went on a quick tour of the property by way of *Tom Thumb* to get our gear for the night, and for the benefit of Jeff and Rosy who wanted to "just make sure you're not kidding us." They were a hard working, salt-of-the-earth couple. Sue looked elsewhere as Jeff slaughtered a sheep in our honor for a barbecue dinner. We all sat on old cast iron beds watching an even older action video, drinking tea and passing the biscuit tin around. It was a memorable night sharing in their outback hospitality. The next morning we waved good-bye to another couple of newfound friends. Our mailing list for Christmas was getting very long.

It was a quick morning's sail across the open 25 miles that are the northern mouth of Exmouth Gulf. Through the haze North West Cape and the town of Exmouth eventually came into view, with the thirteen prominent 1900-foot towers of the joint Australian-American tracking station. It was surreal seeing this technology in an isolated and desolate landscape, like some inexplicable man-made mystery, constructed by civilizations long gone — a Stonehenge of the future. Controversy has surrounded this base since its inception with claims by Australians that it encourages a strike in

Mining and Lobsters

the event of nuclear war. The enterprising local hotel has cashed in on this, selling T-shirts and coolers stating "Come and get bombed at Australia's number one nuclear target!" The American base is totally self sufficient, with their own supermarket and other shops, all off limits to Australian outsiders. There was reluctant acceptance of the base mixed with envy. It provided some work for locals, but those on the inside seemed to have good pay and everything provided for them. Perhaps it was a case of the grass being greener on the other side of the barbed wire fence.

The members of the yacht club were a very hospitable group, allowing us the luxury of cooking in their galley. Although not a sound anchorage, the Exmouth Gulf does provide a beautifully clear and reasonably protected fishing ground. In recent years it has received wide acclaim for its excellent marlin. Bill, the caretaker, talked of his experience working on boats in Papua New Guinea and the Torres Strait. Some unfamiliar faces poked into the yacht club one evening and when we asked them who they were looking for, they responded, "You guys." Kurt, Irene and Casey were from Oregon, sailing on their 40-foot ketch, *Ruby's Rascal*, and had followed us since the east coast of Queensland. We shared tales of each other's adventures, including their recent saga in Exmouth when their boat had broken anchor while they were ashore and was found next morning lying off the town beach, water lapping the gunwales but with no major damage. As it was the end of November, we decided it was worthy of a big Thanksgiving celebration dinner. How strange to be floating on a hot, sunny November afternoon, eating turkey with four Americans at an American tracking station on Australia's most western Cape!

The tides were now getting smaller which meant a lot less work at departure time and less time wasted waiting for the right tide. However, we still waited patiently as wind warnings were common around here and we now had a 30- to-35 knot southwesterly blowing. Around the corner of the Cape we met the full force of the Indian Ocean, as large swells rolled in from the nearby Continental Shelf, 20 miles out where the sea drops to a bottomless 1,000 fathoms. Ningaloo Reef, which lay between 300 feet to three miles offshore, provides a protected passage for the next 200 miles of coast. Strong southerly headwinds of 25 to 30 knots persisted as we sneaked from hedland to hedland. Some mornings we left at 5.00 A.M. to only make six miles before being blasted ashore as the wind howled in at over 30 knots. On the east coast of Australia this would warrant a strong wind warning but in Western Australia it was just their afternoon sea breeze! Equally frustrating and exhausting was that we shivered with cold from the constant dousing of saltwater while sailing, and then spent the long afternoons trying to escape the baking sun behind a sand hill as there was no vegetation over knee height.

Our one consolation was that this slow progress allowed us plenty of time for exploration and, in retrospect, this harsh country and coast rated as some of the most beautiful we saw on the trip. Looking down from the 650-foot-high Cape range, a line of white, foaming breakers paralleled the shore, marking a line between the deep, dark-green ocean and turquoise bays littered with spectacular coral and abundant wildlife. The land was rugged and rocky and we were surprised to find a property marked on the map. The only livestock we could see were herds of straggly goats. In one bay we came across a vast number of mating turtles and sailed very carefully between them. We camped near them that night and witnessed one female come up the beach and lay her eggs, before burying them and leaving again next morning. It was a wonderful experience.

The area also had a rich history. We explored the whaling station at Point Cloates in Norwegian Bay where there had once been a thriving industry at various stages from 1913 to the 1950s. The Norwegian's originally gained a licence from the West Australian government to whale the north west coast. The wide bay use to run red with whale blood as carcasses hauled from the Indian Ocean were cut open and processed. In 1914 over 2,000 whales were caught, mainly humpbacks. Operations came and went with the profitability of whale oil and the introduction of factory ships that could do the work at sea. The scattered ruins were now slowly being swallowed by drifting sand dunes. Bottles and large whalebones lay scattered among the rusting boilers. Access to the Cape Range National Park was restricted to rough four-wheel-drive tracks and we rarely saw any travelers, apart from two caravans in the first few days.

Day after day the wind howled and tormented us. I read four books in as many days trying to dream myself away and conserve energy. We spent more hours on the beach each day than sailing. Most of the time we weren't really even sailing but pounding through the waves and wind with our little outboard working hard to help us through the narrow passages between reefs. We and all our gear were completely soaked after a few minutes of this kind of progress. What we thought would be a quick couple of days and a few hundred kilometers to Coral Bay was taking forever.

Early the next morning we spotted Ningaloo Station in the sandhills, the only property on the coast, and trudged about a half-a-mile up the track to meet a collection of yelping dogs and the station owners' daughter. "Yep, been on the farm for 36 years," she stated casually. We chatted about goats and sheep, windmills and weather before staggering the kilometer back down the road with two 15-liter containers of water. At least we wouldn't die of thirst now. We had to drink so much more to keep our energy levels up because we dehydrated quickly in the afternoon heat. It had not been a problem up to now as we could carry up to 16 gallons, or ten days water. The expected five-day trip from Exmouth to Coral Bay had taken us almost two weeks. We just had to keep pushing on against the odds, hoping that a break would come our way soon. On our ninth day, still short of Coral Bay, we were getting desperate. Food was also becoming an issue. Breakfast had been four biscuits and lunch was a cup of soup and some rice between us. "I could eat a whole loaf of bread," claimed Sue. Our patience with each other was at a snapping point. As we rounded the corner to Coral Bay early the next morning we were so focused on getting there that we failed to recognize low tide and a surrounding maze of coral heads. As we swore at each other we pulled ashore and walked the half-a-mile over to a small caravan park with a service station and shop.

We introduced ourselves to the managers, Keith and Colleen, and asked about trucks and vehicles out of Coral Bay. "Oh jeez, our fortnightly supply truck from Perth just left empty a couple of hours ago. There won't be anything for another two weeks," exclaimed Keith. We sighed and bought a loaf of frozen white bread, butter, cheese slices and a large bottle of soft drink. We didn't have any money for luxuries. We barely said a word to each other as we both devoured four sandwiches and the bottle of soda each.

Sue got up and went over to a phone booth. I just sat there tired and despondent. "What were you looking for, Sue?" I asked on her return.

"I was looking up trucking companies in Carnarvon. I'm not going any farther!"

It was not a good time to be talking this through. We were both still hungry and exhausted beyond belief. Sue had worked herself up to the point where Coral Bay was to be our savior and we would find something or someone to help us. I tried to point out that it was nothing but a small caravan park at the end of a rough dirt track. Carnarvon was the next major coastal town and the only regular transport had just left and wouldn't be back for two weeks. We may just have to sail to Carnarvon under our own steam. I was furious and she wasn't budging. "Fine you catch a lift and I'll sail the boat down and see you in Perth," I yelled. We eventually came to a compromise to at least check out alternatives and see what happened.

The next day we were offered the opportunity to go down to Carnarvon for a day's shopping — a short 250-mile round trip! Herby and Joyce packed us in with Maureen, who worked at the bar and was on a day off, and we headed south. The track out of Coral Bay was rough dirt for quite a way before hitting the highway. Watching the brown, dry country fly by, it again took some time to get used to travelling at this speed. After an hour and a half the wide, dry, sandy bed of the Gascoyne River was the first thing that broke the monotony, followed soon after by banana plantations. I could hardly believe that out of this dry, desert country such swathes of green could appear. Carnarvon even had a few decent trees along the wide streets.

We picked up our mail, got some money and did two weeks of shopping regardless of whether we were waiting for a truck or sailing. As we explored cake shops and wonderful food whom should we meet but the crew of *Ruby's Rascal*. They had given up waiting at Exmouth for the weather to improve and had hired a car and driven down. Their rented car had blown an engine just short of Carnarvon and they had hitched into town for a few days. We commiserated with them but were secretly somewhat relieved that larger yachts also found these conditions tough. Herby had two cartons of beer in the trunk and 12 cans in the car for our trip back to Coral Bay, so he was happy for Joyce and I to drive. Cheered up by letters, some money, good food and being away from the water and *Tom*, we were in good spirits for the drive back.

Mining and Lobsters

"Quick," greeted Don as soon as we arrived back, "There's a guy with a 45-foot motor cruiser anchored in the next bay fixing his exhaust system in our shed. He said he may be able to give you a lift." I found the owner struggling with a welder and a blackened exhaust pipe. "OK, come around tomorrow morning and we'll see if you fit," said Peter. Sue was almost sticking her tongue out in an I-told-you-so mood. Despite being tempted to kick her in the backside, I was also excited at the prospect of our prayers being answered.

We didn't know if we would fit yet, and Peter hadn't talked to the rest of his crew. As we anxiously motored around to the bay at 6:30 A.M. the next morning and saw the boat I knew it was going to be a close fit. The crew were below re-assembling the exhaust system and on a yell of "hello" we were greeted by Peter's wife, Robyn, resplendent in a dressing gown. We had some breakfast with them and then considered how we could store *Tom*. After a quick assessment, Todd, the skipper said, "No problems, we can winch both hulls onto the top deck." I wasn't about to argue and for the first time appreciated the value of *Tom* being totally collapsable. A normal catamaran would not have fitted.

Not only did they have room for a collapsed *Tom Thumb* on their top deck, but the owners, Peter and Robyn Wheatley from Perth, were more than happy to help us out. We had to laugh when we found out their boat was named *M.V Tenacity,* a recent purchase from Sydney that was being brought to Perth for the Cup. Peter was surprised at the amount of gear that came out of *Tom* but managed to fit it into various storage areas. Floating behind *Tenacity* we proceeded to pull *Tom* apart, down to two canoe hulls, and winched them aboard. "Are you sure this is all right," I questioned Peter as *Tom* was lowered onto his teak deck. "Well, we won't be able to have our dance parties at night," joked Peter. After a good deal of rushing around and anxiety on our part, the crew of *Tenacity* then decided that they would not take on the 25 knots of wind already whipping whitecaps across Maud's Bay. We would stay for another day. Rather than explore Coral Bay with the rest of the crew, we decided to stay put talking to Robyn and Mike, just to reassure ourselves that our ticket out would not go without us.

Only one day previously we had been pondering how we could keep going, exhausted in the heat and tired of the sand of the Western Australian coast. Now we were powering down the coast in air-conditioned comfort, sipping ice cold gin and tonics and watching *Dr. Zhivago* on the video! However, we soon had cause to be wary of our luck. The engine problem that had caused their unscheduled stop in Coral Bay continued and the exhaust smoldered down the coast. To keep things interesting we also ran aground trying to find the Carnarvon Harbour entrance at midnight. The washing machine motion of a power vessel combined with the smell of diesel once again did not agree with me. The only time I surfaced on deck was to witness our departure from Shark Bay past Steep Point and to see the start of the Zuytdorp Cliffs, the 100-mile, unbroken section of imposing rocky cliffs that were to have been another major night-passage challenge for us.

The 100-foot high red cliffs stretching off into the distance were an awesome sight and made me appreciate what Paul Caffyn had taken on alone in his small sea kayak. Popping tablets to stay awake, he had paddled solo non-stop for 34 hours in a kayak to overcome this challenge. With no reef or shoaling shoreline, the big green, rolling swells of the Indian Ocean crashed onto the rugged cliffs. I realized it would have been suicidal to take *Tom* out in this in his current condition. I watched in awe until the sun had baked the cliffs a blood red and sank into the sea. The next morning, after four days in a total daze, *Tenacity* tied up at Geraldton Wharf.

We declined the offer of continuing with *Tenacity* to Perth, determined to sail into Fremantle, the site of the America's Cup race, on our own. For the moment we were quite content to relax and enjoy Christmas in Geraldton, reflecting on an incredible year. We quickly found a nearby boat yard that would fix *Tom's* hull and transport us and all our gear down to the local caravan park. After one night in our tent in the heat we struck a deal with the park managers to clean the toilets in exchange for staying in a caravan. Now we could write while sitting comfortably in a chair, read by light at night, have unlimited water from a tap and even ice cubes.

We settled in for the week of Christmas, comforted that we didn't have an option because *Tom* needed repairs. I went down to the local employment office to try to find some work. My first job was as a roadie for the *Toys*, a rock band from Perth playing at the local pub. It was strange to see a group of rockers with long hair and earrings after being in working man's country for so long. They were a good group of guys and serious about their work.

Mining and Lobsters

We unloaded the truck and set up the gear before sitting in their hotel room smoking dope and talking footy. I soon left, not wanting to spend my hard earn dollars on drinking for the night. I returned at midnight as the band was finishing their final number. A young girl staggered past me and threw up on the nearest table and on a couple of her friends. Then a fellow staggered out of the toilet and grabbed me, "I'm having fits in the toilet. Please get me an ambulance." He released his grip and staggered back into the toilet. I suggested to the nearest bar girl that they had a problem and could she call an ambulance as their manager rushed off to the toilets. Ah... nothing like a fun night out. I helped the boys pack up, took my $20 and left. "Come and see the show when you get to Perth," they called. I just smiled and waved.

We were up early the next morning to water the gardens and dig out a site for a caravan annex. In between jobs we wrote our latest series of magazine and newspaper articles and fixed *Tom*. One of the other guys at the caravan park found me some more work at the local abattoirs for a couple of days. Under a large, open, galvanized shed hung 1,500 sheepskins that needed to be loaded onto semi-trailers. By morning tea I had just about become used to the smell and the maggots all over the floor. "Put the jug on for a cup of tea Mark," yelled one of the local lads. After cleaning the maggots out of the jug and mugs I made morning tea. My work mates had a good laugh at this test for the new comer. "Some blokes leave for a smoke after 10 minutes and never come back," laughed the boss. Climbing up and down open pipe racks three stories high and tossing skins to the outside was hot and hard work. Scotty, my Scottish work mate, talked non-stop of his experiences fishing and shearing out in the "GAFA" — Great Australian Fuck All. We started at 6:00 A.M. and knocked off at 5:00 P.M. The smell almost made me dry retch at times and maggots dropped down my back and in my hair. I thought how much I would appreciate sailing after this and how we needed the extra money. The job as a rockband roadie looked far more attractive now. Sue wouldn't let me come into the caravan without having two showers and leaving all my clothing and shoes in a bucket of laundry soap 60 feet away.

Tom was repaired at Horrie and Steve's Fisherman Co-op boat yard, by Horrie's son Shane. The bottom of one whole hull had separated from its foam sandwich construction. Shane cut out the foam sandwich and laid the base as solid fiberglass with some thwarts built in. Along with a bit of spit and polish *Tom* looked like a seaworthy craft again. Our best Christmas present came from the local outboard dealer who serviced our outboard free of charge. "Happy Christmas and all the best with the rest of your trip," he called. With good food and plenty of rest, we were almost feeling human again.

We sailed a reconstructed *Tom Thumb* around the bay for a day just to test him out and parked him at the yacht club. Out of a corner of the club the crew of *Ruby's Rascal* appeared, looking worse for wear.

"We eventually just sailed around North West Cape and headed south as best we could," said Kurt. They described three days of hell as they and the boat pounded into the wind, breaking gear and almost breaking them.

"I nearly turned around. In seven years of cruising it was the worst I've ever sailed in," admitted Kurt. It made us appreciate our lift even more.

On Christmas day our caravan was decked out in Christmas cards and we exchanged presents before spending the day with Horrie's family. When we were so far from our own families it was nice to be with another family who were warm and welcoming. We were overwhelmed with hospitality and good food and drink, but then we received presents from the family — two new T-shirts and a $100 discount on our bill for fixing *Tom*. We were stunned and stumbled over words of thanks, feeling guilty that we were not able to reciprocate in some way. We spent the afternoon teaching Sue the finer points of cricket in a backyard game before being delivered back to our caravan home. It was a touching and humbling Christmas we had shared. It had revived my spirits. Our Christmas gifts had allowed us to throw out our old T-shirts and replace our collection of well-read books.

Preliminary races for the America's cup had now begun and we were following the coverage on television and in the newspapers, knowing we would soon be there. Yachts and powercruisers from around the world were also stopping in the harbour on their way south. We were desperately trying to organize our arrival in Perth to maximize potential publicity and I phoned Jeff Stewart at Grand Prix Sailing in Sydney. We had talked with Jeff in

Mining and Lobsters

Sydney about sponsorship when he was trying to establish a world circuit for 18-foot skiff sailing.

"Mark, you're still alive! Surprise, surprise. And you guys are still together. I can't believe it — I'd written you off ages ago." Then he offered us $500 to sail into Perth with their logo on our sail. That really made our Christmas. Yamaha outboards were also considering our request for a replacement outboard, the most essential item from my perspective. We set our arrival day in Fremantle for the 10th of January and contacted Fremantle Yacht Club and the promoter of the Cup to coordinate our arrival.

The winds south of Geraldton were somewhat more favorable and we actually made progress under sail most days. The cliffs gradually became limestone bluffs and sandhills, but with a tinge of green and a few trees that actually provided shade. The 250 miles of coast to Perth is protected by a series of infamous reefs and islands three to ten miles off shore. The Dutch, including William Dampier and Dirk Hartog, had often run into them on their passage to the East Indies. The most terrible tale recounted in the museum at Geraldton was that of the *Batavia*, in which the shipwrecked crew turned on the surviving passengers, killing them and resorting to cannibalism before being rescued and brought to trial. Many galleons have been found along the coast and people continue to search for the many more that may exist, as well as their treasure.

At times the coast resembled a lake shore, with a shallowing bottom and banks of seaweed. Crayfish are the treasure along this stretch of coast now, it being one of the most popular areas for cray fishing in Australia. Scattered amongst the sandy coves and bays are a colorful collection of small cray communities and towns. Established fishing ports, such as Dongarra, are protected in rocky bays with breakwaters. Others just appear out of the sandhills or the long, flat beaches, a mere collection of weather-beaten wooden shacks. Despite our rush to get to Perth, it was one of the most enjoyable stretches of sailing.

New Year's Eve was spent in Dongarra, sitting by a windy fire on a beach, sipping brandy liqueur and reflecting on the past year. We toasted our achievement this far without thinking too much about what the year ahead might bring. Retreating from the evening cool we slept on the floor of an old, unused fishing shack and tried to keep the rats from running over our faces. "I won't forget this New Year for a long time," Sue announced. An early morning blow the next day forced us back to shore at the Freshwater Co-operative where we met a slightly subdued and hungover fishing crew. Dean, Jack and Barry and their families were all involved in crayfishing, and took pity on how we had spent the previous evening, plying us with drinks before offering dinner and apologizing that it was only Lobster Mornay again. After our staple diet of macaroni and cheese, it was like heaven to us.

While sharing drinks with Dean and Jack we got the low-down on lobstering. "People think you make lots of money but a boat is $200,000, the license for each pot is $2,500 to $5,000 with people operating 30 to 150 pots, and each pot costs $80," rattled off Dean. By my quick sums that ran into hundreds of thousands of dollars, perhaps even closer to a million dollars. "Then we lose pots. I lost, or had cut off, 56 last season," he continued. "Then they have just reduced licenses by ten percent this year, without any warning, to control stocks. With that kind of money invested you can imagine how people get concerned," Jack added. However we also calculated that they could pull in somewhere between 100 to 500 crays of one to four pounds each in weight, at $6 to $7 per pound. That could mean a catch of $1,200 to $7,000 per day during the season!

This explained why we were meeting retired teachers and accountants and other professionals now running a cray license. "It's a long day's work depending on where you fish and how many pots you have," Dean continued. "Off the edge, means 20 or more miles out in up to 80 fathoms, which means leaving at 3.00 A.M. Popular fishing spots were often crowded with colored floats and you occasionally run over someone else's float and cut them off, not by choice! Its a bloody risk wrapping a line around your prop," exclaimed Dean. There was a real skill between skipper and decky to first find your float — a small flag atop a five-foot float pole, bobbing on an open ocean, and then to get it in and winch up the catch and reset the pot as quickly as possible. Over shallow reefs both strong nerves and a lot of skill were required.

The following day we made slow but steady progress sailing in and out of the reefs and small islands down past the town of Lancelin. Late in the

Mining and Lobsters

day as we skimmed close to shore we were surprised by a foaming four-foot wall that broke less than 20 yards away from us. I just had time to turn *Tom's* nose into it and break through as the spray shot us into the air. It was a close call as we could have been driven backward rudders first into the sandbank. Damp and shaken we pulled into an empty isolated beach only to be surprised and welcomed by a couple strolling by. Les and Sue invited Sue over to have a shower at their shack, a hundred yards down the beach. The shower turned to drinks and dinner as we met the whole family of grandfather, daughters and "the skipper, Butch, who's weight lifting and will be over in a minute". As images of a weight lifting skipper called Butch came to mind, a pony-tailed guy in a sarong came around the corner. "Mark and Sue, meet Butch." Never had I met such a gentle bohemian giant. To recover from his physical training Butch cracked a beer and rolled a joint from his homegrown supply.

We spent a wonderful evening with them, laughing and talking and feeling a part of the family. Les and Sue had invested all their money in a cray license and Butch was their skipper. "It's an interesting life, but we've no regrets," claimed Les waving his hand over their shack in the sandiness. After many drinks and stories, Sue offered us a bed for the night, which we gratefully accepted. Not having to repack the whole boat next morning we thought we'd make an early getaway. But just as we readied to push off, there came a cry of "Wait, wait," from down the beach. We turned to see Butch running down the beach in his sarong, with two cups and an electric kettle trailing its electric plug. "You can't leave without a cup of coffee," he said, smiling and pouring hot coffee into a cup for each of us. We laughed, hardy able to refuse such an effort. Les and Sue joined him and, after our warming coffee, helped us push off. We turned and waved farewell until they disappeared from sight. Such friendship and hospitality was almost overcoming and it was hard to say good-bye after knowing these wonderful, caring people for too short a time. The many people we had met had shared so freely with us, yet we always had to leave, knowing we would probably not meet again and never have the opportunity to reciprocate. It was hard not to feel guilty.

It was a calm sunny day as we cruised past continual sand dunes, broken by the occasional bay or small rocky hedland. We pulled into the small beach village of Jurien Bay and slept under a dinghy pulled up against *Tom*. Fortunately the owner was quite understanding when he came to go fishing next morning and found his dinghy in use. Apparently after finding us sound asleep he left and came back an hour later when we were awake and finished with his dinghy.

After a few more frustratingly short days bashing into southerly headwinds past the small fishing communities of Seabird and Guilderton, Perth was at last within reach. We had completed almost 1,500 miles of the Western Australian coast. As we pulled into the port of Two Rocks at Yanchep Sun City we realized that the photographer hanging off the side of the wharf was taking pictures of us. Apparently the Western Mail newspaper had their scouts out following us down the coast and wanted to scoop our story. After several entries and exits from the harbor to get the right shot, we did an interview on the boat ramp. It finally felt like we had made it. After the marina manager offered us a free berth and the yacht club members said we could pitch our tent behind the club, we decided to stay rather than push on to Fremantle, which was now only 30 miles away.

Sun City was the development initially created by Alan Bond to launch his first America's Cup campaign and potentially cash in on its success. He failed with this bid and Sun City is a sad, faded subdivision on the sandhills, still too far north of Perth to be a suburb. The original yacht club building that so proudly hosted an America's Cup challenge was actually now a squatters shack with the electricity disconnected. It was an even sadder irony that Sun City, that promised so much, was now deserted while the America's Cup was being raced in Fremantle, just down the coast.

In preparation for our hoped-for grand entry to Fremantle we sailed a further six miles down to the Perth suburbs of Observation City and Hillarys and called the *Tenacity* owners, Peter and Robyn. The remainder of their journey had been uneventful and Peter and crew were now refitting *Tenacity* at the docks in Fremantle. It was good to catch up with them. However, we found the density of traffic, people and houses in Perth a bit of a shock. This was our first big city since Darwin three months ago. We picked up our fan mail and our sixteenth box of supplies. Our fan club was excited about us having finally arrived in Perth and there were plenty of congratulatory calls and letters. We read our double-page article in the latest issue of *Modern*

Boating magazine, recorded so many adventures ago in Darwin. It was one of the best and most accurate articles anyone had written about us, and it was great to finally get some recognition in Australia. We sorted gear and stuck "Grand Prix Sailing" on our sails as a sponsorship deal for our arrival in Fremantle, called television stations and dropped a media release in all the pigeon holes at the Cup press center. We were about to sail into the greatest yachting event in Australia's history. Here we were, we had made it! After all the ups and downs over the past seven months, *Tom Thumb* and crew were sailing into the America's Cup. It was exciting to be about to live a dream and watch the Cup live. We were anxious and uncertain about the end of our trip. Would we find support and sponsors to help us back to Sydney?

On the day of arrival there was a hubbub of color, with flags and people and boats of every size and shape marking the Swan River mouth and the entrance to Fremantle. As we turned to head into the harbor and the Western Australian Yacht Club there was a great sense of excitement. I was quickly brought back to earth as we were almost run over by media chase boats and Australia's support boat heading out to sea for training sessions. The crowd and boats were not there for us — there was a yacht race on if we had not noticed. We pulled expectantly into the beach next to the club. No one was there! What a let down. As we cursed in frustration a flustered Channel 7 television crew drove up and apologized for their late arrival. We re-arrived a number of times, trying to make sure they captured the "Grand Prix" sign on our sail.

"Welcome to Fremantle and the America's Cup," said the reporter. "With an American and an Australian on board your small boat, who are you cheering for in the Cup?"

Chapter 10

The America's Cup
Perth

Like so many other Australians, I was in awe of the America's Cup. Every four years the international, wealthy elite of yachting, with their million dollar yachts would gather at Rhode Island to do battle over an ostentatious old, silver mug which is the trophy. As a boy I had witnessed black and white television news stories of the graceful Australian yachts *Dame Pattie* and *Gretel* battling the might of America. They did not win, but they made the final and carried the pride of our nation onto the international arena. To beat the Americans at their own game was the ultimate 132-year-old challenge of international yachting.

In 1982 Australia arrived with a number of challenging syndicates and yachts. The attention, however, was centered around a well-prepared crew and revolutionary designed yacht *Australia II*. The secret keel of *Australia II* developed a mystique and media hype of its own. A cloth curtain shielded it from view whenever it was raised from the water and security guards, including scuba divers patrolled their dock. The preliminary races confirmed its ability as *Australia II* swept all before them.

I was following the final races anxiously from the bush of northern NSW while instructing an Outward Bound program. When the American skipper, Dennis Conner, was leading the best of seven series three to one, I joined a despondent group thinking that, yet again, we were so close, but not to win. Then with skill and luck *Australia II* won the next two races to level the series and the nation was enthralled. I couldn't believe that I would be stuck in the middle of the wilderness on the night of the final race. I heard of the result the following morning. With a whole nation willing them on, *Australia II* came from behind on the last leg to win by 27 seconds. The rest is history! People recounted stories of how buses, trains and even planes all tuned in and gave live telecasts or blow-by-blow accounts over their loudspeaker

Keeping Australia On the Left

systems. Australians all over the country and the world celebrated that morning. The Prime Minister, on live television, enthused, "Any boss who sacks their employees for not turning up to work today is a bum!" People waltzed down the streets of Sydney on the way to work with bottles of champagne. Since then, researchers have highlighted the winning of The America's Cup as having a significant impact on Australia's psyche. Australians began to believe in themselves and our potential to take on the world.

All that was four years ago and now here, for the first time in its history, the America's Cup was being raced outside America, in Perth, Australia. Here we were having sailed a 16-foot catamaran half way around Australia to watch! I was living out several dreams all at once. Strangely, if I hadn't been committed to sailing here I don't know if I would have traveled to Perth to witness the Cup. As much as it had intrigued me, the America's Cup had always seemed to be a world away, not only geographically, but personally and socially. It didn't seem accessible to the common sailor. The wresting of it away from Rhode Island by a bunch of Australian lads had broken some of that perception.

The colorful international crowds around the newly renovated port streets of Fremantle were fun and intoxicating after the barren sandhills and deserts of the West Australian coast. We didn't need to expound on the virtues of sailing to anyone, we could just take in the atmosphere. We met up with our Operation Raleigh friends Charles and Clive, who had moved from Queensland to run projects on the rugged West Australian south coast. It was great to catch up and hear how well their projects had been going with international groups of youth. They also introduced us to a wide range of useful contacts. Within days of arriving we had confirmed the donation of a new Suzuki outboard through Pier 21, a local marina complex, on the Swan River near Fremantle. It was not only a relief to replace our struggling Yamaha, but to double our horsepower from four to eight. It was more than we needed, but an eight weighed almost the same as a five horsepower and we were more than grateful.

This newfound sponsorship resulted in *Tom* being stored at Pier 21 with a bright red PIER 21 emblazoned on his sail. We were also on display in the two boat shows during the Cup, so moving *Tom* around Perth and spending four to five days at each kept us busy. The shows introduced us to some great people. Not feeling bashful we put up a sign acknowledging our sponsors, with a map showing the course of our trip as well as a small sign saying, "Donations gratefully accepted to get us back to Sydney." One day we took in over $55, including $20 from an enthusiastic New Zealander, with a "good on ya and enjoy the rest of ya trip." A passing photographer donated five rolls of film and said, "make sure they're good shots." One man had seen us sailing at Cape Bosset near Broome and thought "Nah, that can't be a catamaran this far from Broome." We were glad to confirm that he wasn't imagining things. Fellow sailors who had sailed to the Cup enthusiastically shared their experiences and invited us to their boats. The kindest and most hospitable of all were our fellow exhibitors who shared their television sets to watch the cricket, and regularly brought us beer and food. They also became some of our best sponsors. The Line 7 foul weather clothing exhibitor was happy to give us a set of beautiful bright yellow overalls and jacket each worth around $500.

"Saves me taking them back to New Zealand and you'll certainly need them from here on," he said happily slapping a big Line 7 sticker on both of *Tom's* hulls.

Along with our new O'Neil dry suits sent from the USA we were now well equipped for the cold Southern Ocean.

Our brightest angel was a neighboring exhibitor, Sid Nixon from Classic Yachts. A happy, friendly salt-of-the-sea, Sid built some of the largest round bilge, steel hulled yachts in Australia. While I was telling him our uncertainties about *Tom* making the distance, Sid offered us the use of his workshop. He also organized for a sailmaker to sponsor us with some changes. A larger headsail was fitted to help us run downwind in slight breezes and new furling points in our mainsail would allow us to reduce the sail area by half, yet keep control in strong winds. We spent many happy days in Sid's workshop in south Fremantle. Peter Pool sent over a new trampoline frame, which slipped together surprisingly well, and we replaced every single nut, bolt and rivet on *Tom*. He looked as good as ever.

Peter Pool was excited that we had actually made it to Perth and the Catcan was proving its worth! He had followed our progress through the occasional phone call and letter, more often getting articles and information passed on by my parents. Our interview in Darwin for *Modern Boating* magazine had since resulted in a center page article which added to his scrapbook of promotional material.

"What else do you need for the southern ocean? How are you feeling? Just give me a call." Peter's excitement and concern came down the phone line.

While trying to promote ourselves amidst this international sea of media we dropped off copies of the *Modern Boating* magazine article and a press release in the pigeon holes at the Cup Media Center. This was housed in an enormous auditorium, banked with computers and update screens reminiscent of a NASA control center. People raced to get their stories off to meet deadlines of morning and afternoon print, radio and television all over the world. We heard some funny stories about how such an event, especially in Australia, had promoted some journalists who had only been sailing once, to "international yachting correspondent." Some learned fast, but I'm sure there were others who didn't know much more about sailing when it was all over. The genuinely experienced yachting journalists were scathingly unimpressed at the efforts of these fly-by-night reporters.

An interesting interlude came with a fundraising lunch for Operation Raleigh at the British Syndicate's Club. An old warehouse store in Fremantle had been converted to offices and an entertainment complex for the team and their sponsors. With dark, wooden paneling and deep nautical blue carpet with insignias it had an opulence, in the best America's Cup, Rhode Island tradition but with a British private school correctness. We chatted to the *Sunday Times* gossip columnist and Mr. UK Consulate all being "so awwwfully polite." It was an interesting collection of West Australian millionaires and entrepreneurs, Chris Rowe, Allan Burns, Laurie Connell, Peter Briggs and Kerry Stokes. This was a time of great excitement and prosperity for Western Australia as the rest of the country, and indeed the world, focused on the state for the first time. Dealings between government and business were seen as sensible and few business decisions were challenged. After a wonderful lunch and the appropriate speeches we were introduced to the British yacht skipper, Harold Cudmore. A small, but vocal character, he was casually attired in his working shorts and Docksider shoes. Eyeing Sue he jovially tossed forth, "So why did you bring her on the trip? So you could get into her pants?" in front of the crowded table. I smiled

The America's Cup

politely and said "No" and went off to find someone else to talk to. Take me back to the honest, unpretentious, hard working cray fishermen around a campfire any time.

The gloss of the America's Cup was wearing thin. Perhaps it was naive to expect anything else. This race being about big boys playing with their toys and egos, flashing their dollars and nautical know-how in a crass display of style and wealth was a long way from the camaraderie and fun that I knew as sailing. Crowds of people there to be seen, and "Oh, by the way, aren't there a few boats over there having some kind of race today." Others gathered like vultures, searching for the quick buck to be made from the America's Cup. Maybe we had inherited the whole package by winning the America's Cup. Then again, weren't we guilty of trying to ride this wave too, and get what we wanted by sailing around Australia in our boat? Either way, I was beginning to hope America and Dennis Conner would win it back.

Ironically, as part of our deal with Pier 21, we were asked to help out with the backup of the Grand Prix 18-foot skiff races, our earlier sponsor. It meant steering around race marshals and media representatives in inflatable dinghies during the racing. The competition was held on a tight course in a small, calm section of the Swan River next to the local Burswood Casino. It was a crazy place to sail, with short four-to-five-hundred yards legs between buoys and fluky winds. But it meant there was easy media coverage and a prominent sponsors tent where you didn't have to stand up or put down your drink to see the racing. I'm sure the crews laughed at the thought of this being a real sailing course. Eighteen-foot skiffs are basically sails on water. Their aerodynamic, lightweight hulls cut through the water as the crew of three hang off extended wings projecting from the hull. It is sailing on the edge most of the time. Some of the spectators and sponsors were suggesting that the America's Cup be raced in this type of boat. "At least you can see the race, and each boat is a few million dollars cheaper than the 12-meter America's Cup yachts."

In the end we had an enjoyable couple of days, meeting people and drinking and eating sponsors products. On the final day, Sue and I were asked to take the media chase boat back to Pier 21 at the mouth of the Swan River. People make amazing assumptions when you have sailed in any shape or form, that you have immediate knowledge of all things nautical.

"Sure, no problem," I replied. I'd never stepped foot in, or driven a boat like it! As it had a set of twin 150 horsepower outboards on the back, I was sure it would go. After spending ten minutes working out how to lower the engines into the water we took off down the Swan River. After months of going at *Tom's* steady five-to-six knots it was frighteningly exciting to suddenly be doing 30 knots, but it wasn't sailing.

As extravagant event followed event in and around Perth, the final day of the main race arrived. The Americans in *Stars and Stripes* were beating everyone convincingly and we went out to watch the fourth race against the Australian defenders with the Americans leading the best of seven series three to zero. We were lucky enough to score a ride on the *Sir Walter Raleigh*, the flagship of the Operation Raleigh program, to see the race. It was a converted North Sea trawler, but with some fresh paint it looked proud and had hosted many functions around the world.

It was amazing to cruise out to sea amidst a flotilla of ships and boats of every size, supported by a hovering flock of news helicopters. The course was a triangle with three-to-four nautical mile sides set about three miles off the coast. You could see the yachts from the shoreline with binoculars but you would not have any idea of what was going on. The *Sir Walter Raleigh* anchored at its designated spot near the *Achillie Lara* and across from the *Queen Elizabeth*, both enormous cruise ships. Around us scooted boats and yachts of every imaginable size. We were at the end of the windward leg, furthest from the start line.

All our Operation Raleigh friends were engaged in friendly banter on the top deck. The Americans were keen to see Dennis Conner in his yacht *Stars and Stripes* win to regain some of their national pride. Everybody else was cheering for Australia, just as anxious to see Dennis and America lose. Dennis Conner is the enigma of America's Cup racing. He had successfully defended many cup races, but had been the first American to ever lose it, and now here he was trying to win it back. There was no doubt about his sailing ability, but people either loved or loathed this arrogant sailor. For me he represented everything I detested about the America's Cup: the arrogant, win-at-all-costs, business approach to sailing where campaign costs had risen to tens of millions of dollars per syndicate.

The America's Cup

It was exciting to hear the start and feel the wind on my face and see the big picture, but to actually keep track of the race you still had to rely on the radio or television. It appeared to be a good battle, closer than some of the earlier races. As they rounded our marker for the second time *Australia* had a slight lead with *Stars and Stripes* on their heels. But then, as they beat to windward, *Stars and Stripes* did what it had been doing all regatta. *Australia* covered her tacks, matching them down the course, but *Stars and Stripes* was clearly faster and just sailed up along side, forcing *Australia* to tack away. In yachting terms, unless *Star and Stripes* mast fell over, or they sank, it was all over.

I couldn't watch any longer, feeling slightly ill at the prospect of the America's Cup returning to America so soon. Many of the residents of Perth and Fremantle who had put up with building projects being rushed through, an increase in population, property values and rentals were saying, "Thank goodness it's over and gone." The English crew of the *Sir Walter Raleigh* suggested that we crack a bottle of scotch and we settled into the staff cabin and drank our way back to port, not even surfacing to watch the inevitable conclusion of the race. So that was the America's Cup!

Our month's stay in Perth hadn't exactly been restful, trying to juggle boat shows and sponsorship and finding a place to sleep. Accommodation had been at a premium and newly acquired friends were very generous in their support of floor space or bedrooms. One night while I was visiting friends on board the square rigger, *Eye of the Wind,* the offer came of a free dinner cruise on one of the tourist boats. A group of us jumped at it and I called Sue to let her know I would sleep on *Eye of the* Wind and I'd be back in the morning. As my eyelids closed, my mind tried to adjust to the new surroundings. Every night we had slept in a new place, so why was this so different? Then I realized. This was the first night in thirteen months that Sue and I had been apart! I drifted to a rocking, unsteady sleep.

Making it to Perth and seeing so many of our friends again had lifted our spirits, but we were still tired, emotionally and physically. I also felt we needed a break from each other to put life back in perspective. Although we had shared so much, I questioned whether there was a future for Sue and I after the trip and said as much. I'm sure Sue was equally tired and frustrated with me and ready to move on with life. If we hadn't received the amount of support we did in Perth, I'm sure we would have packed up and gone our separate ways. As hard as the relationship had become however I felt a strong sense of obligation to our sponsors and supporters and all the other people that had believed in us. We were both very stubborn and determined. There was no question of us *not* continuing south from Perth towards the Southern Ocean and the Great Australian Bight. Being realistic however, we decided that we would size up our ability to cross the Bight when we came to it. We had committed ourselves to making Victor Harbor, on the eastern side of the Bight, south of Adelaide, by April. Our friends Jim and Sally from Victor Harbour, were returning north to where we had met them a year ago, at the caravan park in Yeppoon, Queensland and had offered us the opportunity to house sit for the winter. There was no way we would make our original target of arriving back in Sydney within the year. Our immediate target was therefore Victor Harbour for an opportunity to rest and contemplate the final section of our travels.

We gave ourselves two weeks after the final Cup race to make last minute adjustments to *Tom* and get off the two latest articles for *Multihulls* magazine and Sue's hometown newspaper. I looked forward to returning to the quieter and more restful life of *Tom Thumb* cruising. *Let's get out of here, give me room, give me space. Time for a cool change*, I noted in my journal. We took *Tom* for a test sail, along with our friend Nick Horn, up along the Swan River. It was great to be back on board, with a new trampoline, large headsail, reef points in the main and knowing all the nuts, bolts and rivets were new. Nick questioned us about our ability to push on in tough conditions. So we turned into the wind and stuck him up front.

"OK, OK! I get the picture," he yelled as we pounded in to the chop and he got totally soaked for another hour.

After dinners and farewells and many thank-yous we spent our final night ignominiously camped on the North Fremantle oval to get an early start. The next morning we motored past Pier 21 and under the entry bridges to the Swan River with our mast on deck, pulling alongside *Eye of the Wind* to say our final farewell. On the small beach around from the West Australian Yacht Club where we had arrived amidst crowds and a hive of activity only a month ago, there was just us — a small 16-foot catamaran and two ordinary people. A solitary gull danced in the shorebreak, pecking

The America's Cup

indiscriminately at the retreating foam as if passing time. The early morning sky aimlessly tossed dull streaking shadows from a multitude of limp flags, silhouetted on boat and building. The only activity came from a few small fishing boats. Fremantle was awakening to its normal self, a tranquil contrast to the hurly-burly days of the America's Cup, only a week past, but seemingly long gone. We set the mast and sail and pushed off. We now had a new objective, 185 miles to Cape Leeuwin and the end of the west coast. When we rounded it we would be heading east. Toward home!

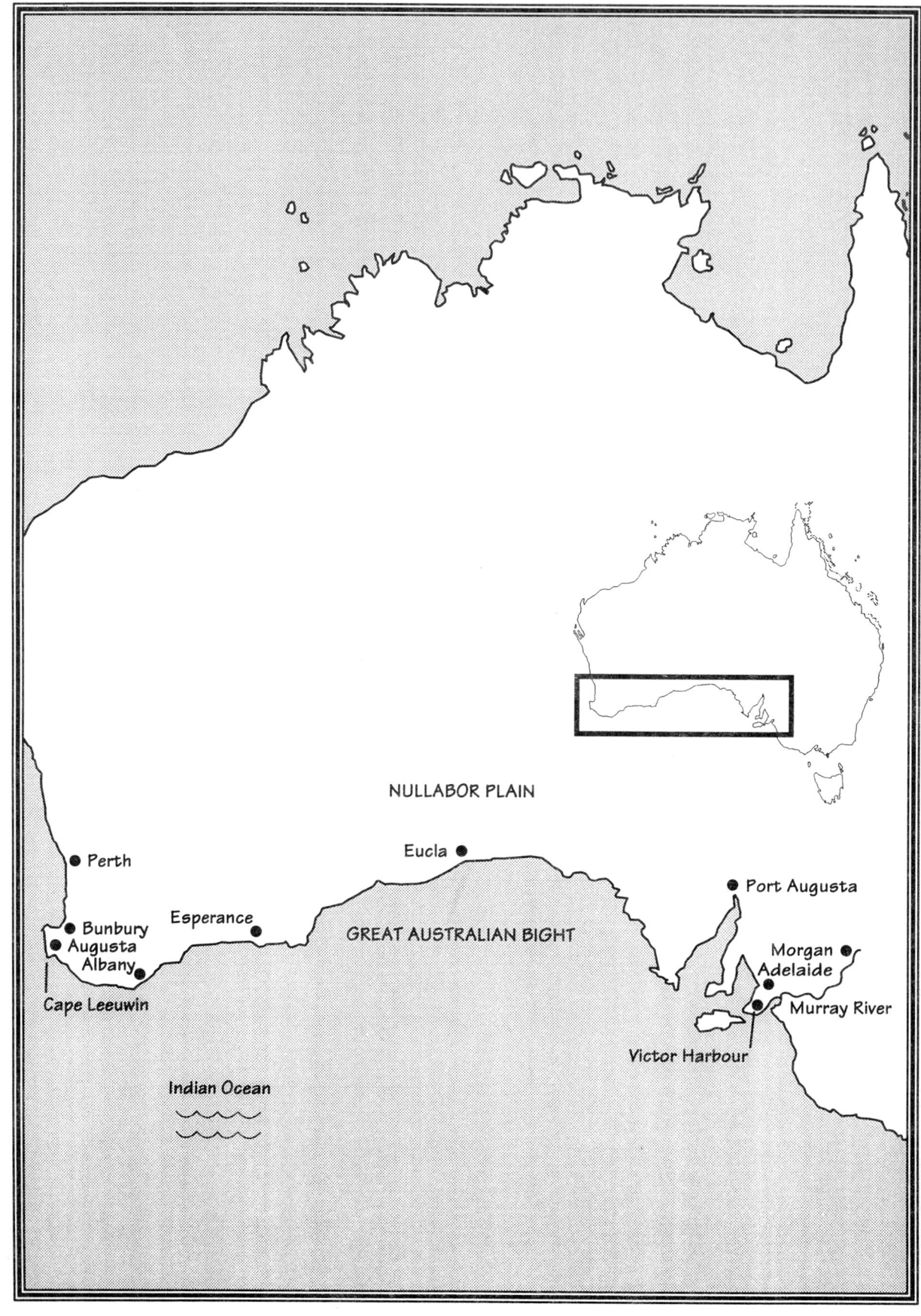

Chapter 11

Windy Cliffs
Perth to Victor Harbour

We set our newly reefed mainsail, confident in the knowledge that if it wasn't blowing on the Western Australian coast now, it soon would be. Sure enough within 15 minutes we were scooting across Cockburn Sound with a 20-knot easterly, both lost in thought reflecting on our enjoyable past month on land, as the familiar landforms of Perth and Fremantle disappeared behind. The long narrow Garden Island, connected to the mainland by a bridge at its southern end, provided six miles of extra protection from the Indian Ocean. *Tom's* new fittings, trampoline frame and rudder brackets gave us a greater sense of confidence as we celebrated being back on the water by racing yachts southward down the wide sound. The hulls sliced through the small swells and spray streamed out behind us as we moved gear and rearranged ropes around the trampoline, settling back into life at sea. *Tom Thumb*'s 22-foot mast skimmed under the Garden Island bridge and we headed for the open sea once more, off to explore the final stretches of the Western Australian coast.

The familiar ocean swell and breaking waves quickly brought us back to reality as we passed outside the line of reefs at Cape Peron and then southwards to Warnbro Sound. Our destination was the holiday town of Mandurah, a short 43-mile hop, providing that the afternoon seabreeze didn't blow us backwards. Signs of civilization gave way to the endless procession of low sandhills stretching south as far as the eye could see. The sea was surprisingly calm, even with a range of offshore reefs. A safe landing was available to us anywhere along the sandy shore.

As the morning breeze died we ran in our new eight-horse power Suzuki outboard to push us through the midday calm. After our poor struggling four-horsepower motor the Suzuki really pushed us along at a steady five-to-six knots without sounding stressed. A five-gallon fuel tank on line from the back deck also made it easier to keep fuel and did not require us to top off the tank every few hours.

In a surprising afternoon calm with beautiful sunshine we arrived at Mandurah in time for a late lunch. The quiet holiday town offered a beautiful protected river inlet with casuarina trees shading green grass, worlds away from the endless beach and usual wind-swept coast. It was so lovely and peaceful after the past months hustle and bustle of Perth and Fremantle. We weren't reliant on anybody else's schedule now — only our own and the weather's. South of Mandurah lies Yalgorup National Park. Fifty miles of unbroken beach backed by high scrubby sand dunes surrounding a network of saltwater lakes provide rich habitats for abundant bird life. On a totally calm day, we motor sailed 150 feet from the beach on what was the equivalent of a lake shore, past Yalgorup Park to the port of Bunbury. Apart from the occasional flock of birds taking off from the lakes we didn't see anything or anybody all day. Our arrival at the local Bunbury sailing club was, fortunately, on club race day and we were formally greeted, directed to hot showers, and then ushered to the bar. Fred and Judy Talbot introduced us to the members before kindly inviting us out to their farm, Wedderburn, for the night. It was a family property beautifully nestled in the nearby foothills, but unusual as it supported beef cattle in a predominantly dairy district. Fred had won the heart of a dairy farmer's daughter long ago and he and Judy both hoped their sons would continue in their footsteps. Four years earlier the Talbots had also met and helped one of our inspirations, Paul Caffyn, as he paddled his sea kayak around Australia solo. It was a small country after all!

From Bunbury we had a choice of a 43-mile shortcut directly south east across the wide expanse of Geographe Bay, or following the coast around the bay to the small town of Busselton. Realizing that these would be the last protected waters we'd sail for quite a while, we opted for Plan B and set off in a stiff northeaster. It was truly amazing to be sailing again with the wind behind us after torrid months of regular headwinds. With our new larger headsail and full main, *Tom* reveled in the fresh breeze, broad-reaching our way down the coast less than 300 feet off a long sandy shore. Throughout this area the coastal waters once again were generally calm, as the combination of shallowed waters and distant reef tamed the mighty Indian Ocean swells.

Windy Cliffs

In the early afternoon we sailed ashore near the long Bussleton wharf and the local sailing club. Busselton, once a thriving port for timber and rural products, is now a sleepy fishing and holiday town, its major attraction being the half-mile long jetty, a reminder of headier days. Its calm, clear, shallow waters resembled a lake more than the ocean and for the first time in ages we felt we were actually on holiday. After inquiring about the possibility of sleeping under the yacht club verandah we were soon swapping yarns with Eric Smyth, a club member and retired chartered accountant. As his bubbly wife Twy said, "Beware, anyone with a foot in the water. Eric will have them cornered and talking till the cows come home." What was to be a shared afternoon cup of tea, then became dinner and accommodation, followed by the offer of a tour of the local area and a reconnaissance of the rugged Margaret River coast ahead. Wanting to see some of the inland we didn't hesitate to accept, although we wondered whether we were becoming soft with all this wonderful southern (Western Australian that is) hospitality.

Armed with a picnic lunch, Twy and Eric drove us off to explore the rugged rocky coast of Cape Naturaliste and assess potential landing points for our next week of sailing. It had been a long time since we'd seen such powerful scenery. The defiant rocky limestone points were pounded incessantly by full-bodied swells rolling undisturbed from the depths of the Indian and Southern oceans. Viewing this spectacle from our detached dry vantage point we were apprehensive yet excited about the prospect of sailing it. If the southwesterly sea breeze suddenly came in as we'd often experienced on this coast (a 180° shift of 20 knots in a couple of minutes), it would probably be a case of turn and run. Our only protection, should we need it, would be from small coves with their sandy beaches which nestled between ragged sharp limestone reefs and headlands every ten miles or so. This is big wave country with surfers and sailboarders making it their territory for much of the year. The names attached to various breaks tell it all — Super Tube, The Guillotine, and Suicides.

Content with our view of the sea we headed inland to the areas Sue and I longed for – forests with huge stands of gums: tuarts, kauri and jarrah. While not quite California redwoods these mighty 100-foot trees were magnificent compared to the stunted scrub we'd seen for so many months. Their lush green canopies and undergrowth provided a tranquillity we'd desperately missed in the harsh north. We also wine-tasted at the popular local vineyards which had started as hobby farms for the well-to-do of Perth and had blossomed into a respected industry.

After saying farewell to Eric and Twy the next morning, a gusty offshore easterly shot us across the calm waters to the eastern end of Geographe Bay. The small bright blue cove of Bunkers Bay provided a stepping-off point for Cape Naturaliste. The afternoon southwesterly sea breeze registered 35 knots (43 miles per hour) at the Cape lighthouse, and convinced us to stay and enjoy the protected bay, shared only with a few salmon fishermen. The limestone cliffs, weathered by wind and waves, presented a variety of shallow caves with stalactites, a veritable smugglers' paradise. Anxious for our welfare, given the weather conditions, Eric and Twy just happened down to our bay with a picnic lunch the next day. "Just wondering if you were OK in these winds" Twy asked, as a 30-knot westerly howled overhead and white caps rolled off ten-foot swells around the corner of the Cape.

The following day provided calmer conditions with strong off-shore easterlies. The rolling six-to-ten foot swells had all but disappeared as we rounded Cape Naturaliste in company with an assortment of recreational fishing boats also making the most of the conditions. Yet again we were grateful for our small reefed mainsail as we cruised at a comfortable seven to eight knots in a 20-knot offshore breeze. We stayed up to a half-mile offshore even though the breeze had all but flattened the swell. It was an exciting morning sail as we cruised past rugged cliffs and picturesque rocky coves rimmed by bright turquoise waters. The regular welcome by people out fishing at each point was comforting after the many lonely miles of travel on this western coast. By early afternoon we made our destination of Cowaramup Bay, a small, rocky cove sculpted into the coastline. A smattering of holiday shacks surround bare hills and provide a popular spot which has one of the few protected boat ramps on that side of the coast. Many of the place names in this area end in "up" — Meclup, Yallingup, Wyadup — this suffix being Aboriginal for a meeting place or water. Our east coast Australian and Californian accents battled to satisfy the locals' pronunciation of these towns.

The following day provided yet another day of surprisingly calm conditions as we enjoyed the sunshine while motor-sailing a further 25 miles down the coast to Hamelin Bay, another small fishing and holiday community protected by outlying islets and a cluster of reefs. Intrigued by

Windy Cliffs

the rocky coast I wandered off to explore and found numerous deep blue pools, potentially loaded with lobster. Curses! We'd sent our diving gear home. The view from Cosy Corner, looking down over a group of honeycombed islets perched amidst deep blue reefs, was spectacular. A steep line of black cliffs lead off into the south with the stark white pinnacle of Cape Leeuwin Lighthouse just visible at the end. This was a long-awaited milestone for us, something we shared with Matthew Flinders. In 1801 he began his dream of charting the Australian coast from that point, naming it after the Dutch ship *Leeuwin*. For us it was the end of an exhausting 2,000 miles and four months of travel down the harsh western coast. Upon rounding it we would finally be heading east and closer to home.

A weather change arrived the next morning, with unsettled showers and strong southerly winds forecast for the afternoon. It was a case of a quick 12-mile sprint round Cape Leeuwin now, or wait for three to four days. We took off motor sailing through the narrow reef-lined passages. I was relieved to have seen them from the vantage point yesterday, as anxiously reading our chart, we slowly weaved through the maze of reef. The southeasterly breeze continued to build as only one to two hundred yards away the high dark cliffs hung threateningly over us. The small white speck of the lighthouse lit by beams of sun shafting down from coal black clouds became our target in the distance. Both of us remained quiet, wishing the lighthouse closer and hoping we could make it before it became too rough. Leeuwin is surrounded by a maze of breaking reefs and ledges, which are usually given a wide berth by all but local fishermen. We gave up trying to identify the reefs marked on the chart and steered by sight between rings of six-to-ten foot foaming breaks that tended to instantly appear from the depths. We were also anxious about huge king waves known to come out of the Indian Ocean and break over unsuspecting boats.

"What's that break over there?" yelled Sue standing at the mast and pointing at six feet of white water that had appeared from nowhere.

"I don't know. It's not even marked on the chart. Just keep looking for the ones in front." I yelled back.

After two hours of anxious progress the cliffs ended and the long narrow point of Cape Leeuwin stretched out beside us. The white lighthouse stood radiant against the black cliffs and increasingly dark sky. We heaved a sigh of relief as we rounded the cape and turned into the relative protection of Flinders Bay and the fishing town of Augusta.

"What do you mean you sailed," the caravan park manager demanded. "I have to see this boat for myself," he said, still not sure of our sanity. We settled into the protection of the campground's natural windbreaks of hardened tea tree bushes. We'd arrived just in time, as the wind was already building to a solid 25 knots. A small town of 1,000, Augusta overlooks the Blackwood River and a wild, desolate coast of sand dunes stretching away for 60 miles to the southeast. This exposed southwest corner of Australia faces the full force of the untamed Southern and Indian Oceans. Wanting to find a local source of knowledge of the next section of the coast, we tracked down a local fisherman, Russell, to get some directions. Rolling his eyes at our plans, Russell did better than give directions, offering to take us out on his shark fishing boat the next morning at 5:30 A.M. His nets were set 28 miles down the beach at a potential landing spot in a virtually unbroken and inaccessible 90-mile stretch of desolate sand dunes. The 40-foot boat pitched and rolled in the heavy swell, while seasick on gas fumes and power boat motion I counted every foot of the six-miles of net as it came aboard laden with shark, groper and assorted other fish. A .22 rifle was produced to quiet some of the larger catches as Russell, Mal and their deckhand Sav, worked steadily. Fortunately for me, the forecast was for rougher weather so we didn't reset the nets but headed for home via Black Point, our next potential landing for *Tom Thumb*. It could hardly be considered a point, being 900 feet of rock protruding from the sand hills and a beach stretching off into the distance, for miles on either side. The surf breaking off the rocky point was a boisterous six-to-nine feet. The waves faded into a deeper channel near the beach before reforming to crash ashore as a six-foot shoredump. Yes, we could definitely get in there, but not in these conditions. We'd have to wait for an offshore northeaster or just calmer conditions. "Not common around here but, possible," said Russell who only fishes 70 to 80 days a year due to rough seas.

While waiting out the blow we visited the Cape Leeuwin lighthouse and chatted with the keeper who had been rather taken aback to see us come around the Cape the previous day. Built of local limestone in 1896, the lighthouse had been witness to many sea rescues and wrecks, some

Windy Cliffs

preserved in photographs around the walls. The weather records graphically underlined Russell's comments with large seas and high winds making a regular journal entry. As we watched, the wind indicator regularly touched 35 knots and black rainsqualls threatened to envelop the lighthouse. Clad in wet weather gear and thermal jackets, we leaned into the gale force winds and walked back to our tents wondering what had happened to summer.

We waited and waited for what seemed an endless week, short of time, patience and money — all necessary when sailing. I had so much wanted to see this unique 600 miles of southern coast of Western Australia through to the small ports of Albany and Esperance. Wild and remote, it features rocky headlands between narrow river inlets, scattered granite islands and long open windswept beaches. It is also rich in southern ocean wildlife of whales, penguins and seals, as well as great white sharks. "Come back in August, it's usually calm for a few weeks then," suggested Russell smiling. We finally accepted that, after nine months of travel, we were not physically or mentally prepared for the coast beyond Esperence that included the Great Australian Bight. Its unbroken sections of 450-foot cliffs towering over this wild southern ocean needed strength and patience that we no longer had. We could have stayed and worked in the area, but felt we had a commitment to be in Victor Harbour in six weeks. After that deadline our friends Jim and Sally would have gone north for winter and our opportunity to house sit for winter gone with them. When considering our options, we realized that going forward could still require a retreat to Perth. "No chance of getting a lift out of Albany or Esperance," shared a local fisherman. "Most produce goes back to Perth and then is trucked or shipped east from there." Only when travelling from west to east or vice versa does one realize that Australia is actually two countries. When ordering a boat part in Perth, I was initially dumbfounded at the response of "We'll have to order that in from the east." I thought they meant Asia!

The wind conditions dropped from gale to a strong wind warning one day in two weeks and were gale-force for the rest of the time! After two weeks we frustratingly retreated, thanks again to Eric and Twy, by car and trailer to Busselton to sort through our options. Sitting by a telephone we put out feelers to secure a ride on any truck, train, boat or bus to the east. With virtually no money it was more a case of hitchhiking with a 16-foot catamaran under one's arm. At times like this, we were grateful for the small size of *Tom Thumb*.

The only export industry in Busselton is timber and we were fortunate to find someone who trucked timber regularly to the east. "Kind of abrupt guy but knows his business," was how the manager of the mill described Bob Guthrie. With our hearts in our hands and a well-rehearsed forlorn look on our faces we went to talk to Bob, who had just returned from his regular five-day round trip to Melbourne. Very non-committal, Bob agreed to come and look at this odd cargo, while contemplating the extra company in his truck cab for two days. Hastily we cleaned the boat and gear, attempting to make it look as compact and easily managed as possible. "It's bigger than you described," commented Bob the next morning and we swallowed hard "but it should travel all right...$300 for you and the boat to either Port Augusta, or think about the Murray River. I sleep in the cab, you two are outside. We leave in three days. I'll give you a call." We quickly said, "Yes." before he could change his mind and agreed to have the boat around at the timberyard to load by forklift. We couldn't believe our luck. Three days later with Tom strapped precariously on top of a load of timber and us high in the cab of a semi-trailer; we rolled out of town. I was trying to come to terms with the thought that in two days we'd be 1,500 miles away in South Australia. Three times the size of Texas, Western Australia had been an all-absorbing experience for the past five months. We were glad to be contemplating a change of coast, even if once again we were getting there by unique means.

With Sue perched cross-legged in the cab between Bob and myself, we hauled through the gears over hill and dale looking down on the world from this incredible vantage point. It was definitely a change from bobbing about like a cork a few feet off the water. Rolling over the Darling Range we passed through grassed, hilly country of dairy, beef cattle and fruit orchards then through to the large merinos and sheep studs as the plains stretched westward. We survived a basic question and answer analysis of our trip with Bob above the roar of the engine, his straightforward practical character obviously assessing us as crazy. Sue and I dozed off and on, not wishing to yell to make conversation and very relieved to be on our way. Across the backcountry roads we headed towards Esperance at a good 60-to-75 miles per hour. Bob was obviously able to drive blindfolded across the familiar

Windy Cliffs

track. I woke from a brief nap surprised to see the Stirling Ranges rising high out of the gray plains. "Yep, those are the Stirlings," Bob answered in his laconic style. We pulled into Ravensthorpe roadhouse at 3:30 P.M. for dinner as Bob explained that the farther out across the Eyre Highway, the more expensive and the worse the food gets. In the roadhouse Bob laughed at the few jibes from the obviously familiar staff about his strange load.

We were "doing" the Nullarbor, crossing one of Australia's best known desert plains in the cooler season but with 85°F temperatures the cab still required air conditioning until the sunset. Nullarbor means treeless and certainly lives up to its name, as moonlit mile after mile of flat nothingness is broken only by the occasional lonely cluster of roadhouse lights every 50 to 100 miles. The road, the Number 1 highway in Australia, had just been sealed all the way to South Australia and Bob recounted when this five-hour stretch to the border used to take two days. There are tales of some truck drivers falling asleep while driving, leaving the road and continuing across the desert. When they eventually woke up they could not find the highway again! We pulled into Norseman late at night where Bob had a shower "to keep me awake." I watched a hitchhiker who was a walking advertisement for body piercing, work the truckers for a lift. "Wrong sex," said Bob returning from the shower. "Had a great trip back from Melbourne last week with two Irish girls!"

On we rolled into the emptiness of the Nullarbor as a couple of small dusty outposts flashed by, the only sign of life through miles of heat and blackness. At about 3:00 A.M. we pulled up by the roadside to grab some sleep, feeling jarred and battered. Bob climbed into the bunk while Sue and I threw our sleeping bags on top of the timber next to *Tom* and took in the hot evening breeze. Another night to remember! The red dusty sunrise found us peering out into the desert scrub with small black bush flies arriving in plagues to help start the day. As the sun rose high in the clear blue sky we pulled into the border town of Eucla and saw the spectacular views of the Great Australian Bight cliffline dropping into the sea. Bob wanted to show us these sights just to see if we really knew what we were up against. We smiled in answer and looked at them in awe. The 300-foot sheer cliffs extending some 90 miles east were breathtaking. It was a stark contrast of nature as the flat yellow desert country extending for thousands of miles just drops off the edge into the blue Southern Ocean, as if someone had indeed taken the great Australian bite. It was beautiful to see, but also sad and frustrating as perfect sailing conditions for *Tom* prevailed. A strong steady northerly provided a lee shore and calm seas producing a small three-foot shorebreak along the lengthy beach sections. I ran through all the research in my mind of how many miles we would have had to sail between these cliffs and small, isolated landings. It was impressive, yet it was possible. But just not this time. As we stood at the top of the cliffs, we both felt that for now we had made the right decision.

Our second day of trucking provided nameless and forgettable roadhouses and gas stations, the only break from the tedious roar of the engine and passing monotony of desert scrub. The coast had once again been left far behind. Later that afternoon, signs of rural life became evident once more as the large beef cattle, wheat, and sheep properties of South Australia took up the horizon. As we listened to Bob's radio calls to invisible trucking mates going the opposite way in the dark, he shared some of the hardships of trucking. "Bored with it. Lousy bloody conditions and pay. Buyin' a liquor shop in Busselton," he stated, with tinges of bitterness and regret. From our high perch in the truck cab the sun set for a second time. The reddish dust was familiar as Iron Knob came into view, an aptly named hill of solid iron ore mined for the local steel industry at Whyalla. As the moon rose we settled onto our familiar bed of timber on the back of the truck. The surroundings were a total contrast to those of the previous evening as a crisp breeze blew off the rich Clare Valley vineyards north of Adelaide. We awoke from a solid six hours of motionless sleep to the crowing of roosters and clink of cowbells. As Bob had predicted, after 48 hours of driving here we were, 1,500 miles and two time zones away, in Morgan on Australia's longest river, the Murray, 200 miles from the sea. Morgan, an historical old river port, provided a strange contrast to the hustle and bustle of Perth. After unloading *Tom* we waved farewell to Bob as his truck took up the entire vehicle ferry across the river headed for Melbourne. I had a new respect for the hours and conditions that long distance truck drivers put up with. We sat back amidst our mass of gear and bits of boat. Gazing down the peaceful section of sunny river we were surprised to see a seagull looking as much out of place as we did, worlds away from Perth, the Cup, and the sea.

Encouraged by the increasing heat of the day, we put *Tom* back together quickly, with only the occasional curse and skinned knuckle. We ate, fuelled and bought a road map of South Australia and a copy of the *Murray River Pilot*. It was to be our sailing guide that described new hazards such as locks, ferries, water skiing areas and bridge heights. We made some quick phone calls to let people know we were on this side of the country and pushed off downstream. Less than a week and 185 miles downstream was Goolwa and the mouth of the Murray into the Great Southern Ocean. From there we would sail 18 miles back around the coast to Victor Harbour. Floating down this clay-colored, 300-foot wide river with not an ocean swell in sight was so calm. We sailed, motored, or just floated with the current. Large gums and willow trees and large orange ochre colored cliffs overhung our passage. The sun was so warm that we had to stop and cool off now and then. No sharks. No crocodiles. Just cool fresh water! Bright holiday houses and shacks floated by as water skiers and houseboat owners waved hello.

We got used to negotiating our new sailing challenges marked on the river map — power lines and ferries. We eventually realized that *Tom's* mast easily made it under the power lines although it took a while to accurately judge our passage around the cables of the ferries. The ferries only exist on the smaller back roads where the building of a major bridge was not cost effective. They seemed to help people slow to the pace of the river and stop for a while in passing. Often, excited children would wave to us from the banks while waiting for their ferry which took loads back and forth regularly through the daylight hours. Long, flat boats shaped like pontoons, they were capable of taking a semi-trailer and a few cars in one trip. Engine-powered winches then pulled them along a cable, which lay slack along the river bottom when not in use. Tom's rudder flicked up once as a tightening cable caught us by surprise.

Arriving late in the evening at Blanchetown, we came across a new hazard, a river lock. It was closed for the evening and after setting up camp we walked up to meet the lock keeper, Tony, and clear our passage for early the next morning. The little country house with its flowering cottage garden was very English. "Where the hell are we? Which country and time zone?" joked Sue, still coming down to earth after our truck journey. There are many locks on the Murray that control the passage of the river and boats downstream. Blanchetown had grown as a stopover and watering spot on the Sydney Road during the 1850s, with its lock built around 1920. Tony filled us in on the details as we sipped on a beer in the evening light watching pelicans playing and feeding.

The Murray River system is the largest in Australia gathering water from hundreds of thousands of square miles across five different Australian states as it runs its course nearly 1,800 miles to the sea. In its glory days as a transport route, the Murray was a regular highway for steamers taking loads of wool and fruit down the river and returning with supplies. History recounts colorful tales of a lifeline and livelihood on the river, long since replaced by trucks and roads. "Mostly it's just people on holidays fishing or in houseboats that travel the river these days," Tony declared. "Tourism is now the saving grace for many of the old river towns," he continued. "You meet some interesting people as a lock keeper. It slows people down to the pace of the river."

The Aborigine left soft marks in his 30,000 years — his sacred burial grounds, scars on the gum trees where he cut his canoes, smoke stains on the yellow cliffs where he camped, and glittering kitchen middens (broken shell piles) where he feasted on cockles and mussels. White man's marks are more easily seen. First he drowned the swamplands and the gum trees with locks and dams to stop the river's rhythm of life which replenished swamp and mudflat, brought breeding cycles to birds and fish. Then he took the wetlands to crop and raise cattle. He dirtied the river with his drains. Today its water has never been more precious nor the burden it carries so great. reads the *Murray River Pilot*.

Early next morning I floated *Tom* into the opening of the lock, as Sue walked off to find Tony. The lock resembled a long Olympic swimming pool next to the riverbank on one side of the concrete weir wall that stretches across the river. Tony waved and Sue climbed back on board as the doors shut behind us and the water level and *Tom* started to sink. Holding tight to the rungs of a steel ladder we descended down, down, down into a black hold, to the point where *Tom's* mast was below the level of the lock. With a groan, the large steel doors in front of us opened to the continuing river. "Enjoy your trip," Tony looked down and waved.

Windy Cliffs

We passed surprised houseboats and a full-paddle steamer that made me feel we were headed down the Mississippi. Past Walkers Flat we met up with a fellow and his teenage daughter in a small half-cabin cruiser, not much longer than *Tom*. Over the past two months they had come from Albury, some 990 miles upstream, armed "with an axe to cut our way through the snags," and were headed for the Murray mouth at Goolwa. "Just for something to do" and "a bloody good trip." It was a way of life for them now, although with the end of their journey less than two or three days away, they were uncertain of the future. We could see from their easy rapport there was obviously a strong bond between them. As we floated down the river I was reading Jonathon Rabin's wonderful book, *Old Glory,* about his trip down the Mississippi in an outboard powered dinghy. I smiled at the way he floated through this vein of the country letting the various scenes and people describe themselves and their land. The Murray certainly does that for Australia.

The days were warm with little wind, and with no tides or afternoon sea breezes to worry about we could leave and arrive when we pleased. Campsites were on grassed river banks in the corner of farming paddocks, or a town park. We set the sail to pick up any breeze and often surprised people as they saw a catamaran come cruising around a river bend. In calm conditions we motored midstream in the river current cruising at an easy ten knots. We passed through Purnong, Bowhill, and the larger towns of Mannum and Murray Bridge. We tied off at the rowing club at Murray Bridge after waving to a couple rowing crews out training. After returning from town for supplies, we got a rundown of the achievements of the local crews from two fellows who were painting the club. "Bloody good club. One of the best on the river," they stated without bias. Apparently competition was fierce between the river town clubs and the annual regatta was well supported.

"Watch out for that Murray mouth! Plenty of people have died on that bar," they warned when hearing of our plans. We thanked them for their concern but the greater and more immediate danger at this stage was Lake Alexandria at the end of the river. A large shallow expanse, it gathered steep sharp swells in strong winds and had taken the lives of a number of school students on a canoeing trip just recently. We patiently waited out a two-day blow before scooting across the open lake into the final port of Goolwa. Crossing the lake we were surprised by a fleet of beautifully maintained gaff rigged cutters, the work of a local sailing club that prided itself on its historic timber boats. There were also groups of assorted outboard powered boats, all headed for the small community of Narrang for Race Day on the local horse track. This was a water-based community where the quickest way between towns and friends was by the river.

We pulled into the Goolwa sailing club and tried to explain how we got there and where we had come from. Our friends Sally and Jim came over from Victor Harbour to help us unpack our gear and transfer most of it to their house. It was great to see them again after almost a year and a chance meeting at a caravan park in North Queensland. We left *Tom* at Goolwa, wanting to sail to Victor when the conditions were safe and after we had made an effort to drum up some publicity. Two days later with the sun shining we pulled through the Tauwitchere lock, the last on the Murray River and came to the Murray mouth. About a hundred miles from where we had started sailing down the Murray and many miles from Augusta we stared out onto the great Southern Ocean. It was a clear choppy passage with only a few foaming waves breaking a couple of hundred yards out. As a surprised fisherman watched, we suited up, set sail, and waving farewell to the great Murray River, headed out to sea. After a couple of refreshing waves had splashed across the deck, we turned the corner and sailed the 18 miles west to Victor Harbour.

As the small bay and town of Victor Harbour came into view, we were circled by a Channel 7 helicopter. It was only after their third pass with a cameraman hanging out of the helicopter that we realized we were their target. I quickly unfurled our larger *Ulmer Kolius* headsail and ensured our Pier 21 on the mainsail was in full flight. We finally surfed into the beach to be welcomed by a rent-a-crowd care of Jim and Sally's friends and the television crew and cameras. It was a pleasure to be interviewed by a sailor at long last when Jon Parrington asked intelligent and informed questions. "So are you getting married after this?" was the only one that threw us and we both stammered for replies. "Welcome to South Australia," he said in parting as the helicopter lifted off the beach, coating our welcoming party in sand and disappearing over the township of Victor Harbour, our new homeport.

Chapter 12

A Winter Port
Victor Harbour

1802 April, Thursday 8

The stranger was a heavy-looking ship, without any topgallant masts up; and our colours being hoisted, she showed a French ensign, and afterwards an English jack forward, as we did a white flag... I hove to; and learned, as the stranger passed to leeward with a free wind, that it was the French national ship Le Geographe, under the command of Nicolas Baudin.

Matthew Flinders.

These words are from Flinders log and were included in a souvenir program I purchased in Victor Harbour which was produced to commemorate the historic meeting of these explorers 150 years earlier in a place they named Encounter Bay. It was ironic that we found ourselves wintering in the place overlooking this bay where what was a brief and chance encounter for Matthew Flinders provided such a cruel twist of fate. Baudin's presence explains the scattering of French place names such as Cape Naturaliste (Western Australia), Fleurieu Peninsula (Adelaide), and Cape Gantheaume (Kangaroo Island) on Australia's south coast. Nicolas Baudin was as distinguished an explorer as Flinders. As a fellow mariner in distant waters, Flinders freely shared some of his new charts with Baudin. Unluckily during his return passage to England the following year Flinders (along with his maps) was detained "as a prisoner of war" on the French island of Mauritius for six-and-half years! He had chosen an unfortunate landfall and paid the price!

Not surprisingly, in his absence copies of his charts which Flinders had shared with Baudin, together with the discoveries of his fellow countrymen Freycinet and Peron, were published by the French. The southern coast was named Terra Napoleane and the two South Australian gulfs Boneparte and

Josephine. If not for Flinders, the majority of our coast would have sounded like a tour through French history. Upon Flinders' release he returned to his wife after a nine-and-half-year absence and published his maps of the Australian coastline. He was welcomed and feted, but never promoted in rank, which would have guaranteed his financial security. Always the perfectionist, Flinders was not happy with the accuracy of some of his charting techniques and set about experimenting with navigational instruments on a variety of ships. Two years later he had developed the Flinders' Bar which allowed systematic correction of a compass to compensate for any iron within the ship and became the standard around the world. Although he was in poor health from his years in captivity and had little money, his three-volume publication, *A Voyage to Terra Australis,* was finally printed in 1814. A copy was laid on his bed, but he never woke to see the culmination of his life's efforts. Matthew Flinders died at the age of 40. His name for "The Great South Land," Australia, was not adopted until 1850.

After reading the plaque on the crest of Granite Island, which commemorates the historic meeting of Baudin and Flinders, I looked out across Encounter Bay. I could visualize those square-rigged ships, both so far from home. Today, a small hill with clusters of houses wraps around the bay. Victor Harbour is now a friendly holiday town but is still in touch with its past. As I reached the wooden causeway at the bottom of the hill I stepped to one side as a horse drawn carriage trundled past carrying tourists headed for the rocky mount which shields the harbor. It felt right. I had a sense that we were predestined to stay here for the winter.

Jim and Sally gave us a warm welcome, introducing us to friends and serving many Devonshire teas. As we settled in, they were packing to head north to Queensland for winter. It was strange to think of them going back to the beach at Yeppoon where we had met a year ago, with us now living in their house! After *Tom Thumb* had been dismantled and stacked together with our gear in Jim and Sally's garage we explored the town. It was strange being able to call a place "home," our first since Sydney.

Our first priority was to find some type of work to sustain us. It wasn't going to be easy during the quieter winter season. "Here are your forms. Just fill them in and the dole will be posted out to you in six weeks. One in 500 chances of getting a job in Victor — no chance out of season," assured

A Winter Port

Tom at the Commonwealth Employment Office (CES), or unemployment office as it is more commonly known. "Why are you out of work anyway?" he asked. I explained and he nodded. "Yeah heard all about it, sounds like a great trip. Just fill out your forms and you will get your checks, don't worry. Sorry, haven't got time to get your names and addresses, got four businesses to run. We'll be in touch," he continued as he ushered us to the door.

Back on the street we considered our next move. While sending off our forms at the post office "to get the checks, no worries," the postal clerk recognized us from our news coverage on television. We started talking about sport and local basketball and he offered to take me over to meet Ron at the sports shop. Ron started asking about our trip and pulled out a map of the Northern Territory. He proceeded to quiz us on the best fishing spots and how to get there in preparation for his next holiday with fellow fisherman Norm, the jeweler. On the way down the street we also met Paul, Aussie, and Jeff and the talk turned to football. "Wonder if he plays. Shit, he's tall enough. Wonder how tough he is?" they commented sizing me up as if they were in a meat market. "Have you played before?" they asked enthusiastically. This was Australian Rules Football mind you, heart of the South Australian league. "Well, yeh, I've played a season as ruck in Queensland," I answered truthfully. I didn't dare tell them how poorly. "Pre-season training tomorrow. See you down there. You probably won't be able to walk afterwards," they said smiling. "Our trainer is Jim," Aussie smiled knowingly. As the name obviously meant nothing to me, Aussie explained in hallowed tones, "He used to be a professional player for Glenelg (a South Australian team)." I left assuring them I'd see them at training later in the week.

At our last stop in town, the Warringa Guest house, we were introduced to Bouc, a fellow catamaran sailor who had a Windrush 24. He was impressed at our efforts. And also knew Sandy and Ginty Anderson, the catamaran sailors who Sue's father had met so long ago in America and who now lived locally on a farm! "Sorry, can't offer you a job, unless you stay around for the year and help set up my school holiday programs," Bouc offered. We declined and went home to cook dinner. What a luxury cooking on an electric stove and then sitting down to watch television without worrying about the wind and the weather!

On Saturday morning I showed up bright and early at the "footy" ground for the pre-season starter. I said hello to a few chaps and met Mark, a dairy farmer who had played for the last five years. It was a relief to see a few older fellows with pale Victorian skin and T-shirt tans, freckled and balding. Surely the training couldn't be that tough! We started kicking the ball back and forward around the field and my knees and legs soon began to ache. A fit, heavy-chested, barrel-thigh fellow strolled onto the ground with a "South Australian National Football League (SANFL) State Team" T-shirt on just in case you questioned his credentials. Jim was introduced "for you new blokes" and we were applauded for our appearance. After more kicking practice we were called in. "We're going to start with 6 x 200 sprints, under 34 seconds, 45 seconds rest after each, then 6 x 300 under 50 seconds, 45 seconds rest after each, then a run around town in teams. Fifty dollars prize for the first in. OK, let's get started." I don't know what I was more shocked at, the physical torture I was about to undertake or the offer of a cash incentive at the end. It appeared cash incentives were introduced when a professional competition replaced the amateur game, where dollars now vied with club pride and personal satisfaction. I didn't have time to contemplate much more as my legs pounded out the yards counting each rest period by the second. While I was recollecting how many years it was since I had run a hundred yards, we sprinted off for the next set.

Two more sets and my legs buckled. I jogged the remaining sets trying to ensure I didn't sustain any permanent injury in my first training session. I was in Jim's town-running team along with Rod and Ruff. Those barrel thighs disappeared over the first hill in front of me and I didn't see Jim until the finish. Ruff and I staggered along together talking most of the way.

"So you are keen to play with us," asked Peter, the president, when we were recovering at the club. I said yes and they immediately retrieved the sign up forms from behind the bar. I didn't realize until later that there were only two local teams and they wanted to make sure I was a member of the Victor Harbor team rather than their staunch rivals at Encounter Bay! I did however recognize my potential bargaining power.

"Well I can only stay around if we can afford to. I need work!"

"No worries," came the reply. "Worked behind a bar before?"

"Yes."

A Winter Port

"Well, what if we try you out there this Thursday?"

The manager of the pub was an avid club supporter. There was also talk of getting some work with one of the local painters. Needless to say, Jim's team hadn't won the $50 and I was not destined for first cut. As the winning money was placed on the bar by the two teams that had tied for first, I took my leave and staggered home. Sue and I had dinner and drinks listening to the cold wind howling outside. Mark, the dairy farmer, had smiled when I said we'd never spent a winter down here.

Sandy and Ginty Anderson's small farm was tucked in behind the exposed hills of the Fleurieu Peninsula and was far from what we had imagined as the home of catamaran sailors. Solar panels adorned the roof of the old stone cottage, and a large wooden barrel served as the rain tank, typical of their recycle-everything approach. The farmyard contained a menagerie of dogs, cats and poultry, and an assortment of machinery, which had more historic than working value. Sandy and Ginty had met Sue's parents in California through some distant family connection, and her father had stunned us with his report of "these Australians who had sailed around in a small catamaran." They had sailed from South Australia up to the Gulf of Carpentaria in Queensland in their Windrush 24-foot catamaran, which had a small cabin. Sandy personified the classic image of a sailor, with his ruffled, willowy figure, appearing to bend in the wind. After brief formalities he hastened to show us his latest project in the shed, a new galvanized structure with power, lights, a collection of the obligatory tools, and a set of near complete sleek wooden hulls. With loving detail Sandy described the Formula 40 catamaran he had built to race. Sailing was his obsession, which determined he and Ginty's total life, from boat to boat and adventure to adventure.

After an hour of talking boats and the important issues of sailing, Sandy rushed us off to feed the animals, then we kick-started the Landrover and, dodging cow patties and mud, we checked out the property. Later that evening, sitting in the warmth by the wood stove with its steaming curry pot "that had been brewing all this week," we shared sailing tales of the east coast. It brought back many memories. "Do you think we'll become like that?" Sue asked anxiously the next day. We agreed that while we both loved the sea, it wasn't in our blood. We were travelers rather than sailors.

Keeping Australia On the Left

As I eased into the enjoyable lifestyle of a small country town with occasional work and football with the boys, Sue sought to escape. I didn't want to go back to Sydney until we sailed in. But Sue didn't want to look for work because on a visitor's visa she would be working illegally and was worried that she might be caught. Despite my suggestions that Victor Harbor was hardly the place she would be found out, she longed to escape to the big world of a familiar city. So she caught a bus to Sydney. I didn't complain and looked forward to some time and space to myself. It was strange to be holding a phone conversation with her for the first time since she had left California nearly eighteen months ago. After being so physically close for so long I could imagine her mannerisms as she spoke.

Sue returned a week later laden with supplies, care packages and presents from my family. She shone with a smile and bounce that I hadn't seen for a while. *We both felt a part of our body or self was missing (while we were apart), but also needed time to find ourselves again*, I noted in my diary. Sue had shared some of our stories with my parents amidst my mother's tears, tales of fun and adventure, tensions and hardship. I could see that it had been good for Sue to talk to someone who knew about the trip and would listen. Our relationship, or its future course, was a cause for discussion and concern. "Perhaps you are just expecting too much of life," suggested my father in a heartfelt letter. Sue confessed to having met someone else. "He made a pass at me and I was so shocked I didn't know what to say or do," she laughed. But she was flattered and wanted to return to attend a major ball in Sydney the next month. "I enjoyed being treated like a woman," she stated. I offered to take her to one of Jim and Sally's local dance hall nights and she threw a book at me.

We talked long into the night about life and the trip. *We had missed each other, for better or worse*, I noted. *We admitted to knowing each other better than we'll ever know anyone else in our lives*. I apologized for being so "trip and sailing" focused and for being stressed, while she expressed her frustration at feeling like my shadow. For the first time we dared to talk about finishing the trip and what it would be like to go our separate ways. Was it just *Tom Thumb* that was keeping us together?

With the Easter school holidays we both found jobs at the local fun park. I was supervising the go-karts and water slides while Sue worked the ice cream stand. We staggered home after long exhausting days covered in ice cream and tomato sauce, deaf from the noise of screaming children and the occasional parent. Sue also had "ice cream elbow" from scooping. We had met a great staff and enjoyed earning money together. The managers, Scott and Allison, invited us for dinner with "I hope you don't mind lobster on the barbecue?" Once again this was cray fish territory. Scott had caught them himself but "some locals get bored with them and prefer steak," he explained.

It was strange to be back in the real world, watching the news on television and hearing about the Easter death toll on roads. For the first time since we had landed, I longed for the natural beauty and ease of life on the sea. It was cold and hard, but it had a rhythm more satisfying than our life in Victor Harbor.

I started painting with Tony, a colorful ex-British Navy "glorified painter." I gave him as much rubbish as he gave me and we got along well. Tony was a local councilor with a no-nonsense, "let's have action" attitude. A woman contacted him asking him to start a petition to improve television reception on Channel 10.

"How is your reception?" she asked with concern.

"Non-existent," replied Tony matter-of-factly.

"Oh that's terrible. Don't worry. You can sign the petition, too," she reassured him. "What for? I haven't got a TV!" exclaimed Tony as he hung up.

We touched up a few houses before he got the major contract for the local high school repaint which kept us busy for the next few months. I soon learned that painting was 95 percent preparation. I became a number one scraper and sander until my hands were numb. Painting with Tony was always entertaining if nothing else. I heard about his previous angelic life as a boy in the church choir. His strong and almost-in-tune blast of *Ave Maria* was quite moving as we painted the local Seventh Day Adventist church. Tony's creative style of planning now saw us going around the high school for a second time doing the sections we had missed, as the school principal had pointed out! At least it kept me employed.

Keeping Australia On the Left

In between six or seven days a week of painting (depending on the weather) I also started pulling beers two nights a week at the Victor Hotel for most of the footy team and their families. I was castigated constantly for not immediately refilling anybody's empty glass when it hit the bar, even if I knew they could barely stand up and had three miles to drive home. So I did and they did! Sue laughed at the sight of me in my black and whites with a bow tie. She insisted I take off my clothes, leave them in the lounge room and have a shower before coming to bed as I smelt like an ashtray.

My sister Kim was in Adelaide making an American television pilot, *Aaron's Way* and we went up to visit her and tour the vineyards. During my work in America she had begun her career in art direction for film and television, and it was interesting to now see her work and the sets she designed. It was also strange to see her in Adelaide, which was unlike home. The warmth of Adelaide as a city struck me. It has an old-world charm and isn't in the least pompous. It is also a citizen-friendly city with parks, wide streets, and sidewalks that encourage people to stroll and live outdoors. Adelaide doesn't apologize like other small cities wishing they were larger. It doesn't suffer from a parochial cringe either, like the distant Perth. It just seemed to stand up and say, "Here I am — enjoy!" Undoubtedly, much of this comes from its history as one of the few early settlements in Australia that was not a penal colony, a desperate port of call, or a forlorn outpost to protect the colonial empire. Free settlers planned it as a city.

Back in Victor Harbor the first game of footy was at Myponga where the slight hump in the middle of the field made play downhill on both sides. "A bunch of sociable farmers," was the description given this club by a teammate. I accidentally elbowed an opponent in the head half way through the game. I checked to see that he was OK as the trainers stemmed the blood flow and carried him off to get stitches. "Don't bloody bother to see if they're hurt," yelled Coach Jim, chastising me at the break. I'd forgotten this was supposed to be serious football. We lost, but it was fun! I enjoyed the running but had forgotten what it was like to feel battered and bruised at the end of a game. A couple of games into the season, just when I was beginning to feel fit, I came down from the bounce up in a screaming heap. I hadn't known pain like it. They carried me off the field on a stretcher explaining it was a torn hamstring muscle. With my leg wrapped in ice I watched the remainder of the game grimacing as we lost by 24 goals! I gave

A Winter Port

up football for a few games and started playing and coaching basketball with a local team. My old sport proved a safer and more casual option. I really enjoyed coaching again and working with a younger group of players to improve their skills and teamwork. We didn't always win but we were getting better and having fun.

In her leisure time, Sue re-read *Tracks*, Robyn Davidson's description of her journey across the Australian desert with camels. "I can understand what they are talking about now," she said having encountered all the Australian slang and nuances for herself. Sue and I grew apart over the month as we led separate lives, me working or playing football and she content to be at home reading and writing and going to Tai Chi classes. She didn't appear comfortable in a small town. She didn't pursue any friendships or outside interests, but caught up on writing articles for her newspaper and the second last one for *Multihulls* magazine. We had a tentative tie to a boat that sat in the garage. We had barely looked at *Tom* for three months as he represented that "unfinished, something we just didn't want to think about." Then the time finally came for Sue to head off for another week in Sydney and the ball with her admirer. I couldn't really say no, but it was hard to see her go. "I have trouble accepting it, but I can understand why," I said in parting.

I sat alone reading and writing, starting to think about the trip overall. The words flowed easily, as for the first time since we had started sailing I could step outside this all-consuming journey and write as an observer. I could see my obsession and feel the stress, much of it self-inflicted. I could also honestly appraise our relationship and the price we had paid, especially for Sue. In her absences, I realized that there was a strong bond between us as good friends having shared such an experience. I didn't want to say goodbye in Sydney! Sue phoned to explain she would be away another week. It appeared she was enjoying being wined and dined by someone else. Sue's mother wrote to say she was sorry to know that I wasn't going to be part of their family. It appeared the end of our relationship was near. Sue's parents had booked their air tickets to Australia to welcome us home in December. My father had applied for his early retirement from the Department of Education and Mum and Dad were planning an itinerary to show Sue's parents some of Australia. I had also sent in a job application for a University tutoring position in Sydney. The end was coming all too fast, compelled by different forces.

Keeping Australia On the Left

I took early leave from work the day Sue came back. When I found her resting on the lounge, there were no hugs or emotional greetings. We needed to talk. For the first time since we had started sailing over a year ago we could talk about the trip dispassionately. We talked of our frustrations, anxieties and friendship. She was finally convinced I was listening. "Yes I want to finish the trip with you, but I can't promise any more than that," was her conclusion. We spent more time together having meals and going for evening walks around the bare winter hills. It was now mid-July and we planned to set sail in another eight weeks, around mid-September. We could now plan the final stage.

We went to the big smoke of Adelaide for another visit and the chance to see Earl Bloomfield's slide presentation of the Australian Greenland Sea Kayak expedition. We had met Earl in Perth and discussed the procurement of sponsorship with him. After he had received the outline of our trip, he wrote a brief letter back saying that to get sponsorship it was essential we return to Western Australia, negotiate from there and then sail the Bight. He apologized for his sharp response but we thanked him as it had clarified for us that we were on a voyage, not an expedition.

To the words of Peter Gabrielle's song, *Don't Give Up,* the slide show told an awesome story of a journey down the east coast of Greenland where support yachts had capsized and dismasted, and the paddlers had nearly been washed to their deaths on a storm ravaged island. The words of the song and the hardships portrayed in the photographs struck home as Sue and I held hands sharing the emotions produced by their hardship. It expressed in a heart-rending manner many of the things we had been through. For me it also said something about our relationship. It was interesting to later meet other members of that expedition and discover that some of them no longer talked to each other because of conflicts that arose during the paddle.

One evening Sue's parents called excitedly about their upcoming visit and the prospect of seeing their long-lost daughter. For 18 months they had anxiously followed our trip by long distance through letters and the occasional phonecall. Sue had mixed emotions about their visit. "I want to see them again, but they will want answers to so many questions, like when I'm coming home. I just don't know." She reassured them we were doing well and due to set sail again soon. Our relationship was strained and we

A Winter Port

both longed to be back on the water to finish the trip. It felt like being frozen in time during a melodrama, tensely waiting to find out what happens. We wanted the answers now! Unfortunately many of these wouldn't unravel until we had finished sailing and moved on to another life. Only *Tom* and a few thousand miles of untravelled sea kept us together.

Setting our departure date for the third week of September gave us a goal to work towards. Victor Harbor was in many ways my savior as it helped me to recharge my emotional and financial batteries. It also gave Sue and I a chance to consider what we truly meant to each other. If we had sailed into Sydney in the state we had landed in Victor Harbor, I'm sure we would have gone our separate ways very quickly. We had reassessed why we were doing this and for whom. We had taken ownership of the trip with enough money to finish and most of our sponsors satisfied. Chasing media opportunities was now an option, rather than a necessity.

The federal election came and went and Labour and Bob Hawke were returned. Sally and Jim came back from their Queensland winter at Yeppoon beach, which they described as "same place, different year" but with no 16-foot catamaran cruising up the coast!" The basketball season was over and, despite Jim's efforts the Victor Harbor team was not in the finals that year. It was time for us to leave. After we dusted off *Tom* from four months of storage, he fitted together easily and we took my painting and football mate, Scot, for a trial sail around Encounter Bay. It was great to be back on the water and *Tom* responded quickly to the fresh south wind.

Despite the thrill of having *Tom* together again, we had mixed emotions about what was immediately ahead of us. The coast to the east of Victor Harbor is bounded by the Coorong and then there is Bass Strait. It was going to be a tough sail. One of Australia's unique and little known wilderness areas, the Coorong features 100 miles of 250-foot high, sand dunes that curve away behind an unbroken beach to Kingston in the southeast. On the landward side of these one-to-two mile wide dunes runs the long arm of a shallow saltwater lake, surrounded by low marsh. Land access to the Coorong is by shallow boat or four-wheel drive track. We would have to sail overnight to make the distance. The chart has the ominous words *Heavy Surf* written repetitively along its length. Mighty swells rolling unhindered from the Antarctic and sudden weather shifts produce large and fearsome seas. A 20-meter yacht had been rolled over and wrecked by a rogue wave a

Keeping Australia On the Left

few miles from the coast just south of here only a few weeks earlier! Paul Caffyn had been swept ashore here by 12-foot waves during his kayak trip. He was lucky to survive. Once again we just had to pick the right weather, but we were at least comforted to know it would be our last overnight trip.

With a mammoth effort, *Tom* and all our gear was transported to the beach. After a couple of hours he was back together and loaded. Vaguely familiar gear fitted into vaguely familiar holds. Dry suits and wet weather gear and spray jackets were a clammy fit. It was all so familiar yet in other ways just a distant memory. The farewell committee headed by Jim and Sally, their friends, basketballers and footy players all assembled for the departure photos. In the cool of the early afternoon we pushed off and set sail once more along the coast of Australia. The waving hands and familiar wharf of Victor Harbor disappeared from view. The long flat sand dunes of the Coorong stretched into the distance as far as we could see. We were sailing again — except this time we were sailing for home!

Chapter 13

The Great Southern Ocean
Victor Harbour to Lakes Entrance

We looked back at our waving friends and the familiar waterfront of Norfolk Pines as they faded from view with some feeling of unease. We'd spent five warm, dry months in Victor Harbour, and life had become comfortable. It was difficult, after more than a year, to believe that this was the homeward leg, with Sydney finally a tangible goal only eight weeks away. I felt clumsy moving about the trampoline with layers of dry suits, foul weather gear and life jackets. We were not relishing the thought of our last overnight sail and had put it out of our minds for the past weeks.

Perhaps we were no longer naive about the Australian coast and the sailing of a 16-foot catamaran along its shores. To be truthful, I was scared and the lump in my stomach tightened like a knot as Victor Harbour disappeared from view. I looked at the endless sand hills of Coorong, all 100 miles of them, and tried to relax, using my vague memory of beginners' Tai Chi to assist in unravelling what now felt like "101 knots you must know for sailing" which were now being demonstrated on my intestines, wrote Sue.

From our prime viewing spot, still a half-mile from the shore of the Coorong, we watched the green backs of monster swells crash ashore on a beach which extended in either direction as far as we could see. From here we felt no desire to inspect at closer quarters! We had left Victor Harbour at midday to ensure we made landfall in the morning light. Now, with the sun setting, we turned off the back of the large mounting swells and set our compass course out to sea. One that would hopefully take us 62 miles southeast, across the curve of the bay by morning and find us at sunrise still a good five miles offshore. The last rays of light disappeared as we sailed out into the dark empty sea. The knots tightened in my stomach, heightened by the cold chill off the Southern Ocean.

Keeping Australia On the Left

The water surface was like dark maple syrup clinging and parting as *Tom* sliced through, with the minutes trickling by through each two-hour shift. Two weeks of patient waiting and careful weather watching had provided this calm clear night. The outboard droned on as we motor-sailed to maintain our course. The constant noise of the outboard and having to concentrate on only faint starlight on this moonless night, induced a hypnotic state. Between shifts we sipped hot coffee from our newly acquired thermos to try and stay warm. When off watch, we huddled in a cocoon of drysuit, thermals, sprayjacket and lifejacket, tied on by our lifeline, searching for sleep. This was different than the Gulf of Carpentaria where the winds were warm and off the land. There was an awesome sense of emptiness and exposure knowing that these swells came from Antarctica.

Just after midnight a school of dolphins joined us, their phosphorescent bodies jumping and diving around the boat. It was like a late night movie as they occasionally splashed or thumped the boat — unnerving since some were half *Tom's* size. They stayed with us for two hours, no doubt wondering what this small boat was doing out in their playground. Our drooping eyes made us change watch every hour after 2:00 A.M., and our bodies ached for the sunrise to warm us and confirm where we were. Luckily, the calm stayed with us all night as the light breeze of five-to-ten knots glided us across an open ocean.

I have never been so glad to see the first faint light of day. A large, brilliant, orange-red orb blazed its way over the calm sea and a loping six-foot swell. Our hearts rose with the sun, but an empty feeling remained in the pit of my stomach. There was no sight of land! I tried to rationalize *that's understandable with such a low-lying shoreline. It should be over to the east somewhere?* For now it was just great to see the sun and I resolved to wait another two hours before panicking about our position. We headed due east and anxiously looked for land. It was nice to pick up some morning breeze and set full sail. After an hour of steady sailing — nothing. Just empty open ocean! Sue turned and looked at me questioningly. I double-checked our compasses to make sure we were going east where the chart said land should be. We adjusted the sails to get maximum speed and *Tom* now slid down the faces of the swells. Another hour and still nothing!

The Great Southern Ocean

I frantically ran through all the possibilities in my mind! Had our compass changed during the night without us noticing? No, we had three compasses and continually checked our direction with them all. Had a current been pushing us out to sea all night? Had we misjudged our distances? So many questions to which I just did not have the answer. Another half-hour later, the hint of cloud rising and morning mist. Out of the haze the dim shape of sandhills appeared on the horizon, followed soon after by the Kingston lighthouse. We had done it. The last overnight passage of our trip was behind us. When I reconsidered our course, it became obvious that our intention to keep away from the Coorong shorebreak had kept us nudging a little farther out all night and we had ended up some 18 miles off the coast by dawn! We must have almost been in the Melbourne to Adelaide shipping lanes!

When we touched shore, the knots in my stomach magically disappeared and we staggered into Kingston to devour a barbecued chicken, six iced buns, and a large bottle of drink for breakfast. It's amazing what sailing does to your appetite! Sue noted, *People just couldn't believe I'd lost 20 pounds on such a diet over the past year — Jane Fonda, look out!* We called Sally and Jim to reassure them that we were still alive and pushed on to an isolated stretch of beach a few miles down the coast. After struggling to set up camp we patiently waited until sunset before collapsing into a deep sleep at 7:30 P.M., and didn't move until 7:00 A.M. the next morning.

An often-overlooked section of South Australia, the southeast corner proved full of surprises. After the Coorong, the coastline is a rugged limestone carving capped with sand hills and fringed by reef. Our chart forewarned of big southerly swells described as "dangerous rollers" and "high rollers in a heavy swell" breaking as far as three miles out to sea. Knowing of a yacht that had recently been tumbled and dismasted at night in that area, we kept well offshore. Inlets, or safe harbors on this coast, were clearly marked with defined fishing holiday villages. Between were 30- to- 100 foot high weatherworn, limestone cliffs pounded by a steady swell. In full dry suits and foul weather gear we had a quick day's sail in 15- to-20 knots of seabreeze down to the next port south, Robe. We kept a constant look out for any rogue waves that might suddenly produce a high dangerous roller on top of *Tom*. A thriving South Australian seaport in the 1800s during the hectic days of wool, wheat and gold, Robe is now a fishing and holiday village, a cross between the quaint New England of America and the wild French coast of Normandy. Restored stone buildings, a colorful lobster fishing fleet, and beautiful craft shops that Sue couldn't resist, convinced us to stay an extra day.

On the 25th of September, my 30th birthday, we sailed south in a choppy sea, the product of the previous day's strong northerly winds. *Tom* did not sail well in the short, steep swells produced by the waves rebounding off the continuously rocky coastline. Even a half-mile offshore the ride was still rough and wet. As the seabreeze increased we were glad to sight Cape Martin and the protection of Rivoli Bay around midday. A long scalloped, western-facing bay, it is partially protected by a series of outlying islands and reefs. Somewhere between the small promontory of Penguin Island on our port and a maze of foaming reefs to our starboard was apparently a safe passage into the bay. With our hearts in our mouths we picked the gap. Large, looming six-to-ten foot swells followed us in, their crests tempting to break and roll down on us. We nervously glanced in all directions, seeking reassurance from our chart. After a hundred yards of anxiety we were clear. The swells petered out and we dodged around the reefs to skirt down along the inside of the bay to its protected southern end. Numerous fishing boats and moorings indicated this was the busy end of the bay. Both of us were shivering with cold and it was with great relief we stepped ashore in the shelter of Cape Buffon. My second birthday present during the trip was yet another memorable day's sail. It was strange to think back to last year when we had been sailing through the heat of Arnhem Land, over 2,400 miles to our north.

Munching peanuts and thawing out in the warm sand, we watched as a young woman ran from a track onto the beach.

> Sue noted, *A pair of Dutch clogs and woolen socks were flung off into a pile of seaweed as she proceeded to run, skip and jump along the water's edge off into the distance. I watched in envy — how could anyone have that much energy and be so happy bouncing down a gray little beach covered with rotting, smelly seaweed. She returned minutes later with a park ranger in uniform. Mark and I both groaned, expecting that we'd be told to move elsewhere. This small spit of beach was, to our disappointment, a National Park."*

The Great Southern Ocean

"Heard about this boat. Where'd you come from? A friend was telling us about this boat of yours."

The questions rambled on, with the excitement of a young child discovering a lost treasure. We were astonished. This was not the typical middle-aged, grumpy, unfit ranger telling us to move. This light agile man was actually glad that we had landed on his beach.

"Come up to the house after you finish dinner, for port and coffee." He leapt up the track with what we assumed to be his daughter following close behind, and miraculously, the beach didn't look gray any more, nor did the rotten weed smell so.

Herman and Colleen proved to be a unique and wonderful couple. A spirited 57-year-old Dutchman and a warm, honey-colored 31-year-old country girl from South Australia may appear an odd combination, but as our stay with them stretched to a week, it became obvious that there was never a pair so well suited to one another. Absorbed in and excited about nature, their enthusiasm for birds, animals, trees, flowers and plants was infectious. Their humor flowed in colorful lively tales, past and present. Herman, in a Hans Christian Anderson fashion, retold tales of his life in Holland and Colleen brought him down to earth by recalling her ice-skating lessons in Adelaide. She got in for a child's price and father Herman had to pay. Hermann and Colleen had worked with Alby Mangels when he visited the Coorong on his world Safari film tour. Herman *lived* his life as a naturalist, so his occasional frustration at working as a public servant in national parks was understandable.

Southend despite its small population of 1,000, produced a Pandora's box of characters. Colleen took us to meet Esmerelda, an 80-year-old whose fishing shack was a treasure trove of shell and mineral collection surrounded by a botanic garden and aviary. We had a personally guided tour of her small house where every available wall was covered in one of the best shell collections I had seen, and that included museums! She could still recall the country of origin of each shell in the South Pacific and Mediterranean. Then there was Bruce, the local shop owner who had retired from the lobster trade, but made the world seem so much smaller by producing his latest copy of *Multihulls* magazine and insisted we fill him in, since in our last article we were still in West Australia.

Herman took us on a tour of Conunda National Park, an amazing collection of sand dunes and rugged, rocky coast stretching south from Southend. This most easterly section of the South Australian coast is beautiful and wild with windswept dunes and a ragged torn coastline of beach and rock. We went to examine and record a dead sperm whale that had washed up on the beach. I hadn't been so close to a wild whale before, and it was with mixed emotions that we helped record the details of this beautiful stranded animal. This was a regular occurrence for Herman and Colleen as they helped gather research for national parks and fisheries.

On the way home Colleen found out it was my birthday and invited us up for dinner and cake. It was a special way to turn thirty sharing it with such wonderful people! We spent five days of waiting out the weather at Southend. It was frustrating to have unpredictable weather forecasts of strong wind warnings and be sitting on the beach in total calm. We began to wonder about our ability to make it back to Sydney before Christmas. At least we enjoyed the Southend hospitality,

When the time came, it was with a new lease on life that we set sail once more. Armed with fresh apple cake, biscuits and coffee, we waved to Herman and Colleen on Cape Buffon as the brisk wind blew us south. We admired the unique cliffs, including arches and caves, along with "sea stacks," pillars of individual rock climbing out of the sea, that showed the uniqueness of this little known national park.

Freshly painted cray floats and clean-cut flag markers dotted the seas south to Port MacDonnell. These marked the newly staked claims on the rich lobster beds, with the seven-month cray fishing season having just begun. The white outlines of Cape Banks and Cape Northumberland lighthouses heralded the beginning of the well know Bass Strait between the large island state of Tasmania and the Australian mainland. It was Australia's most notorious shipwreck coast. The swells were large, solid and imposing, limiting our view with four surrounding walls of water, whenever we were deep in the trough. Our insecurity could have been psychological, knowing there was nothing but water between us and the

Antarctic or Africa. No reefs, no islands, nothing but deep blue sea. After a full day of great sailing on a steady broadreach we gave Breaksea Reef a wide berth and happily scooted in behind the seawall of Port McDonnell to be greeted by the local fishermen. Camped on the small strip of sand in the harbor with our take-out chicken and chips we soon became an evening highlight as the nearby pub gossip spread and a regular procession of visitors joined us for dinner.

Early the next morning a farewell committee helped us launch and we headed back out past the seawall and set a direct compass bearing across the 30-mile expanse of Discovery Bay. There was no retreat today as the wide open bay faced directly to the vast Southern Ocean in the south west and there was no protection until Cape Bridgewater at the eastern end. A third of the way across, the Victorian border, marked by a dotted line on the chart, actually progressed somewhat waveringly out to sea with a procession of lobster pot floats and markers indicating the limits of South Australian territorial waters. Victoria's cray season was not due to start for another month. Sightings of ordinary sea life were often obscured by a solid black feathered sea of short-tailed shearwaters, or mutton birds, floating around us. Having just arrived from their 15,000-mile flight from the Bering Sea in Alaska, they gorged themselves and it was touch-and-go as to whether they could get airborne, or even swim out of our way as we sailed through them. In some places they covered the water's surface for as far as we could see.

The sand dune coast of the Coorong and the later limestone cliffs were replaced by high, hard rocky headlands of Cape Bridgewater and Nelson with south-facing, small sandy coves. Framed by foaming white waves they provided little protection as we pushed on towards the larger bay of Portland along a wild and rocky coast. An inquisitive seal and a few fairy penguins kept us company. As we rounded Danger Point, the last headland before Portland Bay, we hit straight into the face of a 25-knot northerly. With the outboard going flat out we ate salt spray for a half-hour before we finally pulled ashore in a small carpark area near the port. Very cold and wet we were at least grateful to be in Victoria, our last state. Portland was one of the south coast's earliest ports providing a base for early sealers and whalers. Its collection of old colonial buildings contrasted sharply with the new and dynamic port facilities. Grain, live sheep, and timber are the prime exports and the harbor provides a service base, which also supports the nearby Bass Strait oil fields. It was certainly not a quiet location when you are camped in the local harbor carpark! We were impressed with the facility but we didn't get much sleep.

We did a quick tour of the town, anxious about leaving *Tom* and our gear unattended. As we settled back in our tent, feeling a bit like a shag on a rock next to the only tree in an exposed parking area, the rain started to fall. The wind howled and our tent rocked for the next three days as the parking area turned to mud. Our only visitors were local youths looking for a parking lot to drink and find love. I occasionally had to stick my head out of the tent at night to convince them that someone was there and the boat was not to be touched. Our saving grace was a woman who gave us the use of the local Community Room at the Council Chambers with coffee, tea and a heater where we could read and write our next *Multihulls* article. After explaining our predicament she welcomed us in and said, "Make yourselves at home and if any one questions you, just tell them that Anne said."

We read to escape as Sue traveled Siberia with Eric Newby and I admired the skill of Rumpole of the Bailey with John Mortimer. Our lonely tent became rather cramped after four wet days. The council workers and local dog walkers now said hello to us each morning, although they didn't strike up a conversation. Sue was confronted by a fellow at the ladies' toilets one day and, annoyed with the conditions and his affront, yelled at him to "piss off," which he did. Needless to say, we did not fall in love with Portland and longed to move on with the first break in the weather.

The aftermath of a strong, wet southerly change was still playing with the seas when we finally set sail in sunshine, content that moderate winds were forecast to "ease by early afternoon." Clad in thermals, dry suits, foul-weather gear and beanies we were well prepared for a cool, wet day. Well clear of the port, the seas started tossing us about as a six-foot following wind-chop pushed us across the faces of huge 12-to-15 foot ground swells that seemed to tower over our mast. The change may have cleared but the swells certainly rolled on. With only our reefed main we cut back and forth continuously between chop and swell, avoiding the holes in the corner where they met. Caught in one such corner *Tom* seemed to drop in midair and fall down the face of the ground swell. Sue just hung on as I battled with both

The Great Southern Ocean

hands on the tiller. It was exhilarating to have *Tom* sailing in conditions like this. Perching on each big swell was like being on top of the world as we looked down on the windswept ocean around us, with a clear view along the rugged wave-sprayed coast. The only worry was being down in the troughs from where, even when we stood up, the swell was over our heads.

"We'll get some protection from the island over there," I tried to reassure Sue pointing to the rocky outcrop of Lady Julia Percy Island. "By the time we get there, the wind will have started to drop!" Early afternoon came and went and we raced inside the island snacking on a soggy lunch. We didn't have time to appreciate the rich birdlife that call the cliffs home, as the wind was increasing. It had reached the point where we could no longer hold off the back of the swells. I was surfing *Tom* back and forwards down the faces of these huge swells to slow us down and avoid burying his nose in a trough at full speed. It was no longer exciting. I couldn't keep it up for much longer. *Tom's* hull was flexing and groaning at each turn we made and my arm was aching.

"We are not going to make Warnambool, what about Port Fairy?" I yelled to Sue. It was frustrating as we could clearly see Warnambool in the distance on the top of each swell, but then it was renowned for having a difficult harbor entrance.

"I don't care. Let's just get out of here," cried Sue.

We grabbed the chart and started looking at the passage into Port Fairy. It showed some pretty big reef breaks on either side and we knew that if the swell was really big it could break across the whole entrance.

"On the top of the next small swell let's get this sail down," I yelled. After a couple of false alarms when I could feel that *Tom* was not going to make it, we suddenly turned into the wind on the top of a swell and down came the main as I dropped the outboard in and started it on the first pull. Puttering up and down these huge green swells we cautiously motored towards the protection of Port Fairy. Sue stood on the trampoline gripping the mast and called our passage between the reefs. The pounding twelve-foot waves some only a hundred yards away, looked like something out of Hawaiian surf movies. We had been through tighter passages before, just not with this amount of swell. As we came clear of the reefs into the small bay outside Port Fairy, we anxiously sighted the port entrance. Thankfully, the waves were not continuing past the point and seawall. We motored across the foam-covered surface into the peaceful calm of the inlet. I pried my aching fingers from the tiller and stretched in relief.

We motored in bright sunshine up the calm water of the river inlet into Port Fairy. Old wooden fishing boats sparkling with fresh paint lined the wharf. Small, white stone cottages graced the banks and their lush, green gardens, thick carpets of grass and shady trees ran down to the water. The branches appeared to be intermingled with the rigging of a mixture of boats. We could have been at any number of New England fishing ports, quaint and sleepy with life gently rolling by. It was a stark contrast to the high seas that we had just left. We eventually pulled up to a public dock and both clambered ashore, keen to touch ground. As we sorted out our gear some local fellows wandered over to look at *Tom*.

"Have you been out there today?" they asked.

"You're bloody idiots in that boat."

"Where did you come from?"

"Portland, today? Shit, you need your bloody heads read!"

"You aren't seriously going around Australia in that, are you?"

"Where did you start from?"

"Sydney," I replied.

You could see their minds working.

"Which way did you come?"

"We went by Perth for the America's Cup," I casually added. Their minds were working overtime now and I could see them shuffling their feet as they took it all in. "Oh shit. Ah sorry. Ah bloody hell. Congratulations!" as they extended their hands. We shared a few stories before getting the rundown on Port Fairy and the best place for lunch. We introduced

The Great Southern Ocean

ourselves to the harbormaster and arranged for a spot of wharf for *Tom* before retreating to a caravan park up the road. After five nights in the mud in a wet tent we wanted some luxury.

We returned to the wharf the next morning to find a crowd gathered around *Tom* and the local press on their way. Rae Crowley from the *Warrnambool Standard* was so excited about a local news story that we couldn't say no. An ex-publisher from Melbourne, Rae had chosen the quieter lifestyle of Port Fairy and obviously enjoyed it. As the wild weather forced us to stay in another Victorian port, we took in the sights of this pretty town. It was such a welcome port of call in a storm. Its history had been beautifully preserved and its quaintness is appreciated by its many visitors in both the off and summer seasons. At one time this had been the second largest port in Australia, used as a whaling and trading base for the south coast. Beautiful bluestone cottages of the wealthy whalers still provide a strong link with the past.

In her enthusiasm, Rae adopted us, showing us the local sights, inviting us over for dinner, and advising us about writing and publishing. There was something beyond the weather that had called us in to Port Fairy as coincidence after coincidence presented itself. Rae's daughter had worked with my sister Kim on the film just recently finished in Adelaide. A Melbourne fireman, Ivan, who we met at the local lighthouse had helped with the Operation Raleigh sailing ship *Zebu* and knew many of our friends. We met friends of *Paspaley Pearling* from Darwin; and our Operation Raleigh friend Nick Horn's cousin came down to see us after reading the newspaper article. We also met Bob, in his 70's, who learned his seafaring while servicing lighthouses from NSW to Tasmania when he was a lad. "They used to load us with our food, supplies and cleaning gear in a dinghy and pick us up a week or two later," he recalled. He and Ivan had just sailed down in his Clansman from Sydney in an epic blow. "Been married, ...wife died. Had a cat, ...it got run over. Not again, ... got to be free," he chatted in his casual matter of fact way.

We were encouraged to go down to Warrnambool and see the town and get a view of the harbor entrance in its full fury. Seeing its maze of reefs and the various lines required to navigate a safe passage I was glad we had chosen Port Fairy to pull ashore. The museum at Warrnambool, overlooking the harbor, gave an impressive perspective of this seafaring shipwreck coast. Yet another lengthy week's wait through wild and woolly days found us adding up mileage, schedules and dollars. The conclusion was that we would be lucky to see Sydney by late February at this rate. Hesitant after our previously forecast for calm, and a record of one to two days of sailing in every seven for the past month, we felt it was time to reconsider our options. I had a job interview in Melbourne the following week and Sue's parents were arriving from the United States in less than a month to spend Christmas with us.

After a week of agonizing, fate again threw us another option. Ivan, the Melbourne fireman, offered to take *Tom* on to Melbourne by trailer for us and then we could see how we went from there. As we talked over options with the local fishermen, it was considered that we would be going well to get one good day a week of sailing for *Tom* at this time of year. As much as I longed to sail the Great Ocean road coast of Victoria with its spectacular sea cliffs and the well-known sea pillars, the Twelve Apostles, at that rate we wouldn't be home for another six months! We pondered the alternatives. Where did the Gippsland Lakes start? We could sail through those and pop out to the sea at Lakes Entrance back on the east coast of Australia. This would also mean missing out on the southern most point of the Australian mainland, Wilson's Promontory! We would see. The thought of being in Melbourne and catching up with friends was much more appealing than despondently sitting and waiting for good sailing for days every week. Perhaps we had lost our nerve; perhaps we just knew better and had gained in wisdom.

After a week in Port Fairy we packed *Tom* onto a borrowed trailer with Ivan driving and waved goodbye as they went to Melbourne without us. We would follow in a rental car seeing the sights by land. It was strange seeing *Tom* head off down the road away from us. Late that night as my mind went back and forwards through our options, the decisions we had made and the questions still to be resolved, I suddenly sat bolt upright in bed! "Shit — Sue, wake up. We forgot the mast!" Somehow in the hustle and bustle of getting *Tom* off we had forgotten to put the mast on the trailer. It was still down by the boat ramp. I dragged Sue out of bed. At 2:00 A.M. two dark figures struggled down the streets of Port Fairy carrying a mast back to the

The Great Southern Ocean

caravan park, both of us cursing the whole way, me at my stupidity and Sue at being awakened.

We borrowed roof racks and, with mast on top, said farewell to Port Fairy the next day.

The coast was spectacular as we wound around from Petersborough to the small picturesque town of Port Campbell. We sat at the edge of high, orange, sandy cliffs watching the sea break through natural island bridges called London Bridge and The Arch. Brilliant rocky cliffs in earthy creams and reds rose out of a wild blue-green ocean. Long strips of sea weed laced patterns around them. Port Campbell's gentle narrow bay looked very placid until you viewed the boat access from the sea, between reefs with large breaking swells covered in white caps. The seas here in rough conditions required the winching of fishing boats up onto the dock to be placed in cradles stored on shore.

Farther down the coast we joined the tourist groups of honeymooners, busloads of tourists, battered surfing wagons, and rental campervans taking the standard snap shots of Lochard Gorge and the Twelve Apostles. We had never thought of ourselves as tourists before. When we looked back, the rugged rock sea towers stood defiantly in the sea like lonely sentinels guarding the coast. We could have almost sailed that morning, although the afternoon breeze was up over 20 knots. As much as I wished to be out there, I also knew it didn't feel right. The sea taunted and teased the cliffs that dared to defy them.

"We shut prompt at 4:00 P.M. — You should have read the sign on the road. When you leave, take your cigarettes and garbage with you," the sign said in hand-written, black letters on a sheet of tin wired to the security fence. It was hardly the welcome we imagined at Cape Otway. The white lighthouse and surrounding buildings were set on an olive green headland jutting out into the wild blue of Bass Strait. It was also surrounded by a few kilometers of cyclone security fencing topped with barbed wire. Bemused at this unnatural sight we were then stunned by its natural backdrop. A large pod of over 200 dolphins was surfing and leaping around the southern tip of the cape. They were enjoying the wild sea and looked very much at home. From the small isolated lighthouse we felt we were with them although glad that in the 30-plus knots of wind we weren't on *Tom* anxiously looking for our next landfall. We retreated down the eight miles of dirt road back to the highway passing beautiful forest and deep green gullies of fern, amazed at the contrast between the beauty of nature and the crass thoughtlessness of man.

We pulled into Apollo Bay for the evening after an amazing day. We were both suffering from sightseeing overload, having seen so much compared to the slow pace of *Tom*. As we sat eating fish and chips on the headland, dark storm clouds parted allowing shafts of evening sun to spotlight the sea. *I felt this coast was playing with us, teasing us along. But I also felt we were out of our depth!* I wrote. The road continued to follow the shoreline, the Great Coast road hanging to the side of cliffs as they dropped sharply to a deep sea. Sue and I both recalled driving down the Monterey coast and Big Sur in California. As we passed through the beachside resorts of Lorne and Torquay on the remainder of the coast to Melbourne, the wind was howling and we were glad we were not sitting, waiting and waiting. At Point Lonsdale we anxiously looked out to The Rip, where the entire area of Port Phillip Bay exits to the sea through a narrow gap two miles wide. A 20-meter ketch with mizzen and staysail was pounding out through the chop, showing what *Tom* would have faced. We had never planned to sail in here, instead scooting straight passed to the slightly friendlier Western Port Bay further to the east. A plaque stated that someone had swum across The Rip in 61 minutes! Now that was foolish!

Melbourne was a shock after the quieter state capitals of Perth and Adelaide. It was a sudden jolt in the arm that said "Welcome back to the real world." With a population of 1.5 million, it is Australia's second largest city to Sydney. Sue loved its trams and shopping and markets. We stayed with Meg, an Outward Bound friend of mine, and caught up on old times and people, while doing cleaning and repairing gear. Sue confirmed that she could extend her visa to finish the trip and I looked for a job. Teaching Recreation Studies at a Sydney college was a position I had applied for in Victor Harbor and now they were flying me up from Melbourne for an interview. I felt awkward about going back to Sydney without sailing. It was not what I had envisaged, but then the end of the trip was only a month away and we had debts to pay off.

The Great Southern Ocean

It was strange to fly over the coast of New South Wales we had yet to sail. The familiar skyline of Sydney gave me feelings of comfort and uncertainty. It was good to be back. My Mum had developed arthritis during the year and was cramped and in pain, "From all my worrying", she claimed. They were relieved to see me alive and well after a year and half. I left them with a casual, "See you in four weeks." The interview was a blur and despite my research I didn't feel confident. On my flight back to Melbourne I had to think about sailing and *Tom Thumb* again, now knowing that the end was in sight.

We took the option of missing the remaining southern coast of Victoria and heading instead for the Gippsland Lakes, to sail through them and emerge on to the east coast at Lakes Entrance. Australia's largest natural enclosed waterway, the Gippsland Lakes are over 250 miles of linked rivers, lakes and channels, 125 miles east of Melbourne. It was a chance to see yet another unique Australian waterway.

Due to our peculiar transport needs we negotiated a deal to drive an Avis flatbed truck for a one way trip to Sale, "gateway to the Gippsland Lakes." It only took me 15 minutes to find reverse gear and the sweat dripped from me as I double shifted gears crossing the city to pick up *Tom* and our gear. We eventually found our way out of Melbourne and rolled across the open plains of the Yallourn Valley taking in the coal mines and power stations. It was certainly a change from cruising the coast with *Tom*, but not as much fun.

The port of Sale is effectively a basin on a canal that connects to the Thompson River and the Gippsland Lakes. Sale is a pretty town with private schools and was thriving as the Esso/BHP support center for oil and gas fields just off the coast. We met Howard at the local Caravan Sales and Rental shop. *"Yep, fixin' up a river boat. All in cedar. Bit of a project of mine. People always friendly round here. You musta met some great ones. Watch them lakes. Friend of mine drowned on Lake Wellington . Watch that one! It usually blows its tits off here. Eight foot high those waves get. Oh and really watch out on Lakes Entrance it's ... But what am I telling you guys for. Enjoy yourselves. If ya need a hand just give us a call. No worries. Cheers."*

It was great to see *Tom* back in one piece as we finally pushed off. We motored down the winding canal passage, not much more than two boats wide towards the lake. Tea trees heavy in flower and large old gum trees arched over the water as the bird life called us through. It was a strange way to be travelling after the Great Southern Ocean. It was also difficult to have any perception that this was taking us towards the ocean and home. After a meander through the scrub, we eventually emerged in the large open waters of Lake Wellington. We ran with just our jib in a strong wind around to the local yacht club keeping one eye out for Howard's "eight footers." Mosquitoes and sandflies made us welcome as the sun set over this inland sea.

We took a compass bearing across the lake early the next morning with strong winds still shooting us along with just a jib. On the far side we found a forlorn post, marked number six, indicating the further passage through to our next lake. With interest we watched a local fisherman atop the short mast of his boat guiding it towards his nets set in the lake. I was amazed that netting was allowed in what would have been the main breeding grounds for fish in Victoria.

After a day's relatively pleasant cruising in the narrower Lake Victoria we settled for a campsite on the long arm of Loch Sport, a narrow promontory of park dividing two lakes. The most eastern lakes follow the coastline formed by a ninety-mile long beach, with a thin strip of sand dune between lake and sea. It was beautiful watching the birdlife as pipers and herons waded and pelicans seemed to hang glide in group formation. Sailing up these inland waterways was pure heaven after battling with the Great Southern Ocean. Poor Sue was not enjoying it so much with two days of hayfever and an infection that looked like a boil on her leg. "That's what I get from Melbourne," she tried to joke. It was the first ailment either of us had had on the whole trip and it had to come from our experience in a city, not the wilderness.

At the small landing of Ocean Grange we eagerly raced over the narrow strip of sand hills to Ninety Mile Beach and had our first splash on Australia's east coast in a year and a half. On this bright sparkling day it had a welcome familiarity. We were at least in our own backyard again even though Sydney was still 300 miles away. I felt as if a weight was lifted from me after battling the sea, the elements and my own frustrations for so long. It was the first time I let myself believe we were truly going to make it.

We returned to *Tom* to find a young fellow eyeing our proud boat. He had sailed small dinghies called "Moths" around the lakes as well as done some canoeing and he felt inspired by our trip and wanted to read all about it. Only after talking to other people did we start to gain a perspective of what we had done. For us it had been a way of life. What we did, we did. No big deal. We had just reorganized our priorities for two years.

We camped at Steamers Landing that night and I couldn't resist a naked chilly surf to welcome back the east coast. Sue settled for staying on shore and taking photos. We toasted ourselves for Halloween. This time last year we had been in Port Hedland, and the trip had nearly ended! How far had we come since then? Here was Victoria showing us its best in sparkling sunshine. We sunbathed and went over to take in the community of Metung. Billed as Victoria's Riviera it certainly made it in pretence, with the Mercedes and BMW's parked in convoy. When we pulled into the nearest take-out food place on a fishing dock, we were surrounded by three-piece suits and mobile phones! A nearby real estate agent was advertising private islands for sale, and large pretentious homes crowded the waterfront. We motored around the bay to some natural hot springs and soaked our aching bodies before heading over to Lakes Entrance.

The number of shops and take-outs gave some indication of the crowds that must frequent this area during the holiday season. Sue went to the doctor and was prescribed antibiotics for her Melbourne boil, while I bought food and fuel for our next week back on the coast. We celebrated having negotiated Gippsland Lakes with a few cold beers and a barbeque. Early the next morning on the beginning of the ebb tide we sailed out the narrow 75-foot gap that was Lakes Entrance into the Tasman Sea and the Pacific Ocean. It was like being reborn as we were spat back out on our home water. In bright blue sunshine and a calm clear sea we waved hello and goodbye to the surprised crew of the sand dredge, and turned north to Sydney.

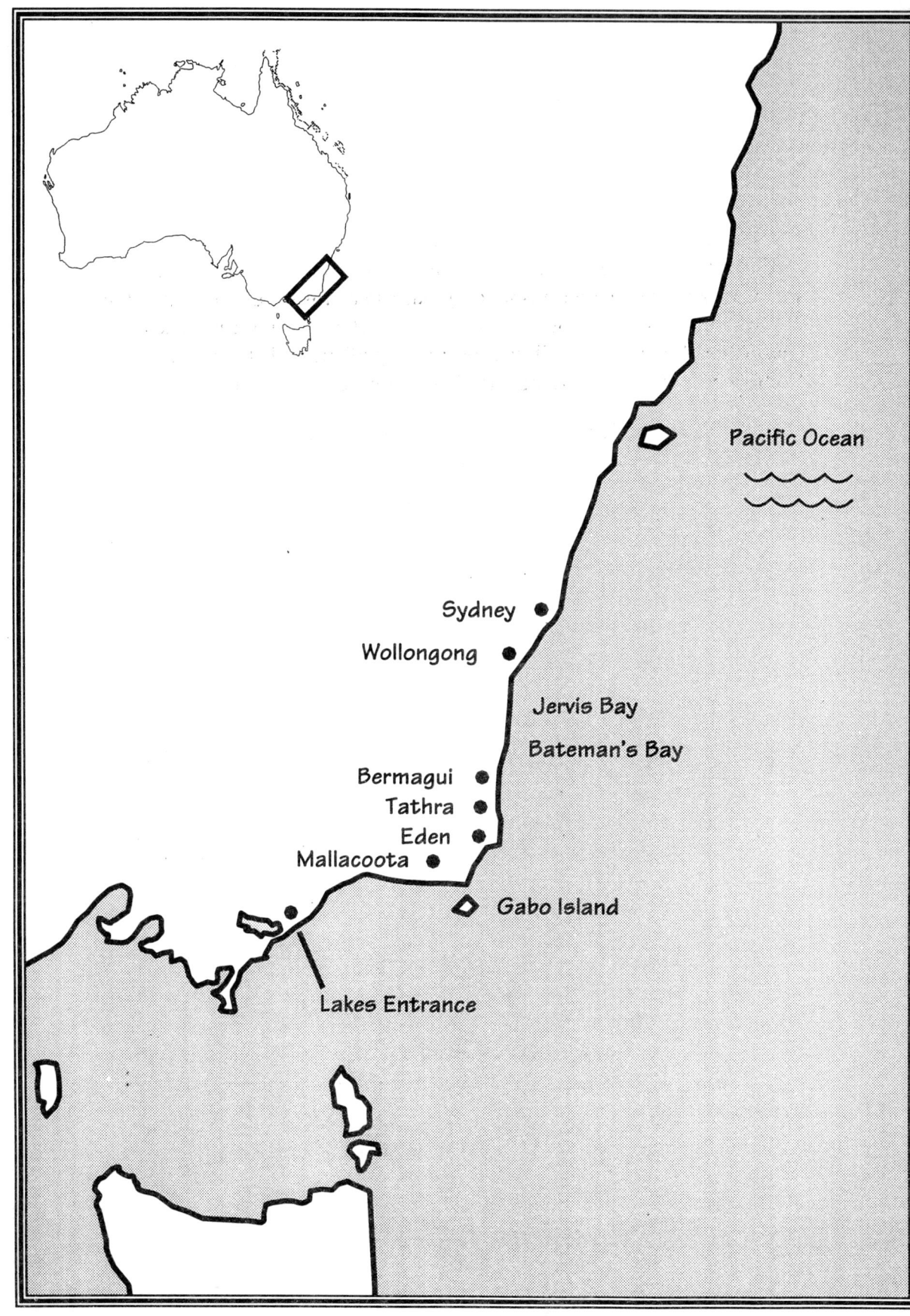

Chapter 14

The Passage Home
Lakes Entrance to Sydney

Lakes Entrance is almost midway along Ninety Mile Beach. It is effectively that — ninety miles or more of golden sand beach that stretches in a huge arc from Wilson's Promontory, the southern most point of the Australian mainland, all the way to Marlo, a small fishing village, east of Orbost. We cruised up the coast sailing only a few hundred yards from shore, taking in the beautiful scenery. Both Sue and I felt calmer, the sea seemed brighter, and the shore more welcoming than ever before.

The wind was offshore, flattening the seas to a bare ripple. The sea was a bright blue green and a group of ten dolphins joined us for a couple of hours. They swam upside down staring up at *Tom's* two white hulls, blinking and trying to understand this new playmate. Rich green forests run down from the mountains to lakes and secluded inlets with not a building or soul in sight. It looked brilliant and exciting after the never-ending harsh sand dunes of the Western Australian coast and the hard rocky cliffs of South Australia and Victoria. Being totally absorbed in the scenery we didn't notice the swell. Only twenty yards from shore I heard the wave before I saw it. I turned *Tom* quickly and tried to get some speed. "Get forward and hang on!" I yelled to Sue. Aiming straight at the five feet of whitewash we plunged through, to be left soaking wet on a calm, flat sea. "Good one Mark!" said Sue with water dripping from her hair. We laughed and steered further out from shore.

We pulled ashore at Marlo for lunch to fully enjoy what felt like holiday sailing again. Unfortunately, it had been a long time since we had landed at a deep-water ocean beach and we didn't have the rudders up in time. Crack! They whipped around and were thrown hard across. It wasn't until we set sail again that I noticed we didn't have much control. Looking down I saw the whole rudder housing had sheered away from the rudder and the stainless steel pin that held it to the boat. "Oh shit," I yelled, "get that jib in and find our next stop quick." It was hanging on by a thread. With light winds we limped into Point Ricardo. We carried a spare bracket but I couldn't fix it without a power drill. I spent the afternoon using creative engineering and our limited supply of rivets and screws to brace the rudder bracket. It would not get us far, but hopefully we could make it to the next township. We spent a beautiful night camped on an empty golden beach that stretched away into the distance lit by a bright half moon and the glow of a warming camp fire.

Early the next morning we had a smooth exit carefully watching our rudder as we cleared the shore. As we turned into the breeze and set sail the makeshift bracket buckled and came loose. "Bloody hell! Let's gets the sail down quick!" I yelled as *Tom* careened out of control and headed for Bass Strait. With only one rudder down and running with the outboard we considered our options. We had to get a major repair job done, but the question was where. Lakes Entrance was too far back so our only option was to keep limping forward until we found our next town. Cape Conran was the next headland only five miles away, but we had no idea of what help we might find there. We limped slowly through the morning haze. After an hour we turned around the Cape and were overjoyed to see a score of small fishing boats. We waved to them and managed to land on an open shallowing shore with *Tom's* rudder hanging limply like a broken wing.

As we were sorting out our gear, a uniformed fisheries inspector came by. He looked us up and down and proceeded to tell us about all the yacht rescues they had to do around nearby Gabo Island. We smiled and listened politely. Then another fellow strolled up with his young son, followed by a steady stream of campers.

"G'day, how ya doin'?"

I mentioned our rudder problem and immediately he launched into,

"G'day the name's Kevin, Dave's got something. Oh, by the way meet Laurie".

The Passage Home

"G'day. Good to meet you guys. I'm off back to Melbourne now. Dave'll fix ya up. Stay in our caravan tonight, it'll be empty."

Kevin took charge again, "This is Jeff. Jeff, we gotta problem. Meet Frank, he's got some silicon gel. Come into town and meet Arthur, he's got a workshop and is a keen sailor."

Within an hour we were standing surrounded by new friends in Arthur's backyard shed at Marlo drilling out a new rudder bracket and sharing sailing stories. Then in no time we were back at *Tom* with Jeff's tool kit and silicon gun admiring the repair job with our rescue crew. We thanked them all profusely and were then helped up with our gear to Laurie's van before having cold beer and chicken for lunch and being invited for a hot shower at Jeff's that night. Sue and I had to go for a cool refreshing surf just to wake ourselves up. Three hours earlier we had been anxious and despondent. Now here we were quietly drunk, very relieved and enjoying the hospitality. Our guiding light was continuing to shine on us.

Dave, Frank, Laurie and various family members were all from Melbourne and had been coming up to this camp for years. Cape Conran was originally a forestry area at the end of a rough dead end dirt track from Marlo. When Arthur had first come to the area as a kid "it used to take days to get here along the track." Jeff remembered clearing a site among the bracken for their tent on his first trip. The site was still little more than a bush camp at the end of the national park track. It was just our luck that it was so popular at this time of the year.

Dave, his wife Lorrie and their daughter Raylene, who had returned to this special spot to restore themselves after a family tragedy, provided an excellent dinner. Once again we shared part of people's private lives and emotions as if we were part of their family. We eventually made our excuses and dragged ourselves off to bed in the luxury of Laurie's caravan. The next morning they wouldn't let us off without a cooked breakfast of bacon and eggs. After Dave had helped me to pack *Tom* and get him down to the water, Lorrie rushed down to give Sue a parting kiss and hug. Then we waved farewell and set sail. It was another place where we wished we could stay for weeks.

Keeping Australia On the Left

Tom and crew had been repaired and recharged in a very short time at Cape Conran. The 25 miles of coast to Mallacoota was magical, consisting mostly of national park with little public access. The area features large coastal lakes, which nestle in between sand dunes and low rocky headlands. Bush comes down to the shoreline, broken only by an occasional sand dune and forest covered hill stretched as far as we could see. Each ridge had a skeleton-like profile of dead white tree trunks, scars from the 1983 bushfires when southern Australia had been declared a national disaster area.

As we cruised along in fresh offshore winds around Point Hicks, a group of abalone boats cruised up alongside. In their high-speed aluminum boats they zapped around us taking photos and shouting out questions. "How's it goin? Heard about you guys. What's taking you so long? Come and have a beer at Mallacoota," then roared off into the distance. The inlet of Tamboon was spectacular as the large, golden sand dunes rose out of the surrounding bush and made a backdrop for a magical untouched inlet, actually the outlet for the Cann River. Point Hicks is the most prominent southern point on the coast and its bright white lighthouse stands proud on a smooth granite point. We dodged around its collection of reefs as a seal came over to play with us.

The rocky outcrop of Rame Head marked the protection of Fly Cove and Wingan Inlet at the end of a long day. Tucked in behind a large scrubby granite island, we were protected from the wind and swell. Set in the middle of a national park, access to the inlet is via a 22-mile dirt road followed by a two-mile walk through the bush. Across the cove a prominent collection of rocky islands called The Skerries are a popular habitat of fur seals and little penguins. Fly Cove had actually provided shelter to George Bass, Matthew Flinders' friend who explored the coast all the way from Sydney to Western Port Bay in a whaling boat in 1799. Rame Head, which provides the shelter for Fly Cove, was one of the first place names recorded by Captain Cook when he first sighted the Australian coastline in 1770.

The early morning weather forecast gave a gale force warning for Bass Strait and a strong wind warning for the rest of Victoria's coast. As wild weather set in, we shared our haven with the local wildlife for the next few days. After a chorus of wrens, whipbirds, magpies, seagulls and oyster catchers woke us up, we found five-foot long goannas and echidnas wandering around our tent and groups of seals playing in the rising swells. We saw only two people in the next few days, a hardy couple staying in their campervan a mile or so up the inlet. The natural surrounds were all ours as we got to know the neighborly birds that would share our breakfast and the seals that would smile over the wind swept swells at us standing on the beach.

As the wind eased and the swell settled, we briskly cruised down the coast to clearly see our goal of Bastion Point that protects the inlet of Mallacoota, backed by the white dot of Gabo Island lighthouse, which marks the state borders between New South Wales and Victoria. As we battled into the wind, totally drenched, a whale sounded less than 500 yards from us with its large tail raised skywards. It focused our attention as we stared out into the empty ocean for the next few hours anxiously searching for his or her relatives. Tales of Moby Dick came back to us as we considered whether whales would take a similar interest to *Tom* as dolphins.

We finally rounded the point, surfed over the Mallacoota bar and motored into a caravan park campsite right on the lake. *Tom* even had his own dock right next to our tent. Mallacoota Lake, the largest in the area stretched out to boundaries of the nearby Croagingalong National Park with the town of Mallacoota wrapped around its western shore.

We decided to celebrate our arrival with a meal and drink at the local pub and found a Maori wake in full swing with guitars strumming and the beer flowing freely. I shook my head in wonder. Had we missed Mallacoota and ended up across the Tasman Sea in New Zealand? It appears that Maoris originally came to the area as abalone divers and now called it home.

The names of the abalone boats tied up at the jetty suggested the abolone divers or owners had a wry sense of humor — with the *Ab Grabber and Ab bortion*. We met Dave, the local fishing inspector, for the abalone co-op and were given the run down on the industry.

"They are limited to 600 pounds a day, that's all they get paid for. That's usually $3,000 to $4,000."

Cripes, I could see why a licence now traded for around $500,000.

"Most of the catch is sold overseas and valued in US dollars or Japanese yen," continued Dave. "We have a hell of a party in town when the Aussie dollar goes down".

Dave was also one of the local sea kayaking crowd and told us about his paddle around Cape York a few months earlier. It was great to share stories of places and beaches that we had both experienced. He had even met some Operation Raleigh friends of ours, Charles and Jasmina, the day they were being married on an island near Cape York. Small country!

The Mallacoota abalone boys and other locals had a reputation for adventure. Some had been part of the Greenland sea kayak expedition on which we had seen the photo presentation in Adelaide. But there were also little casual trips with their mates, including up the east coast to Cape York and across Bass Strait and around Tasmania — just for fun! Anxiously Sue looked at me as I started to talk of future trips "maybe paddling, or hiking." "Mark, let's just finish this one first!" she insisted.

There was a friendly social atmosphere in the caravan park, and on seeing *Tom* people invited us over for food or drinks. We shared our site with a couple we had met at Wingan Inlet, John and Glenda and their camper van. They were off for a five-week trip from Melbourne. They had been married at 21, twelve years earlier, and were now out enjoying travelling. They listed the future trips they had planned. John, Glenda and I listened to Australia win the Cricket World Cup by seven runs as Sue slept. She still didn't appreciate the finer points of cricket. "How can they play a game for five days and still end with a draw?" she always questioned.

I called my parents to try to confirm some work for January. Sue's parents would be arriving in two weeks! Suddenly the end was coming. Our morning farewell to Mallacoota involved an interview with the *Mallacoota Mouth*, the local high school newspaper. Despite some giggling between questions we were impressed with their well-prepared questions. They put many professional journalists we had met to shame.

The final mark we had to round before venturing into our home state of New South Wales was Gabo Island. This low-lying promontory of red granite topped by a lighthouse is barely over a mile long and separated from

The Passage Home

the mainland by a turbulent 400-yard wide channel. Wanting to visit our last manned lighthouse and island, we had planned to drop by. After interviews and shopping it was late morning by the time we had strapped down gear and were ready to sail out over the Mallacoota Bar. It is a notorious inlet which is usually only negotiated by the large powered Sea Cats of the abalone divers. John and Glenda stood on Bastion Point with their video camera recording our exit. With a low swell and high tide just peaking, we surfed out through the main channel under full sail, breaking through a few small waves before turning for a comfortable seven and one-half mile cruise to Gabo.

While waving farewell and feeling proud of ourselves, I noticed the change coming up the coast. "Look at that," I pointed out to Sue. The meanest, darkest, threatening wall of black clouds was swallowing the coast to our south. Like a giant curtain the storm slowly wrapped up the mountains and came across the sea toward us, marked by a line of wild whitecaps. We at first felt confident we could make it to Gabo in time, but as the coast was quickly obliterated behind us, it was a race to find a landing place on the island before we were consumed. Many boats were making a quick dash to Mallacoota. A fisherman came over in his powerboat. "You guys all right?" he asked assuming we would be trying to get back to Mallacoota. "Fine!" I yelled above the increasing wind, "We are staying at Gabo tonight. "OK. Goodluck!" he offered as he spun around and disappeared into the advancing black wall.

The rocky shores of Gabo were still a mile or so away as we searched for the minimal protection of the reported small cove and jetty that would be totally exposed to this south west storm. The chop increased to three-to-six feet as the wind gusted over 20 knots and the steady line of white caps chased us from behind. "Let's get this sail down and just motor in," I yelled at Sue. I dropped the outboard as Sue got ready with the main halyard. The outboard wouldn't start! I tried all our options and still there was nothing. Meanwhile Sue battled with the mainsail.

"Shit! It's stuck," Sue yelled while pulling furiously on the jammed halyard.

"Shut up and calm down!" I replied. "We are going to have to sail in and just run it up on whatever shore there is. Come on. Tie it off and give me directions."

Eyeing off the mad capped sea and black wall behind we sailed towards Gabo with a mainsail halfway down and flapping madly. We couldn't sail *Tom* into the wind now if we tried.

We neared Gabo and spotted the jetty area but I could still see nothing but the rocky shore. It was a case of spinning *Tom* into the wind and grabbing the jetty if we could. Sue got some rope ready and an anchor just in case we had to stay off shore. At praying stage I decided to try the outboard one more time. It kicked and spluttered in protest but kept going. "Come on, Sue. You skipper and I'll get that sail down." She strained with both hands on the tiller and the outboard screamed and slowly brought us round into the face of the storm. As soon as we could hold it into the wind, the sail flickered and came rushing down into my thankful arms. We rolled off the back of swells rather than ploughing into them now and rounded the cove to see a small patch of sand. Without hesitating I ran *Tom* straight up onto it. We both jumped out and hauled him as hard as we could clear of the break. Cast ashore with such relief we were almost oblivious to the hailstones and torrential rain that now hit this small haven.

A truck with two figures aboard appeared at the top of the boat ramp as the rain came down in sheets. Fred Armstrong, the head lightkeeper, and his assistant, Ret, had seen us heading their way and came to inspect. "You can stay here in the boat shed with the rats, or come and have a cup of tea and we'll put you in the spare house," stated Fred. He didn't need to ask twice! In a matter of moments *Tom Thumb* was hauled up the concrete boat ramp, and two drowned rats plus gear were tossed in the back of the truck. Less than an hour later we found ourselves warm and dry inside Janet Armstrong's kitchen, drinking hot tea, eating delicious homemade cakes and sampling the delights of the biggest cookie tin I've ever seen. Fred knew we were coming as Dave from Mallacoota had given him a call. "A bit bloody surprised to see you on a day like this though!" Fred stated. As we started our second cup of tea and began to thaw out, the radio crackled.

The Passage Home

"Fred, did that catamaran arrive at Gabo this afternoon?" It was Dave's voice.

"Oh, those people you told me about," joked Fred.

"Yeah, they left this afternoon headed your way".

"It's OK. They're here drinking tea in the kitchen. Thanks, Dave," said Fred smiling.

As one storm followed another, we settled into life on Gabo Island. After 18 years in the service, throughout Victoria and Bass Strait, Janet and Fred provided a unique insight into Australian lighthouses and their keeping. Not short on words and a good laugh Fred recounted many tales of life on a "light." Fred jokingly refers to himself as a "glorified painter," insisting "you've gotta have a sense of humor if you are working for the government!"

But Ret, the assistant keeper, was quick to point out that there's a lot more to it. He was a qualified cook who had been looking at something different for his family. He was really interested in the radios and weather recording and the variety of maintenance work that continued to keep them busy. Another acquired skill he demonstrated was butchering a cow that had fallen down a fairy penguin burrow and broken its hip and had to be put down. "You certainly don't waste meat out here," said Fred cutting into the carcass suspended from the bucket of the tractor.

A maintenance task unique to Gabo is the care of the airstrip that is the main asset for the two weekly contacts with the mainland. "It's like Christmas when the plane lands and out come the groceries, supplies, magazines, newspapers, mail and even a new pair of shoes for Ret's wife, Carol. Just in time, too, as her toes were popping through the current pair. Shopping like this and planning ahead, is a must since one can't just run down to the local shops when out of milk and weather makes any planned delivery flight uncertain." Unpacking her bundles, Janet found she had six tins of beetroot instead of six cans of tomato paste.

"You can't get upset. You've just got to have a good sense of humor," says Janet, remembering the funnier mixed-up orders in the past. Ten tins of Kitty-Kat catfood came as ten bars of Kit-Kat chocolate — "fine for us, but the cats weren't impressed." An order of hair shampoo became carpet shampoo. "Goodness knows what it would have done for my hair," said Janet laughing. The airstrip was short by any standards, facing east-west across the island with the sea at either end. Departures of more than two people, or heavy loads of equipment required multiple trips to be ferried over to Mallacoota before being reloading to take off on the longer airstrip. After keeping the airstrip in shape, Fred reckoned he might as well be employed as a gardener and greenkeeper.

Fred explained who pays for the lighthouse, "Only the big ships pay. It's a certain price per ton, per lighthouse passed. None of the fishing, yachts or pleasure boats pay, yet they are the ones usually on the radio calling for information or help." The bigger ships don't really need the lighthouse for navigation these days as they rely on their satellite navigation systems and radar. However, they still reset their compasses on the radio beacon off Gabo. It was strange to see them doing 360 degree turns out at sea in the process. Gabo is one of the tallest lights in Australia and is built of red granite rock quarried from the island. That makes for lots of stairs, "187, but who's counting?" One of Ret and Fred's current jobs was scrapping and replacing them. Janet gave us a tour of the light she knew and loved so well. She had started doing miniature paintings of the Gabo lighthouse on red granite pebbles as presents for friends.

They were glad to be on Gabo after being on some of the mainland lighthouses. They recounted tales of tourists "a la terrorists" that were the bane of their lives. "The general person was rude, dirty and inconsiderate," said Fred. "They didn't consider that we had to live there and they would dump rubbish, clean out their cars, dump cats and dogs, and defecate in the bush. At one place we had to cut down the trees, bushes and scrub to keep people from relieving themselves by the busload because it stank so much. We weren't paid to clean up after them!" This was their experience at Cape Otway lighthouse. We now understood the less-than-welcoming signs we had seen at Otway. We could also understand their appreciation of their solitude at Gabo.

The wind continued to blow and big waves rolled by, and for the first time in ages we didn't care. We spent a wonderful five days on Gabo. During this time Sydney was also being battered by gales and high swells

The Passage Home

that even cancelled ferry runs on the harbor. We sent off a radio telephone call to assure my parents that we were not in the midst of those seas. We watched whales breaching and fairy penguins surfing up the beach to their burrows around *Tom Thumb*. We helped take weather reports and listened to radio exchange between yachts that went careening past, roaring down 12-foot swells with the 30- to-40 knot wind behind them. It was a wonderful opportunity to share in yet another unique and interesting lifestyle, a lifestyle that would soon no longer exist in Australia.

Many of the lighthouses were being automated and had caretakers just to maintain the grounds and buildings. In some cases even the historical buildings were going to be demolished as they were considered too costly for the government to maintain. Local weather reports and personal assistance in emergencies were no longer a service to be provided on the Australian coast. "It'll cost lives," claimed Fred. "Nobody in Canberra (the federal capital) really knows what we do in the role of community awareness and service."

It was a sad farewell as both families came down to wave us off. We were not only waving Gabo goodbye, but more than likely Fred's last posting and the last of lighthouse keepers on Gabo Island after a long and proud history. We waved a fond farewell and scooted through the channel between the mainland and Gabo, and headed north.

> *I watched Gabo Island disappear and became lost in thoughts and memories of the past 18 months. We were on the last leg home; our voyage that had become a way of life was about to end, abruptly. The green, majestic shores of the New South Wales coast that I had so longed for, just cruised silently past. Instead of excitement and elation, I was feeling emptiness and sadness,* I wrote in my diary.

Large rolling sandhills descended from green mountain slopes down to the coast at Cape Howe marking the state border. From here it was a rough and rocky coast for a good 25 miles up to the port of Eden. This was our main reason for choosing the best weather to leave Gabo. It was spectacular scenery but it was also rather unsettling to have sites such as Disaster Bay featured on the chart. We sailed and motor sailed to make distance, waving to the Green Cape lighthouse, knowing that Fred had radioed ahead. The sea was empty apart from the company provided by flocks of mutton birds and the occasional group of penguins. Late in the afternoon, we sailed into the large welcoming blue waters of Twofold Bay.

After sailing through Bass Strait, Twofold Bay provided one of the first safe havens on the eastern Australia coast for many of the square rigged sailing ships which bore the early settlers to the new lands of Australia in the 1800s. It still provides a welcome retreat to many a modern day sailor, being a haven in the wild conditions experienced by many crews in the Sydney to Hobart yacht races. In the early-to-mid 1880s, Twofold Bay was also notable as Australia's largest and most important whaling station. It now featured a large stockpile of Japan bound woodchips at the Harris-Diashowa chip mill on the southern side, and the fishing port and town of Eden on the north.

We had heard the story of how a fellow had recently attempted to row across the Tasman Sea to New Zealand and had to be rescued by Eden fishermen, not once, but twice, after he ignored weather warnings and became seasick. Sponsored by *Australian Geographic* and other large companies he was handed a rescue bill of $8,000 and then booed and jeered out of town. We therefore wanted to make our visit as inconspicuous as possible.

After casually pulling up to the local wharf I went to buy some more fuel and food from the dock. Placing the last of our supplies on the counter the shopkeeper turned to me and asked, "How's your trip going?" I was too surprised to speak and then saw his 27 MgHz radio behind him on the shelf. He had obviously been listening to Fred's comments and the Green Cape lighthouse via radio and following our progress all day. So much for remaining inconspicuous! I smiled and exchanged a few brief pleasantries about the weather before Sue and I stole off to a quiet beach and set up camp. We celebrated our home state with fish and chips and a Tooheys (New South Wales beer) and the *Telegraph*, a Sydney newspaper.

It was great to be back on the spectacular, brilliant and diverse coast of New South Wales. With rocky headlands hiding protected beaches and coves we had a daily choice of suitable landing points. Tempted by the beautiful bays and beaches of Pambula and Merimbula, we finally surfed into the beach at Tathra after a long day. The old historic wharf at the southern end of Tathra beach was used when small steamers regularly plied this coast in the 1800s as the one and only highway for supplies and passengers.

Tathra wharf once served the rich dairy area of Bega as the steamers took cheese and milk direct to the Sydney markets. The town is similar to many on the New South Wales coast, with a surf lifesaving club and a holiday caravan park backing the beach. We settled into the comfort of a caravan bed for the night with take-out fish and chips for dinner. Maybe we had softened up too much, or perhaps we were now being realistic about getting away early and not having to pack up gear.

I went down to the beach early the next morning to get *Tom* ready. The sight before me made me sick to the stomach. There was *Tom* half dragged to the water with the sail jammed in its tracks and all our gear pulled out of the hulls and strewn down the beach for hundreds of yards. Welcome back to New South Wales and the populated coast! After one and half years of travelling and many thousands of miles around the Australian coastline, this was the first time that we had had any trouble. Swearing, I started picking up gear and then checked out *Tom*. Luckily the sail wasn't torn and I accounted for the last of our gear buried in the sand. After all the hardships and hazards that we had faced around Australia, it appeared that the prophetic advice offered to us in Queensland of "Don't worry about the crocs mate — it's the people you need to worry about," was justified. It made me furious to think that after all we had been through, we still may not make it to Sydney due to other people's actions. We quickly packed and set sail wanting to leave Tathra behind and return to safe and quiet, unpopulated beaches. A soaking wet exit through the surf did not help to improve our mood for the day.

The coastline north was of beautiful rugged headlands and bays with forest and inlets tempting us to stay longer. We passed Bunga Head and stared at an amazing property with green pastures extending down to the sea and a golden beach, as the mist rolled off the nearby mountains. We spotted the water tower of Bermagui and set that as our target for the day in what had been overcast and wet conditions. In the early afternoon we cruised into the small harbor of Bermagui and tied *Tom* off on some mooring lines, anxious not to leave anything tempting around. The caravan park just up the road from the harbor provided some shelter as the rain settled in and we appreciated a beer and steak at the local pub overlooking the bay. Sue was amazed to find the caravan park was named after Zane Grey, an American author, who had found Bermagui and made it his favorite marlin fishing retreat, returning year after year. The place continues to be popular with fishermen and women as a holiday retreat and is a lovely quaint coastal town. We were stormed in for the weekend and settled into a caravan to write articles and postcards and make calls to plan our arrival.

My Dad retired that day. After his lifetime of dedication to the New South Wales Department of Education I was excited that he would now do something for himself. Sue's parents had arrived in Australia and we chatted on the phone. Sue was already getting anxious and excited about seeing them again for the first time in two years. "We'll have to get you home to learn English again," her mother exclaimed. Sue's parents had also brought over more of her books and clothing as she hoped to stay in Australia "for just a while longer."

We finally departed in calmer weather and sailed in good winds northward past the further coastal ports of Narooma and Moruya. Sunlight sparkled off *Tom's* wet bows as they cut through the small clean swells. With our large Ulmer Kolius headsail and full mainsail *Tom* playfully cruised past untouched golden beaches and green wooded headlands. These were the days we would remember as we touched into the protection of Broulee Island after a day of sailing. A group of power boaters started questioning us about "This around Australia stuff — you bloody idiots," until they found out where we were headed and where we had started. Then they proceeded to eat humble pie and tried to apologize.

We spent yet another three days at South Durras, north of Bateman's Bay at a friendly caravan park on the beach with kangaroos casually grazing the grounds. Sue enjoyed their company as the wind howled in and the swells rolled by. The weather was frustrating! Total calm or howling winds of over 30 knots began to make our arrival date of December 5th in Sydney somewhat doubtful. We made use of our time by finishing off our last *Multihulls* article and cleaning up our gear. If it could just hold out a little bit longer! Our now slightly less-than-new outboard was continually spluttering and coughing and required a regular carburetor service. I could apply for an outboard mechanic's job at the end of this trip.

The Passage Home

Pigeon House Mountain, named by Captain Cook, stands prominent among the beautiful Budawang ranges behind Ulladulla. "It looks more like a breast, or nipple mountain," commented Sue. We discussed the propriety of an English sea captain of the 1800s settling for such a name and considered he had chosen the politically correct option. The Budawangs are an assortment of sandstone peaks, mountain platforms, and escarpments that have survived coastal weathering and now provide a continuous backdrop to this section of coast. We eventually had a great day's sail, even if the only rain cloud of the day found and dumped on us. Getting anxious about the changing winds and still-rolling swells, we all too casually cut into the small port of Ulladulla for lunch, just missing the local submerged reef, or bombora, that we hadn't seen on our chart. This stop and start sailing was not good for our skills or our nerves. Bad forecasts for the afternoon didn't eventuate and we decided to push on. The inspiring scenery of Jervis Bay stood before us.

— Powerful sheer cliffs dropping 300 feet into the ocean depths provided a stunning sight and were to be one of our final, but most memorable campsites, my diary said.

Our campsite quality rating system, developed through many nights of experience was extremely tough, with very few sites awarded perfect scores. *Tom Thumb* always won when we had to choose between an attractive or a safe landing site. Our aching backs did not always appreciate this necessary system of priorities as we slept the occasional night on rocky uneven shores. Whiting Cove, to the south of Jervis Bay, protected by its raking cliffs was heaven. A long narrow cove, barely 25 yards wide, tucked in between fern-covered sandstone ledges and encircled by thick green bush. Fresh water trickled over the cliffs into the sea, and a small creek bubbling along behind the one-tent campsite, then flowed out across the tiny stretch of sandy shore.

Breathing in the beauty of this peaceful cove, I suddenly realized it was Thanksgiving. We ate our feast of beans and rice and toasted our good fortune with a glass of sherry, in a well-worn blackened camp mug. I had a great deal to be thankful for and a feeling of contentment rose with reflection on the months and years past. I had experienced what I had wanted to, learning about, knowing and understanding Australia. It's easy to bask in glowing reflection but I'd been tired, scared, and many times fed up to the point of quitting. It was myself that I'd learned a great deal about, too, and with this I was more than content, Sue wrote.

We sat watching the sun casting its shadows on Whiting Cove, and we both knew it was time to move on. After so long, it would all soon be over. It would be strange living life without *Tom Thumb* and the ocean. We knew there were new challenges and new adventures just around the bend, down the road, or up the river. Our future of jobs and careers was all too frightening to consider. We soaked up the beauty and solitude and gave thanks for our deliverance, almost.

The following day we skirted well out around Jervis Bay with the sheer cliffs and deep sea providing a confusing cross chop. The yachting guide recommends a five mile berth and we headed well out to sea. As we bounced around in a sloppy swell, we saw a navy ship turning circles and making a run along the coast. "They are probably doing training," I explained to Sue as they turned and returned into the bay, one of Australia's naval ports. An unfriendly northeast wind came up again and ended our hopes of making Kiama. Tall water spouts started forming in dark clouds out to sea so we retreated to the shelter of Shoalhaven Heads, at the mouth of the Shoalhaven River. When we were pulling into the nearby boat ramp, a local fisherman said hello and asked, "Did you guys just come past the Bay?"

"Sure," said Sue, "It was a bit lumpy but OK".

"Did you know that the Navy was having gunnery practice and was trying to get you on the radio? They had to abort, and were not too happy!"

He laughed along with us. *Tom Thumb* had redirected the Australian Navy! We were glad that there were no more naval ports or bombing areas between here and Sydney.

The smaller communities of Geroa, Gerringong and Shellharbour floated past as we set our sights on the smokestacks of Port Kembla. For half a day they stared at us before we passed them and pulled into the port of Wollongong. It is one of the largest ports and a steel-making city, but it was a shock to see such huge industrial facilities. Suddenly there were other people and boats and ships all appearing to head towards us! We now had

The Passage Home

more than just the wind and sea with which to contend. With no beach in sight we tied up to the nearest wharf and went for a walk around town. We returned to meet the jolly crowd of the volunteer rescue patrol who invited us for showers and offered us a place to sleep for the night. The local lads shared tales (mainly for Sue's benefit) of an excited American tourist who, while on a whale watching trip out from Wollongong, had rushed back excitedly and said that she had "just seen a short-tailed shearwater!" We laughed knowing how many thousand of them we had sailed past in a week. Sue was suffering from sandfly bites and she was glad to be clean and off a beach for the night. Consuming take-out pizza and beer, while watching television seemed strange.

That night we both slept badly from over-exhaustion and tension. We were anxious about getting home at this stage. We headed out of Wollongong Harbour at 6:20 A.M. to ensure our arrival in Sydney, a good 50 miles away. The coast from there up to Port Hacking is a rugged rocky coast of Royal National Park with deep water and heavy surf beaches. Not the kind of place to stop. The steep 500-foot sandstone cliffs of Stanwell Tops rise as a long bluff directly from the ocean. It was a coastline I had hiked and admired a number of times, but now I was anxiously ticking off each familiar beach and cove. There was only one potential landing area nearest the northern end of the cliffs at Wattamola Bay. It was at this spot that Matthew Flinders with crew aboard the original *Tom Thumb* had been cast ashore during his first explorations of the Australian coast, almost two hundred years earlier.

Around midday, the familiar skyline of Sydney loomed out of a dull-brown, polluted haze, behind the Kurnell sandhills, looking like a picture postcard stuck on the horizon. Whiting Cove, the Barrier Reef, Perth and the America's Cup, were all memories. As we sailed round the last point into Port Hacking, a huge wave of emotion rushed over me. I didn't know whether to laugh or cry. A strange distant sense of deja vu came over me as we at last crossed into truly familiar water. This was where it had all begun, what seemed like a lifetime ago when we test sailed the prototype called a CatCan with Peter Poole. Almost eighteen months later, and after many thousands of miles, here we were sailing back in our *Tom Thumb*. Australia was still on the left and we had done it!

There was an overwhelming sense of relief. To think that we could wake up tomorrow and the next day and not care what the weather was like, or if our worldly possessions were waterproof or not. But there was also a great sense of regret, uncertainty and sadness at the thought of leaving behind this life, these adventures and potentially each other. The ocean was hardly our friend. At times it had appeared a bitter enemy. But we had become part of it, a cork bobbing on an ocean, tossed about with every breath of wind and swell. We had felt, smelt and lived with it for the past two years and it was sad to be leaving it behind. The smog-covered silhouette of the city skyline and the unwelcome smell of Sydney's polluted ocean was a scary, yet familiar sight. In many ways it was much more terrifying than anything we had encountered over the past two years. And what of our futures in the real world?

We looked at each other across the trampoline as we had many times, our eyes showing many different emotions through tears. Without words we crawled across to each other and kneeled to give each other a clammy windbreaker-clad hug that acknowledged the hardships and dangers, the beauty and freedom, and gave thanks for what we had achieved. *Tom Thumb* and his crew had made it home!

Epilogue

Time makes most memories grow fonder. There is a tendency to dwell on the good moments, or selectively shape the memories ever so slightly, until you begin to believe that was what really did happen. This story however, deserves better, for it is a tale of natural beauties, hardship and commitment. The journey was at times spectacular, although often uncomfortable, occasionally frightening and at times, downright monotonous. It is also a story of two people caught up in their own challenges, battling with the elements and each other, yet sharing a common goal. It was a journey that became more than both of us had ever planned. At times it was bigger than both of us and threatened to swallow us whole. At times it was soul tearing, grabbing at our hearts and minds trying to tear us apart. As with many expeditions the goal became secondary as the journey taught us more than we ever imagined it would.

Apart from the crew and *Tom Thumb*, there was the place *Australia*. Its stunning physical beauty, its harsh and wild remoteness, can leave you speechless, at times in awe at its space and solitude. There was also the most unique ingredient of all, the people. From city "yachties" sipping their champagne in a harbor, to the hardy, rugged true "salts of the sea," and all those people making their living by fishing, mining and farming on the Australian coast. It made me proud of this country which I am fortunate to call home.

We did eventually stage a finish to the trip and sailed back in under the Harbour Bridge. *Tom* was on display at Pier One for a couple of weeks. Despite many calls to the media and our sponsors, only a brief Channel 7 television news interview took place. But that was OK, it was our trip by now. A large welcoming group of family and friends waved us under the Harbour Bridge, followed by a support group of Catcan canoes. Our welcome home party for family, well-wishers and supporters was a wonderful day. It allowed us to say a big thank you and present *Order of Tom Thumb* awards to people such as our Post Master, Les, who had made sure that all our supplies arrived safely and Peter Pool who was just glad to see us alive and safe. Our parents received special mention for their encouragement and support.

After one-and-a-half years on the open seas we returned to jobs in Australia's biggest city, Sydney. From a cruising pace of ten knots life now became frantic and fast paced with three million other people. Sue worked as a nanny with her bedroom window six feet from one of Sydney's busiest inner city streets. I started tutoring in Recreation Studies at a local college. We followed up on all our sponsorship requirements and wrote to Marlin to tell them we hadn't drowned in their lifejackets We sold *Tom* and some equipment to pay off our debts. It was strange to see him head off down the road on a trailer into someone else's life. It wasn't too hard to part with him. I could never keep *Tom* stored in a backyard gathering cobwebs, only to be used on the occasional weekend. That would break my heart after what we had been through. Parting with *Tom* was the final sign that we were ready to move on to other things and another life. The hardest adjustment was living without the serenity and beauty of the wilderness that had become a daily part of our lives.

I felt crowded by people, space, noise, and life, all wanting answers and action. The pace was all too fast. We retreated to each other because we were the only ones who understood. We didn't have to explain. We just knew, because we had been there.

"Would you do it again?" many people asked. "Not all at once," was the immediate reply and maybe not for a while. Exhaustion had at times reduced the opportunity for enjoyment and further exploration. However, we now had a collection of well-worn charts with many highlighted bays, coves and beaches marked for further visits.

"What would you do differently?" was usually the second question. To get more favorable winds someone had suggested we start in Adelaide and sail counter-clockwise to Darwin, truck the boat back to Adelaide then sail clockwise to Darwin. From the winds we had experienced it would have halved our trip down the Western Australian coast. However, in truth we

Epilogue

wouldn't have changed much. For an unsupported trip the Catcan was excellent, with ample storage and stability. Racing down twelve-foot swells in the Southern Ocean we had appreciated its sturdiness and quality of design. It would have been good to have spent more time fine tuning its sails and rig to get more speed in slight winds and more control in high winds. The furling points of the main were a major advantage and we would have benefited from a light spinnaker in the light northern airs. We would not take a 27 Mgz radio and the supporting framework of battery, solar panel and aerial. It weighed too much and was not regularly monitored or used outside the east coast. A handheld VHS radio and a mobile phone would probably serve just as well. We had excellent service from our Yamaha and Suzuki outboards, although a better sailing rig would have saved the use of them, especially into the headwinds in Western Australia. Through trial and error we found out what equipment best survived the regular battle with salt and sand. The basic rule was it was better to spend the extra money up front and get the best quality, rather than go through two or three updates. If we could have afforded it, freeze dried foods could have greatly decreased our weight and made storage a little easier. A few months preparation test sailing the boat would not have changed much apart from calming our initial nerves, and saving us buying the odd piece of useless equipment.

Sue and I got married. Living swallowed us up. We got divorced. We should have kept on sailing! Sue now lives in California and I returned to an unexpected place. That gentle rolling green farm that was lapped by the sea near Bunga Head on the far south coast of New South Wales drew me back. This book has been written in my new home, ironically at Tathra, where I often gaze out at the coast we sailed. As I paddle it in my sea kayak and the sea mist rolls off the hills, the mutton birds squawk, or a dolphin passes as the sea rolls and pitches I am momentarily taken back to *Tom Thumb*, Sue and our travels.

WELCOME TO
Hellgate Press

Hellgate Press is named after the historic and rugged Hellgate Canyon on southern Oregon's scenic Rogue River. The raging river that flows below the canyon's towering jagged cliffs has always attracted a special sort of individual — someone who seeks adventure. From the pioneers who bravely pursued the lush valleys beyond, to the anglers and rafters who take on its roaring challenges today — Hellgate Press publishes books that personify this adventurous spirit. Our books are about military history, adventure travel, and outdoor recreation. On the following pages, we would like to introduce you to some of our latest titles and encourage you to join in the celebration of this unique spirit.

Our books are in your favorite bookstore or you can order them direct at **1-800-228-2275** or visit our Website at **http://www.psi-research.com/hellgate.htm**

ARMY MUSEUMS
West of the Mississippi
by Fred L. Bell, SFC Retired

ISBN: 1-55571-395-5
Paperback: 17.95

A guide book for travelers to the army museums of the west, as well as a source of information about the history of the site where the museum is located. Contains detailed information about the contents of the museum and interesting information about famous soldiers stationed at the location or specific events associated with the facility. These twenty-three museums are in forts and military reservations which represent the colorful heritage in the settling of the American West.

BYRON'S WAR
I Never Will Be Young Again...
by Byron Lane

ISBN: 1-55571-402-1
Hardcover: 21.95

Based on letters that were mailed home and a personal journal written more than fifty years ago during World War II, *Byron's War* brings the war life through the eyes of a very young air crew officer. It depicts how the life of this young American changed through cadet training, the experiences as a crew member flying across the North Atlantic under wartime hazards to the awesome responsibility assigned to a nineteen year-old when leading hundreds of men and aircraft where success or failure could seriously impact the outcome of the war.

Gulf War Debriefing Book
An After Action Report ISBN: 1-55571-396-3
by Andrew Leyden Paperback: 18.95

Whereas most books on the Persian Gulf War tell an "inside story" based on someone else's opinion, this book lets you draw your own conclusions by providing you with a meticulous review of events and documentation all at your fingertips. Includes lists of all military units deployed, a detailed account of the primary weapons used during the war, and a look at the people and politics behind the military maneuvering.

From Hiroshima with Love
by Raymond A. Higgins ISBN: 1-55571-404-8
  Paperback: 18.95

This remarkable story is written from actual detailed notes and diary entries kept by Lieutenant Commander Wallace Higgins. Because of his industrial experience back in the United States and with the reserve commission in the Navy, he was an excellent choice for military governor of Hiroshima. Higgins was responsible for helping rebuild a ravaged nation of war. He developed an unforeseen respect for the Japanese, the culture, and one special woman.

Night Landing
A Short History of West Coast Smuggling ISBN: 1-55571-449-8
by David W. Heron Paperback: 13.95

Night Landing reveals the true stories of smuggling off the shores of California from the early 1800s to the present. It is a provocative account of the many attempts to illegally trade items such as freon, drugs, sea otters, and diamonds. This unusual chronicle also profiles each of these ingenious, but over-optimistic criminals and their eventual apprehension.

Order of Battle
Allied Ground Forces of Operation Desert Storm ISBN: 1-55571-493-5
by Thomas D. Dinackus Paperback: 17.95

Based on extensive research, and containing information not previously available to the public, *Order of Battle* is a detailed study of the Allied ground combat units that served in Operation Desert Storm. In addition to showing unit assignments, it includes the insignia and equipment used by the various units in one of the largest military operations since the end of WWII.

Pilots, Man Your Planes!
A History of Naval Aviation ISBN: 1-55571-466-8
by Wilbur H. Morrison Hardbound: 33.95

An account of naval aviation from Kitty Hawk to the Gulf War, *Pilots, Man Your Planes! — A History of Naval Aviation* tells the story of naval air growth from a time when planes were launched from battleships to the major strategic element of naval warfare it is today. Full of detailed maps and photographs. Great for anyone with an interest in aviation.

REBIRTH OF FREEDOM
From Nazis and Communists to a New Life in America ISBN: 1-55571-492-7
by Michael Sumichrast   Paperback: 16.95

"...a fascinating account of how the skill, ingenuity and work ethics of an individual, when freed from the yoke of tyranny and oppression, can make a lasting contribution to Western society. Michael Sumichrast's autobiography tells of his first loss of freedom to the Nazis, only to have his native country subjected to the tyranny of the Communists. He shares his experiences of life in a manner that makes us Americans, and others, thankful to live in a country where individual freedom is protected."

— *General Alexander M. Haig, Former Secretary of State*

THE WAR THAT WOULD NOT END
U.S. Marines in Vietnam, 1971-1973   ISBN: 1-55571-420-X
by Major Charles D. Melson, USMC (Ret) Paperback: 19.95

When South Vietnamese troops proved unable to "take over" the war from their American counterparts, the Marines had to resume responsibility. Covering the period 1971-1973, Major Charles D. Melson, who served in Vietnam, describes all the strategies, battles, and units that broke a huge 1972 enemy offensive. The book contains a detailed look at this often ignored period of America's longest war.

WORDS OF WAR
From Antiquity to Modern Times   ISBN: 1-55571-491-9
by Gerald Weland   Paperback: 13.95

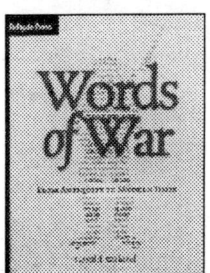

Words of War is a delightful romp through military history. Lively writing leads the reader to an under- standing of a number of soldierly quotes. The result of years of haunting dusty dungeons in libraries, obscure journals and microfilm files, this unique approach promises to inspire many casual readers to delve further into the circumstances surrounding the birth of many quoted words.

WORLD TRAVEL GUIDE
by Barry Mowell   ISBN: 1-55571- 494-3
   Paperback: 19.95

The resource for the modern traveler, *World Travel Guide* is both informative and enlightening. It contains maps, social and economic information, concise information concerning entry requirements, availability of healthcare, transportation and crime. Numerous Website and embassy listings are provided for additional free information. A one-page summary contains general references to the history, culture and other characteristics of interest to the traveler or those needing a reference atlas.

TO ORDER OR FOR MORE INFORMATION
CALL 1-800-228-2275

K-9 Soldiers
Vietnam and After ISBN: 1-55571-495-1
by Paul B. Morgan Paperback: 13.95

A retired US Army officer, former Green Beret, Customs K-9 and Security Specialist, Paul B. Morgan has written *K-9 Soldiers.* In his book, Morgan relates twenty-four brave stories from his lifetime of working with man's best friend in combat and on the streets. They are the stories of dogs and their handlers who work behind the scenes when a disaster strikes, a child is lost or some bad guy tries to outrun the cops.

After the Storm
A Vietnam Veteran's Reflection ISBN: 1-55571-500-1
by Paul Drew Paperback: 14.95

Even after twenty-five years, the scars of the Vietnam War are still felt by those who were involved. *After the Storm: A Vietnam Veteran's Reflection* is more than a war story. Although it contains episodes of combat, it does not dwell on them. It concerns itself more on the mood of the nation during the war years, and covers the author's intellectual and psychological evolution as he questions the political and military decisions that resulted in nearly 60,000 American deaths.

Green Hell
The Battle for Guadalcanal ISBN: 1-55571-498-6
by William J. Owens Paperback: 18.95

This is the story of thousands of Melanesian, Australian, New Zealand, Japanese, and American men who fought for a poor insignificant island is a faraway corner of the South Pacific Ocean. For the men who participated, the real battle was of man against jungle. This is the account of land, sea and air units covering the entire six-month battle. Stories of ordinary privates and seamen, admirals and generals who survive to claim the victory that was the turning point of the Pacific War.

Oh, What a Lovely War
A Soldier's Memoir ISBN: 1-55571-502-8
by Stanley Swift Paperback: 14.95

This book tells you what history books do not. It is war with a human face. It is the unforgettable memoir of British soldier Gunner Stanley Swift through five years of war. Intensely personal and moving, it documents the innermost thoughts and feelings of a young man as he moves from civilian to battle-hardened warrior under the duress of fire.

Through My Eyes
91st Infantry Division, Italian Campaign 1942-1945 ISBN: 1-55571-497-8
by Leon Weckstein Paperback: 14.95

Through My Eyes is the true account of an Average Joe's infantry days before, during and shortly after the furiously fought battle for Italy. The author's front row seat allows him to report the shocking account of casualties and the rest-time shenanigans during the six weeks of the occupation of the city of Trieste. He also recounts in detail his personal roll in saving the historic Leaning Tower of Pisa.